Marxism
AND THE
Human Individual

Marxism
AND THE
Human Individual

ADAM SCHAFF

Introduction by
ERICH FROMM

Edited by
ROBERT S. COHEN
Boston University

Based on a translation by
OLGIERD WOJTASIEWICZ

McGRAW-HILL BOOK COMPANY

New York   St. Louis   San Francisco   London   Sydney   Toronto
Mexico   Panama

Library of Congress Catalog Card Number 68-58510

1 2 3 4 5 6 7 8 9 0 M U M U 7 9 8 7 6 5 4 3 2 1 0

La plus belle, la plus agréable et la plus nécessaire de toutes nos connaissances, est sans doute la connaissance de nous-mêmes. De toutes les sciences humaines, la science de l'homme: cependant cette science n'est pas la plus cultivé ni la plus achevée que nous ayons: le commun des hommes la néglige entièrement. Entre ceux même qui se piquent de science, il y en a très peu qui s'y applique, et il y en a encore beaucoup moins qui s'y applique avec succès.

N. Malebranche: *De la recherche de la vérité,* Tome premier, Paris, 1762, p. xxviii.

[The most beautiful, the most pleasant, and the most necessary knowledge is without a doubt the knowledge of ourselves. Of all the human sciences, the science of man—though it is neither the most cultivated nor the most developed that we have—is disregarded entirely by ordinary people. Even among those who have pretensions to being scientific, few apply themselves to it and many fewer apply themselves to it successfully.

N. Malebranche: *On the search for truth,* Vol. I, Paris, 1762, p. xxviii.]

Contents

Contents

Introduction

The publication of this book constitutes an important event. It was an event first of all within Poland itself, where the original version was published in 1965. One of the most outstanding Polish philosophers, who has at the same time been a prominent political figure for many years, speaks out; he criticizes some of the weaknesses of his own system and more importantly raises questions about man, individualism, the meaning of life, norms for living, which until recently had been neglected in most of Marxist literature.

But the publication of this book also constitutes an event for the non-Communist world, and especially for the United States. One of the clichés in American thinking has been to believe that Marxism is "materialistic," that it subordinates the individual to the state (or society) and that thus it is the antithesis to the values of humanism on which Western society was founded. Schaff demonstrates in his book that this picture of Marxism is wrong; as wrong, I would say, as if during the years of the counter-Reformation someone had believed that the deeds of the Inquisition represented the teachings of Christ. By this analogy I refer specifically to the distortion of "Marxism" which was taught in the Soviet Union under Stalin, during what is called in the socialist countries the years of "the cult of personality." The same distortion, in a slightly diffcrent version, is to be found among most people in the non-socialist world, even among most of those who consider themselves "experts" of Marxism.

In the United States the certainty of what constitutes "Marxism" was, and largely still is, matched only by the ignorance about Marx's writings and ideas. What is believed to be Marxism is essentially a conglomeration of clichés which one writer copies from another, usually without bothering to read or study the Marxist texts. The distortion of Marxism was much more severe in the

United States than in Europe largely due to the fact that one of Marx's most important philosophical texts, the "Economic and Philosophical Manuscripts" of 1844 had never been translated into English until a few years ago. In Germany and France, where these manuscripts were well known, there has been a lively concern with them during the last decades among philosophers, and especially among Protestant and Catholic theologians.

This book deals all the more effectively with Marx's ideas because historical development has proven how dangerous the neglect of certain aspects of Marx's philosophy has turned out to be. Marx was one among the great humanist philosophers who, like the humanists from the Renaissance up to those of our day, have stressed the idea that all social arrangements must serve the growth and the unfolding of man; that man must always be an end and never a means; that each individual carries within himself all of humanity; that human progress in science and in art depends on freedom; that man has the capacity to perfect himself in the process of history. The main difference between Marx and his great humanistic predecessors does not lie in their concept of man and the goals for his life, but in the idea that these aims cannot be realized only by teaching, but that necessary economic and social changes are required which will permit and further the fullest development of man. It is an ironical fact that the main accusation against Marxism in the capitalist countries has been his "materialism"; this is ironical because it was precisely Marx's aim to fight the materialism engendered in bourgeois life and to create a society in which man—the creative, "self-active" human being—is the *summum bonum,* in which the rich man is the one, as Marx put it, who *is* much, and not the one who *has* much.

Our industrial civilization, both in the socialist and in the capitalist areas of the industrialized world, has led to an ever-increasing neglect of man. Man has become alienated from his work, from his fellowman, and from himself; he transforms himself into a thing, occupied with production and consumption. Unconsciously he feels anxious, lonely, and confused, because he has lost the sense of the meaning of life and the conviction of who he is and what he lives for.

By emphasizing the vital necessity of raising these questions, Professor Schaff has a message which is important not only for his own country, but equally so for us. For in spite of all political and ideological differences between the two opposing camps, the need to find a new and authentic frame of orientation and devotion is equally great throughout all of industrial civilization.

This book is one of the first works of a humanist Marxist philosopher from a country belonging to the Soviet bloc to be published in the United States. But it gains in significance through the fact that Professor Schaff is by no means the only Marxist philosopher who stresses Marx's humanism as the basis without which Marxism cannot live. This renaissance of Marxist humanism is occurring with such force and intensity in Poland, Czechoslovakia, Yugoslavia, and Hungary, that one can truly speak of a movement in which the great majority of the philosophers of these countries are participating. They have published many books and articles in which they have expressed their humanist convictions. But little of this has become known in the English-speaking world.[1]

This renaissance of humanism among socialists is part of an even larger movement, the significance of which has not been sufficiently recognized: the renaissance of humanism all over the world, and within different ideological camps. We find this movement among representatives of Christianity as well as among socialists and scientists. It will suffice to mention here only the names of Pope John XXIII, Teilhard du Chardin, Albert Schweitzer, Albert Einstein, and Bertrand Russell, as representatives of this movement.

This humanist movement of today stresses the same principles that have been characteristic of humanism since the Renaissance, and even earlier. It has arisen as a reaction to the ever-increasing threat to man—the threat of nuclear extinction and the threat to all that is specifically human: independence, aliveness, creativity,

---

[1] An international symposium on *Socialist Humanism* (edited by E. Fromm, Doubleday & Company, Inc., Garden City, N.Y., 1965) contains a large number of papers (including one by Professor Schaff) of which approximately one-third were written by authors in Poland, Yugoslavia, and Czechoslovakia; it thus gives a picture of the scope and aliveness of humanist-socialist thought today.

and most of all, to man's being an end in himself and not the means for institutions or purposes outside of himself.

The humanists in various ideological camps do not ignore the important differences that exist among themselves, and they do not want to minimize them. Yet their common concern for peace and reason as the basis for the full unfolding of man constitutes a common element of great importance, and the basis for an ever-increasing dialogue taking place among the various groups of humanists.

Professor Schaff's book represents one significant expression of Marxist humanism. It is not, and does not claim to be, a dogmatic expression of "the" true Marxist humanism. There are considerable differences among humanist socialists themselves; this writer, for instance, would go much further in establishing objectively valid criteria for happiness and the meaning of life. But these differences only testify to the genuine and undogmatic character of the new humanism among socialists.

One last word about the author and his book. There are books which reflect the personality of the author in their content and style; there are others which hide it. This book belongs to the first group. It reflects the courage, honesty, modesty, and humanity of the author. It does not shy away from expressing unpopular ideas, and it does not pretend to have solutions which have not been thought through or which are purely ideological. It is permeated by a spirit of genuine concern for man, for the writer is true to himself, never hiding his doubts, and yet full of hope that mankind can take the next step toward a more human and a happier form of existence.

ERICH FROMM

Marxism
AND THE
Human Individual

Rediscovery of
the Old Content of Marxism

Maximilien Rubel has written in the preface to his biography of Karl Marx that "Despite the reputation he has enjoyed—or precisely because of it—Marx stands in need of rehabilitation." [1] This statement, which at least in the not so remote past would certainly have startled the "orthodox" Marxist, contains a valid point. It is simply that certain basic Marxist truths, long forgotten or passed over, need to be restored to their rightful status and luster. Indeed, Marxists have already set about this task, and with increasing success.

There is no doubt that ours is a time of rediscovery of Marxism both by wide circles of research scholars and by laymen who are the consumers of ideology. Nor is there any doubt that this rediscovery is being accompanied by a revival of Marxism and a growth of its influence in these groups.

"The young Marx is a discovery of our time," writes Erich Thier,[2] and the American Marxologist Robert Tucker says in one of the most recent books on the subject: "It seems fair to say that a change in the generally accepted view of Marx has been taking place in the twentieth century." [3] Countless statements to this effect could be quoted, all of them testifying to a general sense of change in the historical assessment of Marx and Marxism. If they are less abundant in the works of writers who are declared Marxists and who represent Marxist positions, then the often radical change in their approach to Marxism, and thus of their scientific attitude, is much more telling than any mere verbal declaration.

In most cases what the "discovery" simply amounts to is that the traditional image of Marx as economist, politician, and sociologist is increasingly supplemented (and even to some extent eclipsed) by the picture of him as a humanist, a student of the problem of the individual and a champion of his happiness. To anybody familiar with the origins and history of Marxism, this may seem a fairly banal discovery, but it is no more banal than all great discoveries made ex post facto—when the truth is already known. Yet they are extremely important for our knowledge of the world as well as for the way this knowledge affects the world in practice.

Habent sua fata libelli, the ancients said. The destinies of books fluctuate in the course of history, and so does the destiny of their subject matter. This is not only because—to quote another Latin saying—*tempora mutantur et nos mutamur in illis,* and not only because of changes in the perceiving subjects, but also because changes in objective circumstances bring into focus what is particularly pertinent at any give time, illuminate it with a greater clarity, and often make us grasp the importance of something previously underestimated or simply overlooked. This is why every age rewrites history: not only because people learn new, previously unknown facts, but also because they see the old ones in new ways. Naturally enough, their own attitudes and concerns, connected as they are with the existing conditions, tend to direct their attention to similar occurrences in the past that could easily have been ignored in other periods. It is also natural that the course of events should reveal the succession of causes and effects in history—and it is only these causal relations which allow a proper assessment of the meaning and importance of the various facts. Such an assessment is usually impossible, or at least very difficult, before the effects of contemporary developments are revealed.

There is nothing strange or exceptional in the fact that today, in new conditions, we should interpret Marx in a new way, tending to stress those elements of his system that have long remained in the background. But what really matters, particularly from the point of view of theory, is to explain why it is precisely today that this change of viewpoint is taking place.

There is no doubt that a great role was played by the discovery of the young Marx in the most literal sense of the word: the publication of some of his unknown writings, particularly the *Economic and Philosophic Manuscripts of 1844.* If we remember that the first complete German edition both of these *Manuscripts* and *The German Ideology* appeared in 1932 and that of *A Contribution to the Critique of Hegel's Philosophy of Right* in 1927, we realize how defective was the knowledge of Marx and the understanding of Marxism available to previous generations. Unfamiliar with these, as well as with some of Marx's less essential writings, Kautsky and Rosa Luxemburg, Plekhanov and Gramsci, even Lenin, had only an incomplete knowledge of Marxism—a disadvantage that the greatest genius could hardly overcome. What was involved was the genesis of Marxist thought—a genesis which shed a new light on the later development of that thought.

But it is also true that the publication of these writings in the 1930s passed almost unnoticed before the Second World War. The *Manuscripts* did arouse a response of sorts in revisionist circles, but chiefly as a weapon against the official, Stalinist interpretation of Marxism. It is interesting, both sociologically and psychologically, that the use of Marx's own writings apparently to support the revisionist case and to attack the prevalent interpretation, should in fact have resulted in the propagation of Marxism and the spread of its influence. For it is an undisputable fact that the legacy of the young Marx was originally popularized by the opponents of official Marxism; their intention was to undermine Marxism, but unwittingly they were instrumental in furthering its influence. This grew, together with the evolution in the interpretation of Marxism that gradually absorbed more elements of the young Marx's thought, integrating them into the overall picture. Georg Lukács was a laudable exception in this respect—all the more noteworthy because of the price he once had to pay. Whatever objections can be raised by Marxists with regard to his *Geschichte und Klassenbewusstsein,* Lukács was probably the only writer to have arrived at views that later were to be confirmed by the publication of Marx's early writings, particularly Lukacs' views on the question of alienation and reification.

There are many objective reasons why the response to these works was so half-hearted when they first appeared.

In the first place, a few years was too short a period for a sufficiently profound study and proper understanding of these philosophically difficult, not to say esoteric, texts. To grasp their full meaning, it was necessary to acquire a thorough knowledge of the entire Young Hegelian milieu—a terrain with which the Marxists of that time were only superficially acquainted; even today our knowledge of this subject is far from complete.

Second, the dissemination of these writings was hardly encouraged by the generally accepted, traditional form of Marxist theory. There was an obvious reciprocal influence here: since the great writings of the young Marx were unknown, it was possible for the traditional stereotyped image of Marx and Marxism to take root— and, in turn, this stereotype became a barrier to the incorporation of all those features that were considered alien to the theory. For Kautsky, for Rosa Luxemburg, Marx was everything, but not a philosopher. Among important Marxist thinkers of the past, problems of the human individual and the philosophy of man could only be found in a clear and systematic form in the works of Gramsci, who, for that matter, was inspired in this sphere by non-Marxist thinkers—above all Benedetto Croce. That these prejudices were deeply entrenched and seriously hampered the incorporation of the newly discovered elements into Marxist theory can clearly be seen from the fact that the editors of the latest—and most complete— Russian edition of Marx and Engels, begun after Stalin's death, decided to publish Marx's early writings in a separate volume outside the *Collected Works*.

Thirdly, there was undoubtedly the chilling influence of the Stalinist period. In the atmosphere of the thirties, there was no room in official Marxism for the problems of the individual, the philosophy of man and humanism. To illuminate Marxism with the humanism of the young Marx was just as impossible and disagreeable for the leaders of the workers movement in those days as was their policy in the light of socialist humanism and a humanist reading of Marxism. In this climate, and in the context of current political requirements, the traditional, austere stereotype of Marxism—sometimes pushed almost to the edge of a mechanistic conception of man—was not only sanctioned but made even more rigid.

Finally, and this is the most interesting point. It has only been since the last war, in the light of a retrospective assessment of fascism and the ghastly experiences of the war, and more recently —and this is of particular significance for the Marxist in the light of the experiences and lessons of the so-called "cult of personality" period in the world communist movement that there have accumulated sufficient incentives to recognize the problems of the individual, his destiny, and his relationships with society as a question of predominant or at least major importance. And by the same token, there emerged conditions not only for an adequate appreciation of the importance of Marx's early writings but also for a refinement of Marxism with their help, for a reconsideration of its ideas and objectives and its endowment with a clear and considered humanistic meaning. The current "fashion" for the young Marx is not just a matter of snobbism, though this has played its part; nor can it merely be put down to revisionist tendencies, although they, too, have played a certain role; and it is not only the result of confusion or bemusement by a strange ideology, although there was no shortage of this as well. But all these are incidental factors of secondary importance, and to restrict the problem to them is to miss the point, which is that under certain conditions there arose a social demand for the questions tackled by the young Marx; various people, not necessarily Marxists, saw that there was something extremely topical in these issues. And so they began to "discover" Marx. What still remains to be explained is why this happened. How was it possible? Why did it come about today?

Problems of the philosophy of man, and particularly the question of the relationship between the individual and society, become historically important when the stabilized social order begins to waver and when, together with it, the socially accepted system of values is shaken. As long as the social machinery functions without friction, as long as—to use a Marxist phrase—there is harmony between the forces of production and the relations of production, the individual, formed as he is by these social relations, tends to regard them as natural; in the same way he accepts the prevailing norms of social intercourse by which his relationships with society are regulated. This is a very simple process, and in most cases it takes place unconsciously since people, through their upbringing within a social group, receive from society a language, a definite way to see the world, a way of thinking, and a system of values with its habits, customs, and morals. It is only the collapse of the social order, the rise of objective conflicts within the base, and consequently in the superstructure, the upsetting and disintegration of a traditionally accepted system of values that make the individual begin to consider his separate identity and to ask about his relationships with other individuals and with society. What makes a decent life? This is a question that, in various forms, has always faced human beings. But in times of revolution or of transition from one socio-economic system to another, when there is both a breakdown in the traditional relations between the individual and society and also the arduous formation of new ones, this question asserts itself before makind with particular force. People become acutely aware that they are no longer able or willing to live in the old way, without yet knowing how they should live. Such periods encourage the individual to reflect on his status and his destiny; and they stimulate the development of a philosophy of man. Historically, these have been the periods of an "explosion" of this kind of inquiry, when the Socratic current in the history of philosophy, for which man is the primary object, has driven out the Democritean current, the philosophy of nature for which the overriding task is to investigate and formulate the general laws governing reality.

That historical conflicts play an important role in the conflicts of human consciousness was clearly seen in the past, and is also seen today by those thinkers to whom man and his problems are the main subject of inquiry.

The doctrine of an unhappy, torn consciousness was the work of Hegel; today, in quite different conditions, his thoughts are approvingly repeated by Jean Hyppolite:

> But the critical periods in history are those in which the old order is already no more than a semblance, and the new one has not yet emerged. These periods of transition that precede revolution are also periods of spiritual anguish. The dialectic reaches the mind only as a negative dialectic. Its positive side, which is the opposite of the negative, has yet to be perceived. Since the time of Hegel,

attention has repeatedly been drawn to the crises preceding great changes in accepted values. But Hegel's analysis seems to us particularly original for its time.[4]

More than a century ago, in 1845—when Marx was working on his earliest writings—Sören Kierkegaard observed in his diary that periods preceding great changes see the appearance of men who, like plovers, the birds that announce the coming of rain with their singing, are capable of predicting the imminent social storm.[5]

According to Hans Schoeps, this can apply to many thinkers of that period (and, let me add, certainly to Marx) who, long before their contemporaries, correctly foresaw the crisis of the age and the breakdown of the existing system of values.

These sentiments were surely expressed most forcefully and with striking clarity by a contemporary observer of events, Alexis de Tocqueville:

> It is obvious to me that those who for sixty years have been predicting the end of the revolution, are in error. It is quite clear today that the waves are still rising, and the last dams are threatened by the sea; that not only have we not seen the end of that powerful revolution which began before we were born but it is also probable that a child who receives his first glimpse of the light of today will not see it either. What is involved is no longer a change, but a complete transformation of the social system. Where is the world heading? Frankly, I do not know and I think that this is beyond all of us. We only know that the old world is drawing to an end. What will the new world be like? Even the greatest minds of our time cannot tell, just as the minds of the ancients could not foresee the end of slavery, the advent of the Christian world, the invasion of the barbarians—in short, all of those great events which changed the face of the earth.[6]

These words, written by de Tocqueville in 1850 to a friend, vividly convey the state of mind of those people who were then concerned with the question of the individual and his relationship to a rapidly changing society. And their name was legion. It was precisely this problem, under the comprehensive name of humanism, that was the dominant note in the circles in which Karl Marx moved and in a sense it fashioned his attitudes. Feuerbach, Moses Hess, Bruno Bauer, Max Stirner, and many others, including the young Marx, all were preoccupied with these questions, which they regarded as of the utmost importance. How can man, who has been turned into a slave of his alienated products, be made a free creator of his destiny? How can man secure a full and unrestricted development of his personality? How can he create the most favorable conditions for human happiness and transform human existence into something in keeping with the human ideal, with "essence" of man (or, in the language of those days, transform the actual man into the true man)?

On closer inspection, the problems then tackled by the proponents of humanistic tendencies prove to be still extraordinarily relevant. Here is man faced by an alienated world in which his own works—in the field of economy, politics, ideology (particularly religion), and social life (particularly the family)—are acquiring a certain independence; they no longer submit to the individual's power and will but, on the contrary, begin to dominate and subjugate him. Like the devil's disciple, man has unleashed forces he is unable to control. Hence the need is to transform this inhuman world, in which things rule men, into a human world—a world of free human beings who are architects of their destiny and for whom man is the supreme good. A humanism of this kind is a theory of happiness. The prime objective is to make people happy, *to make them capable of happiness*.

In taking up these problems, Marx was in no way breaking new ground; nor was he isolated in his endeavors. On the contrary, in Lenin's fine phrase, he was following the broad highway of the issues and thoughts of his age. This was one of the reasons for his greatness and one of the sources of his relevance today. It explains why he seems so close to us when we ask these questions today.

For while the problems studied by the young Marx and his contemporaries had a wider historical validity, reaching far back into the past, they made themselves particularly felt in his time. It was obvious to everybody—and the memories of the French Revolution were a painful reminder—that the old world was drawing to an end. The new world was still emergent, revealing and aggravating the basic contradictions. The old system of values had collapsed and the new was in a formative stage, provoking protests and conflicts. The problem of the individual—lost and craving stability, oppressed and pining for freedom, exploited and longing to live a full life, lacerated and thirsting for happiness—stood out more sharply than ever in clear and vivid relief. It became the salient question of an age of change and revolution.

And it is this that makes these issues touch so sensitive a chord today, in a situation that is different but similar, in an age of incomparably sharper conflicts and contradictions that are, however, analogous to the old ones.

Marx and his contemporaries—Kierkegaard among them— asked questions about human existence and advanced various humanist programs because this existence was clearly threatened and because society explicitly demanded answers to certain problems. Hegel wrote that no philosophy can go beyond the limits of its age. But this idea can also be put positively: each philosophy, and certainly any philosophy that finds response, provides answers to actual questions and problems. This is why problems of the individual are also tackled by us today in a variety of philosophical guises, and why the young Marx's work seems so close.

The dominance of human themes in modern philosophy arises out of the demand for answers concerning human existence at a time when this existence is in danger, and when, at the watershed between two forms of society, the traditional systems of value have been undermined. On this point there is a consensus of opinion among all students of the subject who are otherwise very far apart, if not diametrically opposed, in their philosophical convictions.

Here is the view of a communist, Roger Garaudy:

> The two world wars have had a decisive influence on the formation and development of the existentialist philosophies. Above all, it was largely due to them that all philosophies—atheist existentialism, Christian philosophy,

Marxism—had to become philosophies of existence because the foundations of human existence had been ques-
tioned and the answer could no longer be delayed. There
is no modern, living philosophy which does not reflect
this human situation, the situation of all men, thrown into
general conflicts and unknown destinies, facing a continuous threat of death, experiencing an anxiety generalized
to the scale of the events which engender it.[7]

At the other pole of philosophy we find Martin Buber, who in
my view has provided one of the most interesting analyses of the
problem—all the more interesting as it was formulated before the
outbreak of the Second World War and thus before the war's consequences for man's situation in the world today were known.

In *Le problème de l'homme*,[8] Buber speaks of ebbs and flows in
the philosophy of man's thought that depend on man's sense of
isolation. If an explanation were added of the source of this isolation and the reason why man feels "homeless" in an abruptly changing world in which human relations and their underlying systems
of values undergo revolutionary changes, then one could fully agree
with this diagnosis.

But it is only in our times, says Buber, that the human problem
has fully matured. He thinks that, apart from the evolution and
crystallization of philosophical thought in general, this is due to two
factors.

First comes the sociological factor: the disintegration of the traditional forms of humans living together, such as the family, the
rural and urban communities, etc., as a result of the bourgeois
revolution.

Second, and this is in my view the most interesting part of his
argument, man has lost control over the world he has himself created—the phenomenon that Marx with Hegel once called alienation.

This concerns the relationships between man and the
objects and relations which arose out of his activity or
with his participation. Man lets himself be overtaken by
his own works—here is exactly how I would describe this

particular feature of the modern crisis. Man is no longer
in a position to take in the world created by his own activity; this world is getting the upper hand of him, slipping out of his hands, opposing him in all its elementary
independence, and man no longer knows the magic word
which could put a curse on the man-made Golem and
make him harmless.[9]

His wording may be different, but Buber is referring to the same
developments that preoccupied the young Marx and his contemporaries when they analyzed the status of the individual in relation
to the great upheavels of their age. He is discussing the same phenomenon when later he speaks of technology, economics, and politics as the principal domains in which the ascendancy of man-made
things and relations over man is revealed.

In Buber's analysis, the problem is placed in particularly sharp
relief in the case of politics—in the light of the experiences of the
First World War. Naturally, his words take no account of the appalling experience of the Second World War and its aftermath, or
of the sword of Damocles now hanging over mankind in the form
of atomic annihilation.

And so man found himself confronted with a sinister
fact: he was giving life to demons which he could not
then subjugate. What was the meaning of this power
which was at the same time powerless? The problem was
reduced to the question about the nature of man, which
was acquiring a new, supremely practical significance.[10]

And surely this is where the essence of the problem lies: in our
days philosophy of man has acquired a practical meaning. It explains why such inquiries exploded after the First and even more
after the Second World War—an interesting socio-psychological
phenomenon emphasized by both Buber and Garaudy.

In the twenties, Martin Heidegger summed up the position in
these pointed words:

In no age before has so much knowledge about man
been accumulated and never has it been so diversified.

> But in no age before have we known so little about man.
> In no period before has man been the object of so many
> questions as in our time.[11]

Symptoms of alienation long have been present in society—probably ever since the inception of social life—but never have they been so drastic and powerful as they are today in all possible forms: economic, political, social, and ideological.

Throughout history, human existence has always been subject to various dangers, but never before has this threat acquired such tremendous dimensions and never has it been fraught with such terrifying consequences for the existence of mankind as today.

Naturally, in the past, too, systems of values have been rocked. But never before has this been so universal and far-reaching as today when in one part of the world the conviction is growing that the old systems of values, though publicly venerated, have outlived themselves and are *no longer* useful, while in the other part men are harassed by a situation in which new systems have not yet been consolidated and thus are *not yet* as useful as they should be.

Small wonder then that the individual feels threatened, insecure, frightened, that he does not feel organically united with society and consequently feels lonely and isolated. These are normal things at a time of change and of a weakening of relations among men. But it is also normal that in such periods man tends to wonder about himself and to ponder questions that are otherwise hardly noticed; it is at such times that the role and importance of philosophical anthropology grow. In Buber's fine words:

> In the history of the human spirit I distinguish ages
> when man has a home and those in which he is homeless.
> In the former he inhabits the world like a house, in the
> latter he lives in the world as in an open field, sometimes
> even without the four pegs necessary to put up a tent. In
> the former anthropological thought is only part of cosmo-
> logical thinking, in the latter it becomes profound, and
> thus independent.[12]

It is precisely at such a historical juncture—when men live in society not as in a house but as in an open field—that our world finds itself today, particularly since the Second World War and the beginning of the atomic age. Given the pressure of the many questions about man that have become urgent, the publication of the previously unknown writings of the young Marx was a genuine discovery. After all, the problems raised by Marx are analogous to those exercising us today, the issues he discussed remain extremely relevant, and the solutions he suggested are bound to appeal to people's minds. Suddenly a new Marx, quite different from the familiar stereotype, was revealed; suddenly new aspects of Marxism, unknown to the uninitiated, were perceived. The fashionable "career" of the young Marx, Marxian humanism, and the philosophy of man, particularly in the last two decades, has not just been a matter of snobbism, or revisionism, or a cunning attack on the scientific character of modern socialism. The chief factor has been the genuine compulsiveness of the problems, the freshness and immediacy of the issues discussed, particularly of the broadly conceived question of alienation. It is precisely these problems that have made Marxism so attractive to the masses of the intelligentsia —particularly young people—and to such thinkers as Sartre, Merleau-Ponty, and even Heidegger. But what is surely most important is that these problems have attracted Marxists themselves, have changed their vision of Marxism, and in the light of the experiences of the "cult of personality" period, have affected not only the theory but also the practice of Marxism. Marxist humanism is becoming an increasingly powerful ideological weapon—both outside and inside the working class movement. It is an element of propaganda for socialism and of the socialist education of men.

But what, in the final analysis, is the crux of the matter? Is it Marxism in general, or merely the theory of the young Marx, treated not only apart from, but even in opposition to, the mature thought of Marx? Or, to put it in a different way: is the recent vogue enjoyed by Marxian humanism and the Marxist philosophy of man, especially of Marx's theory of alienation, a genuine *Marxism* signifying a spreading and strengthening of its influence, or is it something that implies the rejection of what has been traditionally known as Marxism?

This question is by no means fanciful. It is closely connected with the way in which the relationship between the young and the mature Marx is interpreted—not only by revisionists or anti-Marxists, but also by "orthodox" Marxists. This alone would be a sufficient reason for close analysis of the matter. But there are other and surely more positive reasons preeminent among which is surely the desire to penetrate more deeply into the essence of Marxist thought.

But into two different Marxisms, or only one? These questions have serious and interesting methodological implications whose scope reaches far beyond the problem of Marx and Marxism. But they also have a crucial practical meaning; indeed our approach to Marxism, our understanding of its message, has both theoretical implications and practical implications in the field of action.

A study of the *Manuscripts* on the one hand, and of *Capital* or the historical writings such as *The 18th Brumaire* on the other, reveals two obviously different types of writing—with regard both to their content and to their intellectual style. No doubt the same could be said after comparing such philosophical works as the *Manuscripts* and *The German Ideology* with, for example, Engels's *Anti-Dühring* or his *Ludwig Feuerbach*. Taken at its face value, the theory of two different stages in the development of Marx's thought —and thus of two Marxes and two Marxisms—is not without foundation. But this claim can be seen to be superficial and so false, when subjected, as it should be to a historical, genetic analysis, and when it is borne in mind that the elements of a whole cannot be analyzed in isolation, or out of their context. If this background is ignored and if the methodological requirement of historical analysis is not properly understood, the evidence may easily suggest not only differences in the various stages of Marx's evolution but even contradictions.

The claim for two Marxes—the young and the mature—and for two Marxisms—the humanist and the dogmatic materialist—has been argued over the years in various forms and with various motives.

There is no doubt that an important factor in this respect was the spell cast by the new Marxian writings in the first years after their publication. While little was known in those years about their relationship with his later works, people were carried away by the unfamiliar nature of their humanist, ethical, individualist approach to human problems, so different from the stereotyped image of the economic and sociological Marxism, particularly in the rigid and narrow form of the 1930s. After all, such turning points in the evolution of a thinker's work have happened before in history; there often comes a moment when a completely new stage begins, quite opposed to the past. This has, for instance, been the case with religious thinkers turned atheist, or vice versa.

Apart from this fascination, coupled as it was with a poor knowledge of the history of early Marxian thought, there was doubtless, at least in certain cases, a deliberate desire to replace the scientific motivation of Marxism with an ethical, humanist one—in any case with an approach that would shift the emphasis from the sphere of description and laws into that of values and commands. This fitted in much better with the background of idealist philosophy held by some of the supporters of such views about Marxism and socialism. Another reason—perhaps not always fully realized —was that this change of ground facilitated the battle against Marxism. It is one thing when socialism justifies its *raison d'être* merely with the help of moral arguments based on the accepted system of values; when this is the case, it can be rebutted by other reasons based on other systems of values. But the situation is quite different when, to justify its *raison d'être,* socialism invokes the objective laws of social development and thereby takes scientific analysis as the basis for its actions. The latter is certainly a more difficult situation for an opponent of Marxist socialism: to oppose scientific arguments, suitable counter-arguments must be used and this—as history has shown—is not so easy in the case of Marxism. Consciously or unconsciously, the various intellectual adversaries of Marxism were undoubtedly motivated by a class-determined dislike of the revolutionary feature of Marxism.

In the 1930s, this also was the dominant element in the specifically ethical-humanist interpretation of Marxism based on Marx's early writings. Landshut and Mayer, Marcuse, and de Man all display a similar tendency: by attacking the narrow, rigid, official interpretation of Marxism of the communist theorists of the thirties (and these attacks were, unfortunately, not only easy but frequently well-founded), they tried to force through an extreme, moralizing concept of Marxism, which would lead in fact to an elimination of everything known as scientific socialism. This was authentic, classical revisionism.

In 1926 Hendrik de Man published his much publicized book *The Psychology of Socialism* or *Zur Psychologie des Socialismus* (the title of the original French edition is even more emphatic: *Au delà du marxisme*), in which he flatly dissociated himself from Marxism. Six years later, in 1932—the year when the full text of the *Manuscripts* was published for the first time—an article by de Man appeared in *Der Kampf,* the organ of the Austromarxists; its title, "Der neu entdeckte Marx," [13] is particularly significant in the context of our discussion. The initial argument is so characteristic that it needs to be quoted in full. Any attempt to summarize it would be liable to incur charges of bias:

> Early this year an unknown work of Marx was published, and it is of decisive importance for a correct appraisal of the meaning and progress of Marx's teaching. It will force many supporters and opponents of Marxism to revise their opinions, at least with regard to the historico-philosophical foundations of Marx's thinking. For it reveals with greater clarity than any other of Marx's writings the ethical-humanist motivation which determined his socialist attitude and the value-judgments of his entire scientific life-work.
>
> It is true that what is primarily involved is merely a certain phase in the development of Marx's thought; consequently, it is an open question whether this "humanist" phase should be regarded as a preliminary stage which was later overcome, or as a lasting, integral part of Marx's theory. But the question itself cannot be evaded. The orthodox Marxists—who until now have considered the whole achievement of Marx's life (at least since

1843) as one system and supported their interpretation of this system with quotations from both *The Civil War in France* (1871) and the *Critique of Hegel's Philosophy of Right* (1843)—will now have to decide: either this humanist Marx belongs to Marxism, and if so both the Marxism of Kautsky and of Bukharin will have to be thoroughly revised, or it does not—and then there is a humanist Marxism which can be invoked against materialist Marxism.

But the heretics to Marxist orthodoxy (with whom I stand) are confronted with the question to what extent have they the right to invoke Marx himself in their criticism of what in "Marxism" stems from his work? [14]

This is both interesting and reasonable. Incidentally, my study of Marxological literature has convinced me that such interesting and sensible comments on Marxism can often be found in writers who are critical or even deeply hostile to it. In any case, I have learned a great deal from them as far as my understanding of Marxism is concerned.

This does not mean, of course, that the very same writer cannot also be found making obviously false, even ridiculous statements. In the same article, de Man, for example, says that the most valuable achievements of Marx's thought belong to 1843, so the "true" Marx is the author of the *Manuscripts,* not of *Capital.* This idea was reproduced in many variants by other writers in the thirties. There was nothing new or original in similar views propounded after the last war—in Poland it was particularly in 1956–58—when the young Marx was described as "authentic" and the mature Marx as "dogmatic."

What is interesting, however, is that all these writers stress the significance of the young Marx's works for a proper understanding of the essence and drift of all his later work. This view—although it was put forth with distinctly revisionist purposes—I regard as not only correct but extremely important.

De Man wrote in the same article:

It is essential to realize that in the Manuscripts, and

more broadly in his works between 1843 and 1846, Marx revealed sentiments and judgments which are at the basis of all his later work, including his research, and endow it with its proper meaning. Whatever one may think of the intellectual structure of their formulation and their logical position within historical materialism, these value-judgments and sentiments shed light on the motives from which Marxian materialism arose, and thus also on its goals and meaning. If Marxism is conceived as a living force, rather than being restricted to a dogma or system, and if its origin is not treated separately from Marx's personality, or the history of its transformations from the steadily changing world and the resultant objectives, *then the Marx of 1844 belongs to Marxism just as the Marx of 1867, and certainly the Engels of 1890.*[15]

To these interesting remarks on the work of the young Marx as a guide to the motives by which Marx was led and on the goals and sense of Marxism, I intend to return below. They are most significant.

The same trend of thought is even more explicit in the statements by S. Landshut and J. P. Mayer, both of whom are regarded as belonging to the same group as de Man. In their view (as is rightly stressed by a number of students of Marxian thought, and as I fully believe) the key to Marx's economic theory can be found in his anthropology, his theory of man, without which the economics is limited and impotent. Let me quote the relevant passage, since it will help us in the further course of our argument.

In these works of the forties Marx was, step by step, uncovering a whole horizon of historical conditions and securing the human foundation without which his exposition of economic relationships would have remained only the *tour de force* of a shrewd economist. Anyone who has not mastered the inner pattern of the intellectual effort contained in these early writings, pervading as it does the *whole* of Marx's work, will always lag behind Marx in his understanding. These works are of fundamental importance for an appreciation of Marx's inner development.[16]

All these quotations suggest a general observation which, though it may seem a truism by itself, is by no means platitudinous in the light of certain traditions and judgments current among Marxists: the *political* position of a thinker does not necessarily prejudge the question of whether his views on Marxism are right or wrong. Primitive sociologizing, in which the question of truth is made a simple and direct function of class commitment, is here no less misguided and harmful than in other cases.

The view that there are two Marxisms and that the young Marx is different from the mature Marx is defended not only by those revisionists who, denying the scientific nature of Marxism, acclaim the young Marx as the only "true" one, but also by those who, seemingly from orthodox positions, draw a line between the young and the mature Marx. According to this theory, the works of the young Marx were not yet free of the influence of Hegelian idealism and of Feuerbach; and he was only on the threshold of the transition to socialism. His works do not reflect his mature thought and cannot be regarded as part of the finished Marxist system. Such an approach not only sets the young against the mature Marx, but simply eliminates the former as a negligible quality; at the most, some thoughts or expressions are extracted from Marx's early works as predicting his later achievements. Such an "interpretation" of the development of Marxism inevitably leads to a denial of the key importance of Marxian anthropology for the understanding of the whole system, of its essence and meaning. Unfortunately, what was often clearly seen and understood—in spite of all their errors—by writers from the revisionist camp long remained a sealed book to their critics and opponents from the orthodox school of interpreters of the revolutionary spirit of Marxism. This poses an interesting problem in the psychology and sociology of science; and let us illustrate it with a specific example.

The Protestant philosopher Erich Thier published Marx's *Manuscripts* with a lengthy preface that later appeared as a separate book, *Das Menschenbild des jungen Marx* (1957). [17] "The young

Marx is a discovery of our times," Thier says in the introduction to this book.

> While in previous years any argument about or against Marx concerned his later works—*Capital* above all— and was sociologically and economically oriented in its political aspects as well, now it centers around the "real humanism" of Marx. What does this mean? When Marx, in his formative period, went beyond philosophical discourse in the narrow sense and saw that he was above all confronted with social realities, he found man homeless and "a stranger to himself." His concern for this man haunted him; and this concern was the driving force behind his effort to "come to terms with himself." This cannot be separated from his problem of whether and how "self-alienation" can be transcended and man, freed from it, "emancipated." In the course of this coming to terms with himself, Marx's thinking more and more systematically became a highly coherent theory. That this actually was the Marxian system in its original form was only brought home to us in 1932 when many of the previously unknown sketches from his stay in Paris in 1843–45 were published; these are now know as the "Parisian *Economic Philosophic Manuscripts*." [18]

In 1960, L. N. Pazhitnov's work *At the Sources of a Revolutionary Turn in Philosophy* [19] was published in the Soviet Union. It should be stressed that it is a study of sources, written with expert knowledge and historical insight. Among other things, the author discusses Thier's views on the significance of the young Marx's anthropology as a key to the understanding of his later evolution and the meaning of his socialism. (Pazhitnov, it is true, quotes Thier's earlier preface to his edition of the *Manuscripts,* but as already pointed out, the book on the young Marx's picture of man is only an enlarged version of this preface.) Here is what Pazhitnov has to say on the subject:

> So what does this "guiding idea" which, according to

the author [Thier], is contained in the *Manuscripts,* represent for the understanding of the essence of Marxism? It is here that the author has something "new" to say. The "guiding idea," it appears, is that in the *Manuscripts* the *"understanding of the essence and tasks of man as such"* is revealed as the main source of "Marx's whole view of the world." The *Manuscripts* show that in working out his view of the world—"reaching as far as the problems of creation and the ultimate goal in the realm of nature, society, and history"—Marx focuses upon "man and his sense of life," that is upon a "philosophico-sociological anthropology."

A century ago the doctrine of such an anthropologism could be found as a philosophical doctrine in Feuerbach, and later in Tshernyshevsky, as one of the forms of materialism. In modern conditions, however, the anthropological principle as preached by E. Thier has become one of the chief foundations of existentialism—a variety of irrationalist, idealist bourgeois philosophy, very fashionable in the West.[20]

It is not my intention to discuss Pazhitnov's views on the question of philosophical anthropology, its present role in general, and in Marxism in particular; in my opinion they are a collection of errors on fundamental questions in the diagnosis of the modern philosophical situation. I only wanted to illustrate what I have said above. Let me simply add that although I consider myself wholly a Marxist and, politically, am certainly close to Pazhitnov's views and remote from Thier's, it is not Pazhitnov but rather Thier who is right in his ideas of the young Marx's anthropology. I even fear that Pazhitnov's sarcasm with regard to Marx's anthropology and its place in the whole of the Marxist system is proof of a profound misunderstanding of Marxism that can be harmful in its practical effects.[21]

The attempts to contrast the young with the mature Marx— either through acclaiming the former as the only "authentic" one or making the same exclusive claim for the latter—were bound to provoke the counter-argument that the work of Karl Marx is an integral whole, which cannot, without flouting the basic premises of historical study (and I may add, of common sense), be divided into parts that are not so much different as cut off from each other, or even ideologically opposed. It is this position that I intend to uphold in my further remarks. But before I can do so with a clear conscience, I must first radically dissociate myself from a certain regrettable direction that the defense of this case has taken.

According to some students of the problem—and I have encountered such views, although they are relatively rare, both in print and in conversation—in order to demonstrate the integral nature of Marxist thought, it is necessary and sufficient to show that in the various stages of Marx's development we have to do with *the same* themes and *the same* terminology. The following operation is then carried out: a certain problem is selected, for example, the question of alienation or the essence of man; the spiritual development of Marx is divided into periods; and, finally, it is investigated whether the given problem (or even the terminology) can be found in the various periods. In most cases they can indeed —"seek and ye shall find." Only the value of such a "proof" is negligible, if only because similar does not mean identical. Quite different, sometimes even opposed philosophies are concerned with similar questions, such as the problem of man; but far from this being proof of their "organic unity," they are more often poles apart. This is even more true of similarities in terminology. It is common knowledge that the same phonetic form may conceal different meanings and that to discover this primitive homonymity of words is one of the primary concerns of semantic analysis. Such a "demonstration" of the unity of Marxist thought is, consequently, not only methodologically wrong but also based on false semantic premises. As I have said, such views are rare but out of pure caution they should be borne in mind.

The question of unity—or lack of unity—in the development of Marx's theory must be approached historically. "Historical" does not, however, mean only investigation of the *sources* of certain ideas and opinions, although this undoubtedly constitutes a very important element of any historical analysis in this field of research. "Historical" has a far wider significance, tantamount to "evolutionary," "dynamic." Now we know how to study evolution and dynamics—and this requirement is clearly part of the method of Marxian historicism—from the point of view of the *effects* of certain phenomena in the historical process. How often it is that the historical place and importance of phenomena can only be ascertained ex post facto, after the consequences have revealed themselves in certain cause-and-effect connections. This is not only because contemporaries are shortsighted; in many cases the resolution of a hugely confused knot of events simply cannot be foreseen. This knot is one that is, in addition, beclouded by the passions of immediate participation and emotional commitment. As already pointed out, history is rewritten in various periods not only because new sources become accessible, but also because the newly appearing effects of past events make possible a new appraisal of the past. This was the meaning of Marx's metaphor that human anatomy is the key to the anatomy of the ape; what he meant was the methodological postulate that the full meaning of history can only be grasped ex post facto. This approach is in no way teleological; it is not asserted that the character of events is determined by the objectives whose realization they serve. What is claimed is that it is only the fully developed consequences of the given happenings that make possible a proper appraisal of their historical meaning as causes in the chain of events. This is, of course, quite different from teleology, and it is embarrassing to find participants in a discussion missing such an elementary point.[22]

The problem is must better understood by Bogdan Suchodolski, who says in his Preface to *Narodziny nowożytnej filozofil czlowieka* (*The Origins of the Modern Philosophy of Man*):

> The starting point for this selection [of Renaissance ideas important for the further development of the philosophy of man] are the later links in this evolution of the idea of man which carries over into our age and for which even wider horizons have been opened up by the modern era. As in many other branches of history so in

the history of ideas the later stages of development allow
for a better appreciation of the character and problems
of the earlier stages. We understand history not only by
the study of its sources but also by investigating its
fruits.[23]

When "historical" is so widely interpreted, the problem of the
unfolding of Marxian thought becomes relatively simple. Here we
have a thinker who was creatively active for more than forty years.
In this time, he underwent an evolution that led him, in philosophy,
from idealism to materialism, and in politics, from bourgeois de-
mocratism and liberalism to communism. We can easily distinguish
the various periods of this evolution and of the formation of his
views; but at the same time we can see with greater clarity how
they interlock and how each determines the next. The question is:
what is the relationship between Marx's first period of development
and his maturity?

The suggestion that we are dealing with two wholly different
systems of opinions must, of course, be rejected in view of the continuity of development, against which no reasonable argument has
so far been produced, and—the most important point—in view of
the continuity of the basic theme of the system, no matter how the
approach and the solutions offered may change.

Obviously—as has been stressed above—we must also reject
the idea that the views in question remain the same because of the
similarity of the motivation and terms found in the various periods
of their development. For it is always possible for similar topics to
be approached and solved in a different, even opposed, manner.

In my view, there is only one sensible suggestion: the first period
is genetically linked to the later ones, for it was then that the
problems emerged to whose solution Marx's entire life was devoted.
There is, in effect, a continuity of the basic issue that constitutes the
axis of the system—although this is not wholly apparent when the
various parts or phases of this system are analyzed in isolation. If
this is so, as I am sure it is, our thesis has a great heuristic value,
since such an integral approach makes it easier to properly understand the thought of Marx in his maturity; only when illuminated

with the ideas of his youth, the ideas of his philosophical anthropology, does his mature thought show all its wealth and its inherent meaning. This, I maintain, has a fundamental importance not only for the theory, but also for the practice of socialism, which is bound by a thousand threads with its theoretical and ideological foundation.

Marx, let me say again, answered the questions posed by his age and remained within the broad compass of its concerns when, like most of his contemporary thinkers, he took up the problem of the individual and of his relations with nature and society as the chief problem of his philosophical considerations. His philosophical anthropology stemmed from his vision of the conflicts of the individual in a world whose system of values was collapsing, a world shaken by the difficulties involved in the transition from one social formation to another.

In his analysis of man's situation in those days, Marx, naturally enough, echoed the philosophical concerns of his age and the current terminology—humanism, and the concept of alienation. In doing so he wanted to express his absorption with those particular relationships in which man's various products begin to dominate their creator. To Marx these relations, in which man's actions and products become not only objectified and reified but also alienated —that is, they assume an autonomous existence and subordinate man to themselves—were the paramount issue of the age. This was shown by the social realities around him, in which alienation was laid bare with especial starkness by the advances of capitalism. It was so obvious that criticism of these relations on behalf of the human individual was not only undertaken by revolutionary thinkers, but also by such conservative writers as Balzac and Carlyle.

Marx's analysis of the various types of alienation—religious, political, ideological, economic—and their hierarchy is not just an academic exercise of contemplation; his primary concern is to find a way out, to overcome alienation. As a result, he arrived at a position that he called realistic humanism, but I would prefer to call militant humanism. It was in this period that Marx identified the central issues in the sphere of problems that were to preoccupy him till the end of his life and formulated theoretical propositions whose development by the power of their inner logic led him to historical materialism in theory and to communism in politics.

It was then also that Marx saw economic problems, in the widest sense of the word, in their *anthropological* aspect: here was the basic form of alienation underlying all its secondary manifestations; here was the field in which it was necessary to look for the means to its defeat and thereby to guarantee the fullest development of human personality and create the best conditions for personal happiness. At this stage, Marx was only just beginning to study economics, to which he was drawn both for practical reasons (as editor of the *Rheinische Zeitung* he had come across several economic problems with social and political implications) and from theoretical considerations (as a consequence of his speculations about anthropology). His letters from these days contain express references to this gap in his education and to the need to make good his knowledge. So he set about those studies that remained with him for the rest of his life.

But although he devoted his life to it, Marx did not see economics as an end in itself. He had been and remained a philosopher and sociologist for whom the problem of man was a central problem. And it is precisely in this light that his concentration on economics becomes understandable. But in the same light, his creative achievement acquires meaning and importance that are lost when Marx's economic doctrine is severed from the whole complex of his views.

Let us try to follow Marx along the path of his thought and draw the logical conclusions from it.

We proceed on the assumption (and an analysis of Marx's views in those days puts this beyond doubt) that alienation is the chief issue of conflict in society and that our task is to eliminate it. Further investigation reveals not only the diversity of the various forms of alienation, but also their specific hierarchy—a ladder, as it were, with that complex of relations known as economic alienation at its base. The central fact is the private ownership of the means of production, determining as it does the particular forms of the division of labor as well as the alienation of the very process of labor and of its product the commodity. Private property is the pivot of the exploitation of man by man, the class division of society and its resultant political institutions, the state above all.

What conclusions can be drawn from this anthropological argument?

The first is acceptance of communism as a movement bent on the overthrow of a society based on relations of economic alienation. This is absolutely clear: if the aim is to create the best conditions for the development of human personality and its happiness, and if the road to this goal is barred by economic alienation, institutionalized as it is in the form of private ownership of the means of production, the main line of attack must be against the principle of private property. This means acceptance of the communist program as a consequence of a certain anthropological theory and specifically of a certain theory of happiness.

Another consequence is concentration of one's intellectual endeavors on political economy. If the struggle is to be waged against economic alienation, and if the main blow is to be dealt at property relations, then the mechanism of these relations with all their concrete social manifestations have to be known with precision. In other words, as Marx himself declared, it is necessary to examine the anatomy of bourgeois society. But at the same time this means that economic studies are not an end in themselves but only a means to an end; and thus the effort to solve economic problems and to settle the political issues so closely connected with them are only a means of fulfilling the central aim—*the liberation of man.*

Seen thus, the humanist meaning of Marxism stands out in all its clarity, and it becomes possible to illuminate the later works with the humanism of the young Marx. Such a genetic analysis is of great heuristic value, since, instead of the ludicrous doctrine of two Marxisms and the equally nonsensical claim that Marxism is one and invariable, it yields us a moderate and fruitful proposition about Marx: that in the course of his development the problems he studied and the manner in which he treated them changed. But since the question of the liberation of man remained the chief object of research and action during his whole life, his mature thought can and should be interpreted in the light of his philosophical anthropology, whose premises and principles were consciously formulated in his youth. This anthropology explains Marx's later interest in various problems such as economy; it also provides a key to the humanist meaning of the later statements of scientific socialism, such as the theory of class struggle or the dictatorship of the proletariat.

It does not follow from this that the work of the young Marx can be regarded as a mature and self-contained form of Marxism, that can easily be separated from the context of his later doctrine. Far from it: to the over-enthusiastic "admirers" of the young Marx, it must be emphasized that this early work, though unquestionably stamped by genius, lacked maturity, and so was often eclectic and certainly confused and imprecise—which indeed was typical of the intellectual atmosphere among the Young Hegelians. If Marx had stopped writing in 1845–46, he would not—in spite of those who hold the young Marx to be the only "true" one—have found a place in history. All this means that Marx's texts from the 1840s cannot be quoted indiscriminately alongside those from the 1870s as if they carried equal cognitive weight as parts of one and the same doctrine. On the other hand, the work of the young Marx can and should be employed as a clue to the interpretation and illumination of the humanist meaning of the specialized parts of his mature theory.

It is in this sense that the young Marx's anthropology can be considered a key to his economics and analogously to his whole mature work. This view is shared by serious students of Marx's thought belonging to various schools and trends.

Thus, for example, Jean Hyppolite discusses in his essay on "Marxisme et philosophie" the two possible approaches to the problem of the relationship between the young and the mature Marx. He rejects as untenable any attempts to interpret Marx's views after 1847 as self-contained and lending themselves to separation from his earlier views; in contrast, he advocates an integral treatment of the whole opus and particularly an interpretation of Marx's economics from the viewpoint of his philosophy.

It can indeed be assumed that Marx only becomes intelligible on the basis of his philosophical works. . . .

> An economist who is ignorant of the dialectics of *aliena-tion* as shaped by Hegel and Feuerbach, like a philoso-pher unfamiliar with the *economic writings* of Engels which had so powerful an influence on Marx, cannot comprehend the dialectical movement which constitutes the essence of Capital. . . .[24]

Similar opinions are voiced by de Man, Landshut, and Thier, the last of whom adds a very interesting and, in my view, stimulat-ing remark: not only is the understanding of the mature Marx de-termined by his early writings, but vice versa; the meaning of the philosophical anthropology of the young Marx can only be grasped in the light of his later works.

More recently, the same attitude has been expressed by the American Marxologist Daniel Bell:

> The question why men were propertyless turned Marx to economics. For a man whose name is so inextricably linked with the "dismal science," Marx was never really interested in economics. His correspondence with Engels in later years is studded with contemptuous references to the subject and he resented the fact that his detailed ex-plorations prevented him from carrying on other studies. But he continued because, for him, economics was the practical side of philosophy—it would unveil the mystery of alienation—and because he had found in the cate-gories of political economy the material expression of that alienation: the process of economic exploitation.[25]

Thus there is full agreement as to the unity of Marxian thought among such diverse authors as Erich Fromm, Robert Tucker, Kostas Axelos, Pierre Bigo, and others, even though they do not deny that there are important differences among the various stages in its evolution. There is surely no need to mention Marxist writers for whom the matter should be completely clear.

I would like, however, to adduce the opinion of one more author: the Protestant philosopher Erwin Metzke, since it seems to add a new element to the discussion. Metzke wants to refute the charge that the role of the *Manuscripts* and other previously unknown works from the same period has been exaggerated because they were published only in 1932 and so could not have influenced the development of Marxist thought. This is his answer—which in my opinion is unassailable.

> It is precisely because of this that an important ob-
> jection is usually raised against invoking these manu-
> scripts and treating them with special attention. For since
> they were unknown before 1932 they could not have had
> any historical influence and are therefore, or so it is main-
> tained, without any importance for the understanding of
> Marxism. This somewhat rash opinion seems to overlook
> the fact that it is in these writings that we get to the roots,
> the deeply buried roots, from which Marx's thought drew
> the sap for its farthest ramifications. That the manu-
> scripts had not been brought to light does not reduce
> their fundamental importance, but in fact confirms it.
> Hegel's thought was also originally bred underground,
> and his example has taught us to understand how produc-
> tive and influential is the force of such a growth, invisible
> from the outside and only later revealed in its fruits, and
> how a new, integral approach to Hegel's philosophizing
> was later developed from this growth.[26]

This judgment applies remarkably well to the influence of the early Marxian writings on the present development of Marxism. One further point, though: this usually happens only when ob-jective conditions create a demand for certain ideas and encourage their renewed reception and dissemination.

We have already spoken of two consequences flowing from the anthropological thought of the young Marx—acceptance of com-munism and concentration of creative effort on analysis of the anatomy of bourgeois society. But there was a third consequence: a focusing of attention away from the problems of the individual and upon mass social movements. Paradoxical as it may seem, this transition from philosophical anthropology to sociology is not only a logical outcome of Marx's interest in man, but amounts to its consolidation.

Let us once more make an attempt to reconstruct the thinking of the young Marx. The task is to overcome economic alienation in all its various manifestations and effects and thus to ensure the best conditions for a development of the personality and happiness of the individual. But economic alienation has taken on the institutionalized form of property relations with their whole subservient apparatus for the defense of the class interests of those who have made these relations the basis of their rule in society and their exploitation of the propertyless classes. To liberate the individual and to overcome alienation, it is, therefore, necessary to effect a change in social relations and institutions, to overthrow them by overthrowing the prevalent pattern of class relations. Here economics is closely intertwined with social problems and politics. In this context, the problem of liberation of the individual can no longer be viewed in terms of spiritual self-improvement, although the significance of this requirement cannot be denied. But the problem has now become a social issue—the *struggle of social forces* committed for and against the existing relations of domination. For surely only an incurable dreamer or incorrigible optimist could believe that the rule of the exploiting classes can be overthrown and economic alienation eliminated in its most drastic form merely by moral self-improvement, by the preaching of virtue. Marx is a realist in this respect; he analyzes history, and on the basis of this analysis rejects the idealist mirages of his former philosophical allies: the objective can only be accomplished by the revolutionary struggle of great social forces. He builds uncompromisingly on this struggle and finds within bourgeois society a social force destined to carry out this task by its objective condition and its interests: the proletariat. It is then that Marx coined his famous dictum that philosophy is the ideological weapon of the proletariat—naturally a revolutionary philosophy—while the proletariat is the material arm and executor of the directives of this philosophy. In this way, proceeding from the problems of the individual and philosophical anthropology, advancing certain propositions concerning human happiness, Marx logically shifts his focus to the question of class movements, the question of class struggle. This is not only a corollary to the increasingly strong emphasis put on the economic analysis of bourgeois society, but also to his ever more profound anthropological self-knowledge. Less and less is said now about the individual, and what is said is put differently than before. Marx even ridicules his own way of philosophizing on the subject two or three years earlier, indeed less than a year earlier (after all, this can already be found in *The German Ideology*). But problems of the individual remain the dominant note; *they endow Marxian socialism with its profound sense*—if, of course, this socialism is properly understood and interpreted. And this precisely is the crucial point—from the viewpoint both of theory and of practice.

In some studies of Marxism, this approach has been clearly emphasized—and whatever we may think of their authors' views as a whole, scientific integrity enjoins us to give them due credit for this. Here is one of them, Kostas Axelos:

> However this may be, one must not forget that Marx, particularly in his youth, was capable of perceiving certain problems concerning the essence of man, his agonized humanity; the advocate of universal collectivization, of radical socialization, often paused to reflect on the drama of man, the wasted lives of individuals and of the individual within society. Human existence—and not only social structure or the stifling superstructure—was in his eyes a bleeding wound. *But Marx never dwelt on this vision—he was in a hurry to forge such weapons and tools as would eliminate the causes of suffering and, by shock treatment, to heal what required healing* . . . When the objective is reached human life will be transformed, all alienations giving birth to differences between private and public life will disappear, world history will become the history of men's polytechnical and universal activities. In this way the individual will cure his ills and society will no longer be based upon the exploitation of man by man. The reciprocal opposition between individ-

ual and society will disappear and so will the contradiction between spirit and matter, subject and object, nature and history.[27]

How true. Taking the problem of the individual as his starting point, Marx, in his search for a solution of the issues confronting him, concentrates all his attention on the social forces and movements that can provide this solution. The problem of man is no longer viewed in the same form as it was in his youth, and further analysis of his work may give rise to doubts whether the current of humanism and philosophical anthropology was not interrupted at a certain moment. Abundant evidence of such questionings can be found in contemporary literature of various schools and trends, the Marxists included.

The underlying reason for these doubts is to be sought in the fact that in its historical development Marxist thought for many years abandoned its direct interest in the philosophy of man, in philosophical anthropology.

This was so originally because the concretization of this anthropology—among other things, of the concept of the individual as enmeshed in society through the medium of classes and other social groups—as well as the fulfillment of its requirements demanded a closer association with economics, sociology, and politics, and this resulted in a natural shifting of emphasis to these fields.

A further reason was the shortage of qualified experts particularly in the field of theory, which forced the revolutionary workers movement to concentrate its efforts on those domains that were directly connected with the struggle of the masses.

Finally, when conditions were ripe for the cultivation of the previously neglected fields of thought (and this was made possible by the victory of the revolution) new barriers appeared in the form of ideological habit and tradition that had discarded questions of anthropology and of the individual—all the more so since this sphere of inquiry had become the domain of alien ideology and even was a platform for attacks on Marxism.

These were the reasons why anthropological issues were temporarily relegated to the background in Marxist theory. But all the complex problems of the individual were bound to explode when the working class movement passed from destruction of the old life to the construction of a new one. With the emergence of socialist states, the stabilization of the new system, and the transition from revolutionary heroism and war communism to everyday socialism, the problems of the individual, with their subtle philosophical questions of life and death, the meaning of life, and happiness, etc., began to assert themselves with ever greater force and insistency. It was found that a man could be unhappy under socialism too, or in any case that socialism was unable to guarantee personal happiness to everybody, even if it could completely eliminate the causes of collective unhappiness. It turned out that under socialism, also, people were mortal and that this was the most important problem that even philosophy was unable to solve; that under socialism questions about the sense of life were also meaningful, that men were stirred by the problems of freedom, and that socialism might even create certain worries on this point that could not be "talked away" by the most beautiful words. And that under socialism, too, people were preoccupied with the problem of personal happiness. In a word, the philosophy of man began to knock ever more insistently at the door of socialism. And when knocking proved insufficient there came the pressure of needs—growing along with the protest against the distortions of socialism known under the cover name "cult of personality"—which simply broke this door open. Whether we like it or not, whatever name is given to this type of problem and whoever criticizes it in the name of Marxism, the wave cannot be checked by anybody. In any case, who in the workers movement today would dare oppose Marxist humanism? Who would dare deny that the problem of the individual and his happiness is the paramount issue of Marxism? China's distinctive position in this respect is due to the specific conditions and the stage of development of that country.

Is it strange that this natural revival of anthropological interest within the workers movement is accompanied by a growth of interest in the young Marx and his writings? Is it strange that in a new situation Marxists display a growing humanist self-consciousness and a tendency to reappraise their own ideology? And that in this situation the value and importance of the problem of the human individual are rising among Marxists, both in practice and in theory?

Maximilien Rubel, whom we quoted at the outset, says that Marx requires rehabilitation. Anyone who is shocked by this statement should recall a much more thoroughgoing rehabilitation that the communist movement has been carrying out with full candor— the sometimes very painful reinstatement of certain basic values in our whole life. In the final analysis, this is a rehabilitation of the problem of the individual men in the construction of socialism; and from a certain, and surely correct, point of view, it is *a practical rehabilitation of Marx and Marxism.* For the matter is not limited to the appraisal of the young Marx; it concerns the whole Marx, the *vision of Marxism* and its content.

The restoration of the problem of the individual to its proper rank within the Marxist system and the interpretation of the whole Marxist theory in the context of humanism are above all of essential importance for practice, specifically educational practice.

The role of ideas and their influence on human life should not be exaggerated, but not discounted either—particularly when ideas make their appearance among people in an acceptable form transmitted by education and public opinion. A Marxist should find it ridiculous to claim the role of Jehovah writing a new decalogue on stone tablets. In any case, we know today that even Jehovah was at best a plagiarist. No system of morals can be made to order and those who want to save us by means of codification are simply foolish. On the other hand, the problem of public opinion is extremely important; shaped as it is by actually existing social relations, it is the actual codifier of moral commandments. Today it is codifying a new, modern decalogue of socialist society—and this creates a completely different situation, since public opinion, once it has crystallized, is a mighty force. This does not exclude the possibility of abuses, of transgression of the accepted norms; but it certainly means that no such transgression is possible without a sense of guilt, a feeling of having committed something wicked or indecent. This is the crux of the matter.

But public opinion is not only formed spontaneously, as a superstructure reflecting changes in the base of society. Its shape can be consciously influenced—and so certainly can the direction and tempo of its evolution. This is precisely the object of the ideological struggle within society—and it is often waged with a full awareness of its objective. Such, at least in principle, is the case with socialist ideology. The point was made by Marx in his youth (when he described philosophy as the ideological weapon of the proletariat), and it was later repeated by Lenin with great caution and deliberation. At a new developmental stage of the working class movement, he insisted that its socialist consciousness was brought to the movement *from the outside*. This is applicable not only in the earliest stages of the workers' movement, but in a changed form, this problem is also evident in the process of building a socialist society. This is what the role of ideology in society primarily amounts to—provided, of course, that among the many meanings of the word "ideology" today, we use it to denote the whole of the opinions and attitudes that determine the social actions of men, as well as the system of values that lays down and defines the purpose of these actions.

Which vision of Marxism is inculcated into the minds of men by education, propaganda, art, and so on is not, of course, irrelevant. Is it a clearly humanist vision in which the problem of the individual and his happiness is placed in the foreground as the supreme good, the object of all activity; or another vision in which this is in the shadows, or even simply rejected by *opposing* the public welfare to individual interest? It is this problem of educating the members of a socialist society—including the present and future holders of the highest offices in this society—*in the spirit of Marxist humanism* that is important as a factor in the formation of public opinion. What matters is not undue attention to the momentary interests of this or that individual, or even of a group. Sociologically, this would be nonsense, out of tune not only with Marxism, but simply with common sense; it is normal in society to find conflicting interests between various individuals, and there may often be a conflict between an individual and society. What matters is something else: that people under socialism firmly believe that man is the supreme good, and that the ultimate goal of human actions is to achieve the happiness of men, who do not exist in any other form except as individuals. When in a social emergency, for the sake of a higher goal, action must be taken against the momentary interests of one or another group of people, this must always be accepted as a necessary evil that should be kept to a minimum in time and scope. This sounds modest, but it would be a great deal if public opinion could actually be shaped in this way. In this lies the *practical* importance of the humanist vision of Marxism—and, as its main element, of the Marxist concept of the human individual.

This concept, however, has also a great *theoretical* significance for the further development of Marxism, particularly of historical materialism.

It would be a commonplace to say that more profound research into problems of the individual, within the framework of Marxism is essential for the Marxist interpretation of those humanistic disciplines that are directly connected with these problems—such as psychology, education, philosophical anthropology, etc. But it becomes less platitudinous and less simple when linked up with the question of the role played by the subjective factor in its broad sense in the various domains of our knowledge of social realities. Thus when the problem of the individual receives its proper place in the system of Marxist thought, it is possible to introduce this subjective element in the field of knowledge, a psychological factor in sociology and an individual factor in politics—without which all these fields might easily be treated in a mechanical and simplified manner. And so a more intensive interest in problems of the individual opens up new possibilities of a deeper development of Marxist theory.

The problem of the role played by the subjective factor in knowledge has penetrated into modern epistemology in a variety of ways —above all in the form of an all-round study and discussion of the role of language in cognition. For epistemologists the subject-object relationship—a problem without which no sensible discussion of the cognitive process is at all possible—has always been the essential, but also the most difficult issue. This question has always invited one-sidedness, ranging from subjective idealism in which only the subject mattered to the vulgarized and mechanically interpreted theory of reflection with its exclusive emphasis on the object. Marxist writers have as a rule criticized both these extremes, offering instead of a very convenient formula: the process of cognition is objective but includes a subjective element. Unfortunately, in default of closer definition, this formula remained a cliché, lending itself easily to more varied interpretations. It has been made concrete to a certain extent by modern research into the role of language in the process of knowledge, which, acknowledging the active contribution of the subject to the process of cognition, makes it possible to reject the simplified interpretation of the theory of reflection. This brings to mind the remarks of the young Marx on the humanization of nature, the humanization of the object of cognition, the historical nature of human senses and so forth, in their close connection with his concept of praxis. This does not mean that one can simply take over all of his ideas here or that they provide a sufficient basis for a reconstruction of his epistemology. But they certainly contain some valuable hints that fill out what Marx had to say in his *Theses on Feuerbach* about the active role of the intellect and the relation of idealism and mechanical materialism in this respect. In any case, further analysis of the problem of the individual from the viewpoint of the role of the subjective factor in cognition opens up new possibilities and prospects for the Marxist theory of knowledge, enabling it to reassess many traditional problems (like the theory of reflection) and to tackle new ones (like the role of language in cognition) and equipping it with a modern apparatus of issues and ideas.

The question has even more important implications in the field of Marxist sociology.[28]

"Social existence determines social consciousness"; this is its basic contention about the relationship between base and superstructure. By pointing to the connection between changes in a society's mode of production and the evolution of its consciousness, Marx laid the foundations of the materialist conception to history and of that line of enquiry into human knowledge known as the sociology of knowledge. His claim that changes in the mode of production determined historical development and that the movement of social consciousness depended on changes in the economic-social base was originally most vigorously combated; the struggle between the materialist and the idealist concept of history had far-reaching implications in the sphere of ideology, and thus in politics too. It is, therefore, all the more significant that it is precisely this part of Marxist sociology that has been most fully assimilated by modern social science; there is hardly a school today that has not made it, with this or that modification, part and parcel of its own doctrine. In most cases, if not in all, this has been done without acknowledging the source or the author—but after all this is not what matters most.

The heuristic value of the theory of base and superstructure and of their interdependence is now incontestable—and the further development of this theory is, therefore, all the more important. One of its elements should be a better understanding of the way in which base affects superstructure.

The primitive distortion of historical materialism, which once even made Marx himself quip that he was not a Marxist, has a long history, but there are also two correctives to such a simplified treatment of the relationship between base and superstructure, both due to the authors of the theory. One is that this is not a one-sided relationship; that is, the evolution of the base is also affected by the already shaped superstructure; and the other, that changes in the base do not directly cause changes in the superstructure—but rather by a number of indirect and intermediate links.

Here we have the crux of the problem: what are these indirect links?

Nowadays we laugh at the "Marxism" that sought to explain the origin of Mickiewicz's *Forefathers' Eve* by relating it to the rise and fall of grain prices in Lithuania. Nobody would dream of such antics today, but—historically speaking—they were actually indulged in, and not by cranks, at that. We know now that the issue is much more complex, that economic developments do not (invariably at any rate) directly affect the sphere of ideology, that there exists a relative autonomy of the development of the superstructure—and a subtle filiation of ideas within the framework of this autonomy. But the actual mechanism of the influence of the base on the superstructure is something we are unable to explain specifically. And the missing link here is man—the human environment in which certain stimuli springing from the social base cause the appearance, or change, of a certain consciousness. For there is no superstructure, no social consciousness "for itself," apart from the men who create it; if it exists, it is only as the fantasy of a certain kind of idealist. Incidentally, without this human environment there is no base either, for it, too, is a human product; or, more accurately, it is the sum total of certain relations among men who transform nature. It is thus obvious that there cannot be any relationship between base and superstructure unless there are men who create both of them, and men are always the intermediate link between any relationships between the two.

It is common knowledge today that psychology is the Achilles' heel of Marxist research into social problems. One reason for this is surely to be sought in the simplified approach to the base/superstructure relationship that seemed to eliminate the operation of the psychological factor. The Marxist lexicon includes, it is true, such categories as "national character," "national mentality," "cultural tradition," etc., but these can hardly be said to have been seriously considered in analyzing questions concerning the ideological superstructure of society.

Yet the problem is quite evident. Some self-determined changes occur in the base of society—such as, for example, a radical revolution in production brought about by new technological inventions. These changes should result in corresponding transformations in the sphere of social consciousness in general and particularly in the ideological superstructure (involving both ideology and the institutions it breeds). But even a superficial observation shows that in different social environments similar changes in the base cause different transformations in the consciousness of a given society.

Why? And how does this happen? These are not purely academic questions. They also concern such issues as the reasons why similar changes in the base of socialist societies lead, in some of them, to a relatively smooth and rapid collectivization, while in others they fail to transform the obstinacy of social consciousness.

That man is the *creator* of both base and superstructure, as well as an *intermediary* in their mutual relationships, means that concentration on the individual or groups of individuals can play an essential role in the further development and specification of the theory of base and superstructure.

But since our knowledge of society teaches us that the same causes give birth to different effects according to the environment in which they operate, we are entitled to advance the hypothesis that there is a social system of filters that sift and steer the action of the base in the sphere of the superstructure. These filters are without doubt connected with man, since man is in this case the only go-between. But what are they? Metaphors are picturesque; they help to convey certain ideas, but they do not clear up the matter.

Whether we speak of the psychology of a given society, or of the historically formed character of men—in fact whatever we call this issue—we shall still remain within a sphere of rather vague definitions each of which requires further clarification. What matters in all these cases is certainly the entire range of mental attitudes, the emotional dispositions of men, their readiness to accept certain systems of values, and even the irrational component of the human mind which may be rationally explicable from the viewpoint of its genesis. If all this, and perhaps something else as well, makes up what we call the human "character," it is something that varies in the course of history and has been shaped by society. It consists of two factors: the psychosomatic, which is a social product in phylogenesis, and the effects of social stimuli in the life of the individual, which are the product of ontogenesis. Their sum total constitutes the filters that sift and direct the stimuli of the base. Knowledge of these filters is essential for our ability to predict the influence of the stimuli and thus for conscious planning of our behavior. It is also important as far as changes of the "filters" themselves are concerned, since, however reluctantly and slowly, they too are susceptible to such changes.

All this is, of course, purely hypothetical and has not been accurately stated or clearly delineated. It is simply a suggestion for the researcher that psychology, particularly social psychology and the general theory of *behavior,* might be incorporated into the analyses of historical materialism. This can only be done by taking into account the problem of the individual and his manifold links with society.

Finally, there is a third field—politics—whose development by Marxist thinkers is most immediately connected with the proper approach to the problem of the individual.

The postulate that the individual's interests should coincide with those of society is one of the characteristic features of the struggle for a harmonious relationship between individual and society. It is closely linked to the struggle against all kinds of alienation, particularly economic alienation. It is only in a society in which private ownership of the means of production—and with it the possibility of exploitation of man by man—has been eliminated that the individual's private interests can avoid conflicts with the interests of other individuals and of society as a whole. This does not by any means signify that the individual's distinct character disappears into society, that he ceases to exist as an individual. What ceases to exist, and is transcended, is only the individual's economic conflict with society. His desire to improve his living conditions can be only fulfilled through improvement of the community's situation, but his individuality and his distinctive character remain intact.

This has not always been appreciated—either by opponents or by supporters of the socialist program.

With the former, this lack of understanding is not so dangerous, although it is characteristic. Many anti-communist utopias are based on the allegation that the individual and human personality have to be destroyed in a collectivist system. This is the underlying idea of Zamyatin's novel *We,* which was probably the pioneer of this kind of literature; and it is also on this idea that Huxley's *Brave New World* and Orwell's *1984* are based. In each of these novels —perhaps the most extreme and horrifying example is Zamyatin —the blending of individual with social interests has been reduced to the limit of absurdity, falsely interpreted as meaning a fusion of the individual with society in which the individual disappears and human personality is demolished for the sake of a homogeneous group. Worst of all, this fiction (particularly in the case of Orwell) has a basis in truth; and this is why the more one knows the reality, the more horrifying this fiction becomes—since after all, it is not pure fiction.

But far more distressing is the fact that the demand for the unity of individual and social interests has been misunderstood by the supporters and builders of socialism.

It is natural that a militant, revolutionary movement, forced as it was by the objective conditions of the struggle to adapt a semi-military organization and discipline, should have recoiled from the excessive individualism characteristic of bourgeois society in general and its intellectuals in particular. Individualism, particularly that of the intellectuals in a bourgeois society, can be variously assessed as a rebellion against the rule of the Moloch of capitalism or conversely as a sign of conforming to its rule, often going as far as counter-revolution. Both assessments are true, but it is also true that both forms of this individualism were unacceptable and objectively hostile to the revolutionary movement.

With its built-in concern for the complete flowering of human personality, socialism is by definition a system in which every individual is entitled to genuine, full development. This has always been proclaimed and propagated by its attack on the conditions of life under capitalism. In practice, however, it did not check the spreading of anti-individualistic tendencies—not only in the sense of combating the psychological legacy of capitalism, but also in the wrong sense of denying the right to individuality; and it was this denial that provided the fertile soil for Orwell's type of utopia. If this had no basis in Marxism itself, there were certainly grounds in the anti-intellectual spirit of the "workers' opposition"—and this will not die out as long as the anti-intellectual bias characteristic of the working class under capitalism, particularly in underdeveloped countries, is still alive. *This* anti-individualism does not further social progress; on the contrary, the resentments arising from the old system hamper the development of socialist society.

With the stabilization of socialist society, this problem, too, asserts itself. Old traumas disappear, resentments lose all sense as a new intelligentsia comes into being from the people. The desire for a better and happier life becomes a more urgent problem of theory and this means that a man needs a measure of individuality that grows together with the economic and cultural standards of the community. It is then that there begins a spontaneous growth of those tendencies and attitudes that further the revival of certain forgotten aspects of Marxism. If it were ever distorted by tradition, there is now a greater chance for a renaissance of the proper interpretation of Marxism. The young Marx and the humanist approach to the *whole* of Marxism have a host of potential supporters in such a society; a spark can cause an explosion, and the possibility can become reality.

With growing emphasis on the problem of the individual, the socio-political concept of Marxism is increasingly more concerned with human individuality. This issue carries enormous educational weight and is of great practical significance for everyday life in socialist society. This is probably why the revival of the problem of the individual is of such crucial importance—as is the renaissance of the idea of the young Marx: it is a perspective from which we can view Marxism in a new light. Consequently, what is historically oldest in Marxism makes it possible for us to detect the hidden meaning of its most recent layers.

The renaissance of the young Marx's world of ideas is inseparably connected with the dissemination of his early writings. But this has its hazards, which are all the more worth stressing since the consequences are already making themselves felt.

In the epilogue to the first volume of *Capital*, Marx wrote of his "flirtation" with the style of Hegel. This is quite obvious, and Lenin even said that the structure of *Capital* cannot be understood without a knowledge of Hegel's *Logic*. But in his early works Marx did not so much model his style on Hegel, he simply made it his own. This is only natural if one bears in mind the atmosphere of the age in which Marx's mind was formed and the environment in which he lived. At that time, Hegelianism, particularly in this circle, was not only the vogue, but the reigning philosophy, above all as regards the style of inquiry. This weighed heavily on Marx's works in his youth and clearly distinguished them from the literary style of his mature writings. This magnificent writer, equipped with an accomplished and concise turn of phrase, considered one of the best German stylists of his time, nevertheless wrote in his youth in an unbearably stilted and verbose manner that makes his early writings hardly, if at all, readable for the modern reader who has no special familiarity with the period. Worse still, the young Marx was woefully obscure—if this may be said of a great man whom we esteem and love. Of course, he was obscure in a truly Hegelian fashion—something absolutely unthinkable in his mature years when he became scrupulously precise. Marx himself, as I have already pointed out, later ridiculed his style, and in some cases, as with the word "alienation," he even went so far as to abandon his early terminology. The influence of Hegel's philosophy can be assessed in various ways; but I think that no unprejudiced student of post-Hegelian philosophy can deny that this style of philosophizing not only vitiated German philosophy for a long time but also affected philosophical trends in other countries that fell under its spell.

The matter is even more involved since problems of philosophical anthropology—of the so-called philosophy of man—by no means lend themselves easily to accurate and precise thinking. This is simply because it often deals with questions to which—when they are posed in a certain way—there are no answers, or perhaps because answers are closer to poetry than to science and strict reasoning. For a long time these awkward problems were appropriated by those schools of thought that promoted the unscientific (as in the case of the various trends based on religion) or the muddled (as in the varieties of existentialism) way of thinking as a matter of principle. This was by no means accidental; on the contrary, it was rather a case of birds of a feather. The boundary between philosophy and *belles-lettres* was radically blurred—according to some this was a good thing—but this was harmful both to *lettres* which ceased to be *belles* and to philosophy which ceased to be a science.

This was a situation in our Marxist milieu when the need for a renewal of anthropological studies was dropped on our doorstep: on the one hand, we were faced with the Hegelian and early Marxian style and approach to these studies; on the other, there was the religious or existentialist tradition. Is it, therefore, to be wondered that so many fell victim to this field of enquiry, particularly among the young who plunged into it with such enthusiasm? And is it any wonder that attempts were made to interpret Marxism in an existentialist context, even to make an existentialist of Marx himself? Is it strange—and this I think is the biggest danger—that tendencies emerged with programmatic approval of confused thinking and tortuous language in the development of the Marxist theory of man, as well as the conviction that precision would mean a loss of some important elements? And that, finally, the boundary between philosophy and literature should in this case be confused and *scientific* philosophy abandoned?

As I have said before, the consequences of this situation have already made themselves felt, particularly in the manner of philosophizing adopted by certain circles of young Marxists. In Poland, it is very noticeable. And this is a serious matter. We shall continue to develop the science and philosophy of man, and we will not renounce this road just because of the threatening dangers. But the threat to the *scientific character* of philosophy must clearly be seen and energetically counteracted if we do not want to harm philosophy in general and philosophical anthropology in particular.

Let me begin with the claim that the philosophy of man can be studied and developed with all the rigor of philosophical thinking and without detriment to the scientific character of philosophy; and that it is both possible and necessary to distinguish between philosophy and literature—each of which handles these problems in its own way, particularly as regards the style of approach.

The problems of man, of the individual, are the focus of literature, and it is only natural that the main questions of the philosophy of man should have been so widely deployed in fiction, drama, and poetry. But in my opinion their role there is not the same as in philosophy, if only because in a work of art solutions of general questions are arrived at from a basis in the concrete particular, that is, the individual; while philosophical method is the reverse: from the general to the particular. It is often asserted that this difference is obscured by borderline cases, such as philosophical fiction (Kafka). This is true, but the principle remains and all the more so when the problem of *style* is borne in mind. In fiction and poetry metaphors can and should be used, and it is also legitimate to visualize a strange new world if this promotes insight into what can be experienced but is difficult to express—particularly emotions. This is exactly the case with Kafka's world and his literary style, which conveys his emotional experience. But this discursive style must not be used in philosophy; this, I feel, is simply inadmissible. It has been attempted by the existentialists, but the resulting hybrids are neither good philosophy nor good literature. And when finally a program is formulated in which confused thinking becomes a principle of philosophy, which must be observed unless some of its important messages might be lost, it becomes clear that the advocates of such opinions are muddle-headed themselves and want to present their confusion as something valuable.

In my view, there are at least two demands concerning precision of expression, and one concerning the matter itself, that should be made of the Marxist philosophy of man.

In the first place, it is necessary to draw a line between questions to which answers can be provided and those to which there are no answers. This distinction (and it is by no means identical with the logical positivists' division of statements into meaningful and meaningless, since some of the statements defined as meaningless by this school involve questions to which answers can be found) is of extreme importance. How many philosophical controversies owe their long life merely to badly formulated questions! But one must always remember that to say a question cannot be answered is also an answer—sometimes a very significant one.

As for the way in which anthropological thought is expressed, it is only necessary to reaffirm a generally valid rule: in employing a certain expression, the maximum effort should be made to invest it with a precise meaning. This is not merely an appeal for definitions, but above all for the elimination of ambiguity of words; this can be achieved if care is taken to state their meanings precisely and the various senses are not confused with each other. This is the very common procedure known as semantic analysis, often wrongly identified with logical positivism. It is true, historically, that it was the logical positivists who mainly contributed to its spread, but because the process is of a technical nature it cannot be claimed by any single school. If we were to apply this technique scrupulously, we could knock more than one "problem" on the head and pull the ground away from under many a school. Indeed such a reduction in the number of "problems" and schools would not be a disservice.

And finally, one general postulate concerning the merits of the case: philosophical anthropology should make the greatest possible use of the results achieved by the various special sciences which deal with man. And the philosophy of man should always avoid contradicting the data of the individual sciences. This is a modest demand to be sure, but unless it is respected, no inquiry can claim the name of science.

Chapter 1
The Marxist Concept
of the Individual

Let me begin with a hackneyed truth: for any brand of socialism —both utopian and scientific—man and his affairs are the central problem. And it is not an abstract man, not man in general, but the concrete human individual.

In certain circumstances this undoubted commonplace acquires, paradoxical as it may seem, the nature of an important discovery. For without it, the meaning of socialism cannot be grasped, neither its theoretical premises nor its practical import.

Socialist currents of thought have always arisen from a protest against an inhuman reality, a revolt against oppression, exploitation of man by man, hatred in relations among men. "Liberty, Equality, Fraternity"—these watchwords of the French Revolution —express eternal human aspirations, which, in the course of centuries, have been endowed with various meanings and have been stated in various ways. The roots of these tendencies and attitudes could perhaps (as Kelles-Krauz thought) be traced back to the times of the primitive community and its struggles against the first disruptive elements of the class system. In any case, whatever their form—whether religious or secular, utopian or scientific— they have always been an expression of protest, although not necessarily of struggle; and it was always the living man, with his suffering and his hope for a better tomorrow, who has been the point of departure for this protest. This is precisely why every socialism is a theory of happiness, although it is not always a theory of struggle —authentic struggle—for this happiness. Moreover, when man is not seen as the central issue of the socialist ideal, its essence is lost and its meaning is beyond understanding.

Far from being an exception in this respect, Marxism is part of the historical development of socialist ideology. In a new and more developed situation, when the character of human relations was becoming ever more clearly understood and when the advance of technology made feasible what had previously been utopian, socialist thought could take on a new and more developed form. This was Marx's scientific socialism, which, while basically overhauling much of the socialism that had existed before, nevertheless retained its point of departure: the human individual and his problems.

In a polemical article in 1844, Marx wrote:

> *Social* revolution concentrates on the whole because it is . . . a protest of man against dehumanized life, because *its point of departure is the particular, real individual,* because it is the protest of the individual against his isolation from the *community* which is the *true* community of men, that is the essence *of man.*[1]

Enmeshed in society, the individual has a social origin and nature, but in a sense he remains autonomous. And whatever the topic under discussion—be it the class struggle or the laws that govern history—it is the real, concrete individual, the true maker of history, that remains the foundation of all analysis; for he is the true object of suffering and the true object of action. This was never doubted by Marx, neither in his youth nor in his maturity.

From the outset of his theoretical inquiries, living human individuals were Marx's point of departure. It is precisely in this sphere that Marx, following Feuerbach, declared war on idealism, particularly the Hegelian; his first concern is the living real man.

> In direct contrast to German philosophy, which descends from heaven to earth, here we ascend from earth to heaven. That is to say, we do not set out from what men say, imagine, or conceive, nor from what has been said, thought, imagined, or conceived of men, in order to arrive at men in the flesh. We begin with real, active men, and from their real life-process show the development of the ideological reflexes and echoes of this life-process . . . Life is not determined by consciousness, but consciousness by life. Those who adopt the first method of approach begin with consciousness, regarded as the living

individual; those who adopt the second, which corresponds with real life, begin with the real living individuals themselves, and consider consciousness only as *their* consciousness.[2]

And another passage from the same work:

The premises from which we begin are not arbitrary ones, not dogmas, but real premises from which abstraction can be made only in the imagination. They are the real individuals, their activity and their material conditions of life, including those which they find already in existence and those produced by their activity. These premises can thus be established in a purely empirical way.

The first premise of all human history is, of course, the existence of living human individuals.[3]

The individual is a social individual and accordingly is invariably involved in social conditions; this Marx grasped very early, but the point of departure is always the *individual*.

"Individuals have always built on themselves, but naturally on themselves within their given historical conditions and relationships, not on the 'pure' individual in the sense of the ideologists." [4]

From the time of *The Holy Family* (in the introduction to which Marx and Engels described spiritualism as the worst enemy of real humanism, since it substituted "self-knowledge" for the real individual man) they kept repeating what they wrote in that book: that history is made by real individuals, and that it is not history that makes use of man to accomplish its ends; it is man who makes history, which is his activity.

This notion was stated tellingly and explicitly later on in the introduction to *A Critique of Political Economy* of 1857. In his discussion of production, Marx says:

"Individuals producing in society, and therefore a socially determined production by individuals, naturally constitute the starting point." [5]

That Marx, both in his youth and later, regarded man as the

starting point is incontestable, best shown by his writings. But it is a different matter whether the place allotted to man in Marx's system, both as a point of departure and a goal is theoretically correct. In other words: does Marxism, in treating man as its cornerstone, possess a conception of the individual, and can it, in the light of its system, have such a conception at all? The question may seem a strange one, but it cannot be ruled out—if only because it is an actual subject of controversy.

By way of example, let me quote a Polish neo-Thomist who questions this thesis, although he does not expressly reject the views of such of his companions in arms as Jean Lacroix, Calvez, Cottier, or Pierre Bigo, all of whom consider humanism as a characteristic feature of Marxism. It may be even added that to Calvez Marxism is a complete and systematic theory of man.

> It is therefore no wonder that the modern materialist does not recognize or offer any philosophical concept of man, not so much because of his philosophical, materialist approach, but in view of his methodological principles which, in their essence, do not differ from the methodology of positivism and neo-positivism. This is in contrast to classical materialism where it would be difficult to find a separate philosophical anthropology since in its view man is not essentially different from the animals. However, modern varieties of materialism give first place to a methodological argument which basically denies the possibility of a philosophical theory of man and rejects metaphysics as a relic of a bygone age and a great mistake of mankind.[6]

This is a startling proposition—unless of course it is assumed by definition that a concept of the individual is only possible on the basis of Christian personalism—but it is also a significant one. The total absence of Marxist writings on the subject for several decades helped to implant a certain stereotype of Marxism in human minds, one which has no place for the problem of the individual.

Non-Marxists can hardly be blamed; similar doubts can also be observed among Marxist thinkers—and not only among those for whom the established traditional interpretation has become a sacrosanct dogma and who are incapable of grasping the humanist meaning of the Marxist sociological conception of human history. What is also involved here is a tendency, often described as revisionist, that harks back (in my opinion, without any justification) to Lukács's *Geschichte und Klassenbewusstsein*. Since such a "Lukács family," as it is sometimes called, exists in both Poland and France, and perhaps elsewhere as well, it is probably advisable to say a few words about the subject in order to clear up something that, in my view, is an obvious misunderstanding.

In *Geschichte und Klassenbewusstsein,* Lukács argues that the "totality of the historical process" cannot be grasped *from the position of the individual* conceived to be isolated from any social group (as in existentialism or personalism). This is correct from the Marxist point of view, since such an individual is a social fiction.

On this basis, it is now suggested that, according to Lukács, Marxism has no place for a concept of the human individual but only for such concepts as those of groups, social classes, etc. This claim is completely wrongheaded since it does not follow from Lukács's contention. To conclude from his view that in Marxism there is no room for the concept of the individual is a *non sequitur*. Even less can this be inferred from Marx's well-known dictum— also sometimes invoked by the supporters of this view—that man's essence is not an abstraction inherent in an individual, but an ensemble of social relations. This was only his protest against the one-sidedness of naturalism and cannot by any means be interpreted as a denial by Marx of the concept of the individual.

Nor can this view be upheld by invoking the assumption that under communism the interests of the individual fuse into, become identical with, those of society. This identity of interests does not mean that the individual ceases to exist in the sense of his very being (this would be strange indeed!) or his aspirations, but only that he would not regard as good for himself what is not good from the point of view of society (which does not, of course, rule out the further fact that an important part of individual life is beyond the reach of such evaluation being socially neutral).[7]

This controversy, however, brings the problem of the individual in Marxism into particularly sharp relief. This will be the central issue in the following pages.

Feuerbach's thesis that philosophy's point of departure is the living human being, the flesh-and-blood individual who is part of nature, *today* sounds banal. Historically, however, it was a bold discovery, which, as Marx used to say, turned the Hegelian philosophy of that time the right way up. Many statements, which were once eye-openers, ring trite after the years, having simply become recognized, easily accepted truths.

Feuerbach's theory of man made its radical transition from a God-centered to a man-centered anthropology. Though criticized by Marx for a narrow naturalism that lost sight of history, Feuerbach's philosophy played an essential role in the development of materialism. True, in its conception of the individual this anthropology accorded too little a place to the social and historical factor; this was its failure.

But it is also true that it made a thorough-going breach in the God-centered and thus heteronomous interpretation of the human world; and without this breach it would have been impossible to overcome Hegel's influence and consolidate materialism. No wonder that it played such an important role in the intellectual evolution of the founders of Marxism, a role that was later to be emphasized by Engels in his book on Feuerbach. And no wonder that—notwithstanding his critique of Feuerbach's theory of man—Marx fully subscribed to *this aspect* of his views.

The starting point is thus the human individual conceived as a flesh-and-blood specimen of a biological species, as a part of nature. This is the first element of Marx's materialist conception of the human individual.

> *Man* is directly a *natural being.* As a natural being, and as a living natural being he is, on the one hand, endowed with *natural powers* and *faculties,* which exist in him as tendencies and abilities, as *drives.* On the other hand, as a natural, embodied, sentient, objective being he

is a *suffering* [*ein leidendes Wesen*], conditioned and limited being, like animals and plants. The *objects* of his drives exist outside himself, as *objects* independent of him, yet they are *objects* of his *needs,* essential *objects* which are indispensable to the exercise and confirmation of his faculties. The fact that man is an *embodied,* living, real, sentient, objective being with natural powers, means that he has *real, sensuous objects* as the objects of his being, or that he can only express his being in real, sensuous objects. *To be* objective, natural, sentient and at the same time to have object, nature and sense outside oneself, or to be oneself object, nature and sense for a third person, is one and the same thing. . . .

A non-objective being is a *non-being*.[8]

So Marx wrote in the *Manuscripts,* and although he later made fun of the influence of Feuerbach and his terminology on his own early writings, this influence, visible as it is in Marx's concept of the individual, lingered on—as indeed it had to in a materialistic philosophy. Apropos of materialism, the above quotation is significant in view of the tortuous attempts that have been made to deduce a subjectivist epistemology from the young Marx's views. It has even been alleged that in the light of his early philosophy the world could not be said to exist *independently* of man and so it could not be asked whether the world existed *before* the appearance of man. From the point of view of the mature Marx—who, as even a superficial study of the history of his thought will show, cannot be separated from the views of Engels in, say, *Anti-Dühring* —this is sheer nonsense, as indeed it would be for any materialism. But the young Marx was not yet a full-fledged materialist and he said various things—he spoke of humanizing nature and described consistent naturalism as humanism. On the other hand, the same young Marx who so emphatically stressed the *active side* of human knowledge was a materialist in his ontology; and there is no doubt that when his work is approached without bias no idealistic conclusions can be drawn from his ontology. It is also obvious that his theory of knowledge should be read and interpreted in the context of his ontology, not against it. In this respect, Marx's words about objects that exist *independently* of man and outside him, although man is an active being, leave no doubt whatsoever.

Thus we begin with human individuals living, embodied, objective beings, which, belonging to nature, are objects to other individuals—even though they are objects of a peculiar kind.

Marx was quick to realize that the problem of the individual could—and should—be used as a weapon against Hegelianism, although it was not until the *Manuscripts* that his case was clearly stated. In his *Contribution to the Critique of the Hegelian Philosophy of Right* (written in 1843), Marx argued that if Hegel had set out from actual subjects as the basis for society, he would not have had to resort to a mystical transformation of the State into the subject. "As a consequence," Marx wrote, "the real subject later appears as the result, whereas it was necessary to set out from the real subject and consider its objectivization. With Hegel it is thus mystical substance which becomes the real subject, and the real subject appears as something else, as a moment of mystical substance." [9]

Marx follows up this demystification when he writes:

> In this way an impression is created of something *mystical* and *profound*. It is a very banal statement to say that man is born and that this existing being, determined by physical birth, becomes social man, etc., reaching so far as to include the citizen of a state; man by his birth becomes everything that he becomes. But it sounds very profound and impressive when we say that the idea of the State is born directly, that in the birth of the ruler it gave birth to itself and was given empirical existence. No new content is gained by this, only the *form* of the old content is changed. This content has received a philosophical form, a philosophical confirmation.
>
> Another consequence of this mystical speculation is that a certain *peculiar* empirical being, a certain individual empirical being is conceived, unlike others, as the *existential being of the idea*. Once more a profound, mys-

tical impression is created when we have in front of us a certain *peculiar* empirical being created by the idea; and so, on all levels we meet the hypostatization of God in man.[10]

Naturalism is materialism, but it is a limited kind of materialism, incapable of reconstructing the whole realm of human problems. And so it is not surprising that if Marx comes close to Feuerbach in his theory of man, it is also in this that they part company. But in revealing the failures of Feuerbach's anthropology, he also laid bare the weak points in Feuerbach's materialism in general. It is in the course of this criticism of Feuerbach that Marx arrived at the other side of his conception of man, his own and original view.

The German Ideology was written only two years after the *Manuscripts,* but it already contained a fully developed critique of the naturalist conception of man and the foundation of its social aspect.

> Certainly Feuerbach has a great advantage over the "pure" materialists in that he realizes how man too is an "object of the senses." But apart from the fact that he only conceives him as a "sensuous object," not as "sensuous activity," because he still remains in the realm of theory and conceives of men not in their given social connection, not under their existing conditions of life, which have made them what they are, he never arrives at the really existing active men, but stops at the abstraction "man," and gets no further than recognizing "the true, individual, corporeal man" emotionally, *i.e.,* he knows no other "human relationships" "of man to man" than love and friendship, and even then idealized. He gives no criticism of the present conditions of life. Thus he never manages to conceive the sensuous world as the total living sensuous activity of the individuals composing it; and therefore when, for example, he sees instead of healthy men a crowd of scrofulous, over-worked and consumptive starvelings, he is compelled to take refuge in the "higher perception" and in the ideal "compensation in

the species," and thus to relapse into idealism at the very point where the communist materialist sees the necessity, and at the same time the condition, of a transformation both of industry and of the social structure.

As far as Feuerbach is a materialist he does not deal with history, and as far as he considers history he is not a materialist. With him materialism and history diverge completely, a fact which explains itself from what has been said.[11]

I have quoted this passage in full because of its fundamental importance for our purposes and because it provides an excellent commentary on certain of Marx's statements in *Theses on Feuerbach* that are conceptually abbreviated and difficult to understand.

This is how Marx's argument runs:

1. Feuerbach is a materialist, whose superiority to other materialists lies in the fact that he also interprets man materialistically, *as a sensuous object.*

2. The narrowly naturalistic approach to the analysis of man allows man to be seen only as a specimen of a biological species, but not as he really exists and acts in society. Hence Feuerbach's naturalism stops at the abstraction "man" and knows nothing of the real, concrete man; and among the various types of human relations Feuerbach perceives only love and friendship.

3. The charge of abstractness in his conception of man is in principle reduced to the fact that Feuerbach analyzes man only from the point of view of a biological species, not from the aspect of the social bonds among men and of those conditions of life which make man what he is.

4. Feuerbach's interpretation of the world of men is contemplative; he does not see it as a totality of the human actions that create this world.

5. As a consequence, Feuerbach's naturalism is helpless in the face of all social problems; he invokes principles and ideas, not the activities of men, which transform reality. Hence Feuerbach, when confronted with history, is forced to fall back on idealism, and when he is a materialist, his materialism is divorced from history.

This critique of Feuerbach's naturalism is dominated by two basic ideas:

a. the social involvement of the individual through membership of certain social groups within the framework of human relationships

b. the interpretation of the world *as a product of human activity* and, since this world in turn *creates* man, understanding the independent power of social man through the intermediary of social *praxis*

We shall deal with the first of these elements in the further course of our analysis; here let us take up the second.

Man is part of nature as the species *Homo sapiens,* of which human individuals are the specimens. But if the *ontological status* of the individual were confined to this problem only (although this is the most important issue in the struggle against an idealistic, God-centered or, more generally, heteronomous conception), it would be reduced to the existence in every individual of a number of specific species characteristics that are here promoted to the rank of man's "essence"—if the term is taken to express those characteristics that distinguish man from the animal world, that is, are attributes of man, but not of other parts of living nature. In that way, "being human" is reduced to a set of abstract features that are supposed to be "inherent" in every individual, peculiar to him as an element of a class.

Marx protests—and rightly—against this conception of the human individual, for its naturalism is limited and one-sided: it only takes note of the biological aspect as the constituent element of man and ignores the social aspect. Yet the species *Homo sapiens* is distinguished not merely by its biological features but also—and, in a sense, primarily—by its socio-historical characteristics.

In his criticism of Feuerbach, however, Marx uses an inappropriate line of argument (both in *The German Ideology* and the *Theses on Feuerbach*). The point is not that, as Marx expressly states in the sixth "Thesis" by conceiving of the human essence as a species, as a purely natural entity, Feuerbach reduces it to an abstraction inherent in each individual. This would mean that when social bonds appear the situation would change in this respect. But this situation will only change insofar as the constituent features of the individual include not only those arising from the *biological* bond but also those due to the social bond. The sum total of the constituent features will grow and there will be a qualitative change, but the logical status of the conception of the individual will remain the same: each individual will still have a certain set of abstract features which constitute the species, but now these will be not only biological but also social in character.

But this is not what matters most in this context. For, in effect, when the social factor is introduced, the conception of the individual acquires a different *quality;* it becomes *concrete* as compared with the abstract character of the purely biological view that ignores the social involvement of man. Yet man is not only a product of biological evolution, but as a result of this evolution, he is a historical-social product, varying in certain respects which depend on the developmental stage of each society and on the different classes and strata of society. When construed only on the basis of the general biological features common to all human beings, as distinct, for example, from other mammals, man is only an "abstract man," a "man in general"; this is opposed to the concrete interpretation of man on the basis of his social involvement, as a member of a society that has reached a certain stage of historical development, and as a member of a class with a place in the social division of labor, in culture, etc.

Feuerbach's discovery that the human individual is above all a part of nature, a specimen of a biological species, was, in its simplicity, a stroke of genius, banal as it may sound today. No less inspired though its impact still remains fresh was Marx's simple discovery, so closely connected with the further development of historical materialism, that the individual is part of society, enmeshed in concrete human relations—particularly in the field of production—and created by these conditions.

This Marx saw as early as *A Contribution to the Critique of the Hegelian Philosophy of Right,* and expressed it quite clearly in the *Manuscripts* of 1844. Man is both a *product* of society and its *maker,* he says, and because of this he is a social individual:

The individual *is the social being*. The manifestation of his life—even when it does not appear directly in the form of a *communal* manifestation, accomplished in association with other men—is therefore a manifestation and affirmation of *social life*. Individual human life and species-life are not *different,* even though the mode of existence of individual life is necessarily a more specific or a more *general* mode of species-life or that of species-life a more *specific* or more *general* mode of individual life. . . .

Though man is a *unique* individual—and it is just has particularity which makes him an individual, a really *individual* communal being—he is equally the *whole,* the ideal whole, the subjective existence of society as thought and experienced.[12]

Later, in *A Contribution to the Critique of Political Economy,* Marx gave an excellent commentary of the above exposition. Explaining that the starting point for analysis of production is always the producing individual (in stressing this Marx dissociated himself from every form of what he described as fetishism—a situation in which relations between men are externalized, particularly in the economic market, into relations between the things they produce), he emphasized the point that it is always a *social individual;* and that all the Robinson Crusoes, so fashionable in his day were pure fiction. He did not, however, simply reject these desert island tales, but gave a sociological explanation of their origin. The vision of an *isolated individual* could only have come into being in an atomized free-competition society, but once it did come into being it was easily accepted that this had been the natural state of the individual man. The idea was then read back into the "golden age" of the past. Thus what was a product of history was presented as its point of departure. In reality, however, the individual is always a social individual and all these illusions about him first appeared in the eighteenth century, in the newly emerging bourgeois society.

But the period in which this view of the isolated individual becomes prevalent is the very one in which the interrelations of society (general from this point of view) have reached the highest state of development. Man is in the most literal sense of the word . . . not only a social animal, but an animal which can develop into an individual only in society.[13]

But the conclusions to be drawn from this as far as the concept of the individual is concerned are not restricted to the general statement that man is a part of nature and a part of society; they also require specification of the socio-psychological structure of the individual. "But the human essence," Marx says in the sixth *Thesis on Feuerbach*, "is no abstraction inherent in each single individual. *In its reality it is the ensemble of social relations.*" [14] This statement—often quoted but seldom appreciated, and I fear, seldom understood—I regard as one of the most momentous achievements of Marx's youth, one that paved the way for the further evolution of historical materialism.

Before we deal in more detail with Marx's description of the individual as the totality of social relations, it seems essential to make two points concerning method that should make for a better understanding of the implications and meaning of his statement.

In *The Holy Family*, in a section entitled "The secret of speculative construction," [15] there is an arresting methodological argument about the relationship between the abstract and the concrete, which is of immediate relevance to our subject.

The essence of Hegel's method is to create abstract notions which we absolutize—that is, we imagine them to possess an existence which is independent of us. Then, standing the problem on its head, we try to construct the concrete from this abstraction.[16]

Marx analyzed the predicament of the speculative philosopher, who tries to find a way from the abstraction he has himself created to the concrete and who confuses the normal products of perception with spontaneous mystical processes of abstract ideas. Thus he in effect undertakes the defense of a method whereby the concrete particular is made the basis of analysis. This premise is also valid in the case of anthropology—here it is concrete human individuals that should be the starting point of analysis.

But it is here that we come across a crucial problem in the critique of naturalism: it is not the abstract "man," but living, particular men who should be the point of departure. And yet what does "particular" mean in this context?

Marx gave an explicit answer much later in *A Contribution to the Critique of Political Economy*. But his methodological statement sheds interesting light on the important question of how the notion of the individual should be theoretically constructed in order to achieve a maximum degree of concreteness.

In *A Contribution,* Marx's problem was the specific starting point for an analysis of production. It might seem that the population was a concrete enough basis. But on second thought it becomes clear that this is only apparently so, since the population turns out to be an abstraction if we do not know the classes of which it is composed. In its turn, a social class is an abstraction when we ignore the elements on which it is based—such as hired labor, capital, etc. In a word, if we began our analysis with the notion of population, its more detailed definition would lead us to ever simpler concepts, and so to abstraction. We would then have to reverse our tracks, going back from the abstract to the particular, and this time the latter would no longer be a chaotic mosaic of many terms, but their rich comprehensive whole. Marx thinks that the latter method is correct, and says in conclusion:

> The concrete is concrete, because it is a combination of many objects with different destinations, i.e., a unity of diverse elements. In our thought, it therefore appears as a process of synthesis, as a result, and not as a starting point and, therefore, also the starting point of observation and conception . . . the method of advancing from the abstract to the concrete is but a way of thinking by which the concrete is grasped and is reproduced in our mind as a concrete. It is by no means, however, the process which itself generates the concrete.[17]

This methodological postulate of the intellectual reconstruction of the concrete is reconstructed through the abstract and can also be applied to the concept of the human individual. Here the starting point of observation is, naturally, the real human individual. Thus, when defining the ontological status of the individual, it is necessary to start from the existence of individuals as specimens of a biological species and parts of nature, just as was done by naturalism. When, however, we have the task of further particularization of the concept of the individual, we have to ascend from what is abstract, and therefore simple, to what is concrete, and therefore complicated. According to Marx, it is only by this method that we can obtain a picture of a complex concrete individual not as a hodgepodge of speculation but a coherent whole. Consequently, observation begins with the real individual whose social analysis should reveal the whole of the relationships that are our frame of reference in intellectual reconstruction of this concrete individual. By his condensed description of human essence as the ensemble of social relations, Marx wanted to explain why a given man, formed as he is by specific social condtions, is characterized by specific attitudes and views.

The above remarks were intended to introduce the climate of methodological presuppositions of Marxian analysis—since this may contribute to a better understanding of the problem. Now let us revert to the main theme of our discussion.

The logical point of departure for Marx's analysis is the conviction that man, both as a species and as an individual specimen of this species, is a result of historical development, that is, a social product. In stating this conviction, Marx does not simply echo Aristotle's truism (for such at bottom it is) that man is a *zoon politikon*—in other words, that he always lives and produces in conjunction with others and is, from his infancy, dependent on society, without which he could not survive. He says much more— that man is a *product* of society, that it is society that makes him what he is. This Marx saw and understood at a very early date; at any rate he was already writing to this effect in *A Contribution to the Critique of Hegel's Philosophy of Right,* and in a more profound and developed form in the *Manuscripts.* But having decided that man is not just a product of nature, that his is not some immutable "human nature" that was given him at birth, that under the impact of historical conditions he changes his attitudes, opinions, evaluations, etc.—in a word, that he is a product of society, he had to explain precisely what all this means.

In the Preface to *A Contribution to the Critique of Hegel's Philosophy of Right,* Marx points out that the critique of religion has posed the problem of man more sharply and writes:

"But *man* is not an abstract being, squatting outside the world. Man is *the world of men,* the State, and society." [18]

The point is not only that man is *linked* with the world and society but—and this is to go much further—that he is also constituted, *created* by this world.

The *Theses on Feuerbach* are another step forward in the deciphering of this proposition: the essence of man = the entirety of social conditions.[19]

From the point of view of historical materialism, the idea is relatively simple and clear. If consciousness does not determine being, but being determines consciousness and if human attitudes, opinions, evaluations, etc., are a historical product and result of mutual interaction between base and superstructure—except however, that over longer periods the movement of the whole is ultimately regulated by the movement of the base—then the general psychological structure of men under given conditions depends on the pattern of social relations, particularly in the sphere of production. These relations are the basis of his consciousness—they *create* it—although this creative process is an extremely complicated one. What philosophers call "human nature" or the "essence of man" is thus reduced to the status of a product—or a function—of social relations.

What is, however, so clear and simple when the existence of a developed theory of historical materialism is taken for granted seems much more complicated at a time it does not yet exist. It is a historical fact that the concept of the human individual in the Marxist theory was not deduced from the premises of historical materialism, but on the contrary, Marx's sociology was developed from the problem of the individual. But this only concerns the ways of reaching the final formulations and not the substance of the case. This was expounded clearly enough in the passage from *The German Ideology* quoted above.

Man is born into a definite society under definite social conditions and human relations; he does not choose them: rather, they exist as a result of the activity of earlier generations. And it is on the foundation of these and no other social conditions—which are based on relations of production—that the entire involved structure of views, systems of values, and their concomitant institutions is erected. Views of what is good or bad, worthy or unworthy, that is, a defined system of values, are socially *given*—and so is knowledge of the world which is determined by the historical development of society. Through the prevailing social consciousness, social relations give shape to the individual who is born and educated in a specific society. In this sense, social relations *create* the individual. This can only be denied by asserting nativism—something that nobody but a racist would publicly risk saying today as of any scientific value. This is a result of the advance of psychological knowledge, but also of Marxist-influenced sociology.

Man is not born with any innate ideas about the world and certainly not with inborn moral ideas—as is proved, at the very least, by the tremendous variability of such views not only over the course of history, but even in the same period among different societies, evolving under different conditions. On the other hand, men are born with certain possibilities of development and these depend on their historically formed psycho-physical structure. This is a result of phylogenesis, which in its turn is also historically determined. But at a certain level of biological evolution, which changes very slowly, man—in the sense of his attitudes, opinions, value-judgments, etc.—is a product of ontogenesis, a wholly social product. For what he becomes in ontogenesis is fully determined socially; and this in a way that is quite beyond his control—through language, which embodies a certain type of thinking, and education, which imparts certain customs, modes of behavior and of ethics, etc. Education does it so thoroughly that even after we realize their origins and their relative nature, we usually remain unable to free ourselves of them. Indeed, even our ways of hearing and seeing—our response to music and art, our literary tastes, and so on—are formed in the same way, in most cases independent of our more mature and conscious reflection on these matters.

Thus man's mental outlook, his consciousness, is formed as a result and expression of certain social conditions. His ontogenesis, which is a function of the whole of social conditions in a given period, can indirectly be described as a whole. This is, naturally, a figurative way of speaking, but the meaning of what we want to convey by this metaphor is obvious.

This description of the individual does not conflict with the statement that the individual is a specimen of a biological species, since neither claims the role of a definition. When dealing with such a complicated entity as man, an analysis only of some of his many aspects or elements is attempted. Now if the statement that the individual man, as a specimen of a biological species, is part of nature settles one aspect of the problem by separating it from the theocentric or heteronomous, then the statement that man's consciousness is in its many forms a function of social relations as a whole takes care of another sphere of problems and queries. There is no competition, no mutual exclusion here. On the contrary, both spheres of investigation are complementary, although even when taken together they do not exhaust the whole of the problem. Some essential questions remain unanswered—and we shall try to take up at least a few of them in our further considerations. These too will be directed toward completing the concept of the human individual, as here set forth, rather than putting forward any competitive formulations.

It may be useful at this point to consider the heuristic value of the description of the individual (in the sense of his attitudes and his consciousness) as a function of the dominant social conditions.

In at least two senses this allows the notion of the individual to become concrete.

First, in the sense of the methodological requirement that the concrete should be arrived at through what is abstract and simpler. There is no doubt that the concrete human individual, from whom any social analysis must start, is structurally a most difficult entity. If the material and spiritual components of this involved structure were to be left aside, then the designations "man" or the "human individual" would be too abstract, and of such generality as to be of little use. But if we begin with the component elements, and an analysis of them can be carried out by their reduction to certain social conditions, then we may arrive at an incomparably richer reconstruction of the concrete individual. Moreover, this brings clarity to such cryptic, often mystified spheres of human life as systems of values and patterns of evaluations and behaviors based on these systems. We shall return to this when we discuss alienation and fetishism.

Second, when problems of the individual man are interpreted as a function of social conditions, then the conception of the individual can be particularized by clarifying his relationships with groups and with society. This is undoubtedly one of the key issues of any philosophical anthropology—and in Marxism it finds an unambiguous solution on the basis of the interaction between the individual and society (or social group).

The individual is in a quite specific sense a function of social relations and social conditions; that is, he is a product of society in the concrete form in which a given society exists. If social relations are class relations, as determined by the mode of production, then the individual is a product of these relations, conditioned by his class membership. But the problem cannot be reduced to broad social classes; it also involves social strata, occupational groups, etc., which depend upon the structure of a society and the role this specific arrangement plays at a given time and in given conditions. The concept of the individual thus acquires a much more concrete shape and becomes more firmly rooted in society, in its separate parts which are the results of the existing conditions.

When this aspect of the question is brought into focus, the heuristic significance of the Marxist conception becomes obvious; it is shown by the fact that it has been ever more widely accepted by modern anthropology.

Critics of this idea have yet another argument. Since the individual is thought to be reduced to the ensemble of social relations, he is thereby entirely reduced to the group; consequently, although the theory indeed has room for social groups, no genuine concept of the individual can be constructed on its foundation.

I have already made a passing reference to this argument and I can only say again that it is a pseudo-argument. It only makes sense

if we accept by definition either the standpoint of Christian personalism, which rests on a distinction between the physical individual
and the spiritual person, or the existentialist concept of the individual as a spiritual monad of free will, which, in the final analysis,
does not differ from the personalist view. The problem belongs to
the sphere of the individual's *ontological status,* a sphere in which
Marxism radically differs from both personalism and existentialism.
Here nothing can be *tacitly* assumed; each point of view must be
made explicit—all the more so for personalism, since there is a
musty flavor of metaphysics about this theory, which when clearly
stated shows its anti-scientific and metaphysical character. It must
be rejected not only by Marxism but by any school of thought
that is unwilling to be at odds with modern science. And this is
something that no philosophy that cares about its influence can
afford.

If, however, this theory is not accepted by definition, the whole
pseudo-argument collapses. For why should the human individual,
as a specimen of a biological species, cease to be an individual if
his views and opinions are genetically conceived as socially determined, and so as a social product? Unless I *assume*—on what
grounds other than metaphysical faith could I do so anyway?—that
what I call an individual cannot be so determined, the whole argument falls apart: the scientific data supply evidence of this social
conditioning, and that settles the matter. But if I do make such an
assumption, then from this point of view of the scientific argument,
attitude can be rejected as metaphysical speculation and the problem regarded as closed.

Let us now consider the third essential element of the Marxian
concept of the individual.

The interpretation of the individual both as part of nature and
as a function of social relations fits into the man-centered, autonomous, conception that takes the human world for its point of departure, remains within it, and dissociates itself from all theories
that hold that man's destiny is governed by the influence of any
extra-human factors. To complete the picture, one more question
must be answered: how did social man come into being and how
did he develop? For to say that man has a link with nature and

with society does not in itself give a complete answer to the question: what is man?

Where is the answer to be sought? Marx thought that it was in human *labor*, in human *practice*—conceived as a process in which man transforms the objective reality—and, with it, himself. *Self-creation*—this is Marx's answer to the question, and without this answer it would be impossible to grasp the basic characteristics of his concept of the human individual.

Marx did not invent this answer—here too he is indebted to Hegel and through him to the English economists (notably Adam Smith). Naturally, Marx did not take over Hegel's idea of self-creation as it stood: in this case, too, he "turned the Hegelian theory right side up." And he also differs from the English economists.[20] What is important is that Marx's point of departure is an individual who not only thinks and reasons but also *acts* consciously and rationally.

Labor is the fundamental form of this transforming activity—because man, unlike mythological forces, creates everything from something, not from nothing. Human labor *transforms* the objective reality and thereby turns it into *human* reality, that is, a result of human labor. And in transforming the objective reality—nature and society—man transforms the conditions of his own existence, and consequently himself, too, as a species. In this way, the human process of *creation* is, from man's point of view, a process of *self-creation*. It was in this way—through labor—that *Homo sapiens* was born, and it is through labor that he continues to change and transform himself.

Marx formulated and developed this point in the *Manuscripts of 1844:*

> The outstanding achievement of Hegel's *Phenomenology* . . . is, first, that Hegel conceives the self-creation of man as a process . . . and that he thus grasps the essence of *labor,* and comprehends objective man—true, because real man—as the outcome of man's *own labor* . . . Hegel's standpoint is that of modern political economy. He grasps *labor* as the *essence* of man . . .[21]

Though Hegel did not conceive labor as concrete practice but transformed it into a spiritual activity, this misconception was by no means general in those days. Goethe, for example, gives Faust a beautiful and profound speech on this theme (vv. 1224–37):

Geschrieben steht: "Im Anfang war das Wort!"
Hier stock' ich schon! Wer hilft mir weiter fort?
Ich kann das Wort unmöglich so hoch schätzen,
ich muss es anders übersetzen,
wenn ich vom Geiste recht erleuchtet bin.
Geschrieben steht: im Anfang war der Sinn.
Bedenke wohl die erste Zeile,
dass deine Feder sich nicht übereile.
Ist es der Sinn, der alles wirkt und schafft?
Es sollte stehen: Im Anfang war die Kraft.
Doch, auch indem ich dieses niederschreibe,
schon warnt mich was, dass ich dabei nicht bleibe.
Mir hilft der Geist! Auf einmal seh' ich Rat
und schreibe getrost: Im Anfang war die Tat.

An English translation for the above passage follows:

It is written: In the beginning was the Word.
Here I am stuck at once. Who will help me on?
I am unable to grant the Word such merit,
I must translate it differently
If I am truly illumined by the spirit.
It is written: In the beginning was the Mind.
But why should my pen scour
So quickly ahead? Consider that first line well.
Is it the Mind that effects and creates all things?
It *should* read: In the beginning was the Power.
Yet, even as I am changing what I have writ,
Something warns me not to abide by it.
The spirit prompts me, I see in a flash what I need,
And write: In the beginning was the Deed! [22]

The philosophy of the deed—involving both the categories of doing and of working—was in those year predominantly the concern of idealist thinkers, Cieszkowski among them. In this respect

Marx had learned a great deal from them—as he himself loyally acknowledged in his *Theses on Feuerbach,* in which he also critically assessed the idealists' narrow approach.

In the first Thesis Marx criticized all previous materialism because of its contemplative character, its concentration on the object, and its neglect of the subjective aspect. This was why the problem of human activity, the active side, was developed by idealism, although it did not conceive activity as practice.

But it is the third Thesis which is particularly illuminating in the context of our argument.

> The materialist doctrine that men are products of circumstances and upbringing and that, therefore, changed men are products of other circumstances and changed upbringing, forgets that it is men that change circumstances and that the educator himself needs educating. . . .
>
> The coincidence of the changing of circumstances and of human activity can only be conceived and rationally understood as *revolutionizing practice.*[23]

This brings out the most profound idea inherent in the notion of man's self-creation: in changing the conditions of his existence, man also changes himself, creates himself. In the further course of these discussions, we will try to show how fruitful this hypothesis has been for the solution of the problem of historical progress and of man's boundless possibilities of improvement.

It is precisely in reference to the content of self-creation that the significance of the category of practice (*praxis*) becomes clear. This category has multiple meanings and applications in Marxist philosophy in general, and in anthropology and epistemology in particular. But its historical origins are bound up with the sphere of politics. Marx came to his interpretation of human activity as practice through understanding the role of *revolutionary practice* in human life. I do not agree with Auguste Cornu that Marx's *praxis* is a substitute for the notion of alienation. It is in fact connected with alienation but the links are different: investigating alienation from the point of view of his search for ways of overcoming it, Marx came to the conclusion that this can be achieved not by speculation but only by human revolutionary practice. "The weapon of criticism," he wrote in *A Contribution to a Critique of the Hegelian Philosophy of Right*, "cannot, of course, replace criticism of the weapon; material force must be overthrown by material force." [24] This appreciation of the role of practice came from Marx's philosophical inquiry into alienation and into the means of overcoming it, and from the political activity that was pushing him step by step towards radical communism. His mental evolution—particularly in the field of philosophy—cannot be understood if it is examined out of the context of his practical activity and his political experiences.

The notion of man's self-creation through labor is an utterly radical denial of theocentricism and its related heteronomy. In Gramsci's fine phrase, [25] it is only in the light of this concept that "we are the blacksmiths of our lives, our destinies," and it is only in its terms that we can call "man a process, or more strictly, a process of his actions." How broad and hopeful are the horizons inherent in such a philosophy of man!

The human individual as part of nature, as an object; the individual as part of society—whose attitudes, opinions, and evaluations are explained as a function of social relations; finally, the individual as a product of self-creation, of the practical activity of men as makers of history—these are the foundations of the Marxian concept of the individual.

This picture does not contain *all* the elements of this concept; it is neither possible nor necessary that it should. Nor is it an attempt at definition—despite Aristotle, this is not always of primary importance, nor is it essential—even though all the ingredients for such a definition are given. But what probably matters most is that, as a result of this concept, the problem of the ontological status of the human individual can be solved in a way that makes it radically different from the rival anthropologies of personalism and existentialism.

Our remarks on the Marxian concept of the individual would

not be complete without consideration of such concepts as "human nature," "human being," "species-being," "real man and true man," "integral man," etc., all of which appear in Marx's early writings. Regardless of the merits of the arguments in which they are embodied, they certainly add to our appreciation of the humanism of the young Marx and make us aware of a number of questions that, even if we reject the form in which they are couched or the solutions advocated, enrich our vision of the individual. Many of these questions are organically connected with the preceding analysis of the concept of the individual. But while previously they threatened to disrupt the structure and blur the clarity of the argument, they will now serve to cast additional light on what has already been analyzed—or at least to make this analysis more complete.

We have already pointed out that a concept of the individual is not tantamount to a definition and that definition is not what matters most here. Yet it is a definition we want when asking about the meaning of the phrase "to be human" or the more traditional term, the "human essence." Personally, I would prefer to avoid the notion of "essence," because of its metaphysical burden. But it was used not only many times but unfortunately in more than one meaning by the young Marx; besides, it conceals a meaning that deserves reflection. Let me go into this point more deeply.

The most penetrating and painstakingly scrupulous analysis I have seen of the notion of "human essence" in all the many senses in which Marx employed it can be found in Marek Fritzhand's essay " 'Istota człowieka' w ujęciu Marksa" (" 'Human essence' as Conceived by Marx").[26] It relieves me from having to undertake a similar analysis—all the more because this is not strictly a "Marxological" study. I shall therefore dwell on that aspect of the problem of "human essence" which is directly connected with the concept of the individual.

When asking about "human essence," we want to learn about the entire complex of characteristics that make it possible to distinguish man, as a class of certain individuals from other parts of reality. In other words, we want a definition by which we can tell man from non-man. What is required is a set of peculiar features— so general and universal as to be applicable wherever the species

Homo sapiens has come or will come, regardless of the differences arising from time, space, level of development, race, etc. In blocking out such a definition along the classical lines *per genus proximum et differentiam specificam,* we want to distinguish our class of objects—the species *Homo sapiens*—not, say, from minerals, since this would be trivially simple, but from another class of objects which, as a type, is closest to man, namely from animals.

Among the many senses that the question about "human essence" has for the young Marx (in his maturity, he carefully avoided this phraseology, which he had already ridiculed in *The German Ideology*) *this* particular meaning is, in my view, of special importance, since it provides a better insight into Marx's concept of the individual. In any case, *this* element is even today indispensable for the structure of such a concept and is closely connected with what has been previously said on the subject.

Marx sees the "human essence" in the process of production.

> Men can be distinguished from animals by consciousness, by religion, or by anything else you like. They themselves begin to distinguish themselves from animals as soon as they begin to *produce* their means of subsistence, a step which is conditioned by their physical organization. By producing their means of subsistence men are directly producing their actual material life.[27]

Thus Marx does not deny that man is distinct from animals by various manifestations of his consciousness—apart from religion, there are many others, language above all—but he reduces all of them to productive labor. In any case, in so far as the origins are concerned, they are all inseparably connected with each other: labor, conceptual thinking, and language.

This interlinking is not only genetic, but also actual. *Productive* labor is a conscious process—and this distinguishes it from the behavior of animals.

> The animal is immediately one with its life activity. It does not distinguish itself from this activity. It is *its life activity.* Man makes his life activity itself the object of his

will and of his consciousness. He has conscious life activity. It is not a determination with which he directly merges. Conscious life activity distinguishes man immediately from the animal life activity.[28]

After many years, Marx repeated this in the first volume of *Capital*—in the famous comparison between the bee and the architect. The bee makes a better honeycomb than the most talented architect could. But the architect is superior to the bee in that he *plans* what he wants to build *before* beginning his work. Or, to put it in psychological terms, the activity of the bee is instinctive, that of the architect conscious.

It is precisely with this character of human labor that production of the tools of production is connected. Tools, in the proper sense of the word, are linked to *conscious* productive activity. In *Capital,* Marx quotes Franklin's dictum that man is *a toolmaking animal,* but—as Fritzhand points out—this is not a definition of man, nor an attempt to *reduce* the peculiarity of human labor to production of the means of labor; what it means is that such production *characterizes* human labor (that is, it is characteristic of this labor, and only of it, but it is not its only characteristic; it is a necessary, but not a sufficient condition).[29]

In Engels' essay on "The Part Played by Labor in the Transition from Ape to Man" (1876), the idea that productive labor was the essence of man was extended to cover the genesis of man.

Semantic analysis of the phrase "human essence" as used by Marx shows, as I have already pointed out, that it has other meanings as well. According to Fritzhand's analysis, it may be tantamount to society, the human world, human needs, etc. These meanings are interrelated, but still different. Thus, when seeking an answer to the question about what distinguishes man from the animal—what are the most general features characteristic of *Homo sapiens* throughout the history of his existence (regardless of any internal differentiation of the species), we follow Marx in pointing primarily to labor in the sense of conscious productive activity.

Such an approach to the problem of "human essence" brings us closer to a proper understanding of the notion of the expression "species essence" and of its problems and implications. In passing, two warnings need to be given: first, against terminology inherited from the metaphysical tradition, and second, against the danger of linguistic hypostases related to such usage. Thus "essence" has various meanings, both in "human essence" and in "species essence."

In *The German Ideology,* Marx clearly dissociated himself from this phraseology, although he had employed it freely only a year or two earlier:

> Since use was still made of philosophical phraseology, such philosophical expressions as "essence of man," "species," etc., which had slipped in there, provided the German theoreticians with a coveted opportunity of misunderstanding the actual development and believing that all that was needed was to turn their worn theoretical clothes. . . . It is necessary to "leave philosophy aside" . . . to get rid of it, and, as a normal man, to investigate reality; for this purpose there is an enormous amount of material in literature, which, naturally, is unknown to philosophers. . . . Philosophy is to investigation of the real world what masturbation is to sexual love.[30]

Here is why Marx abandoned this "philosophical" jargon, although in no way did he disparage the problems that it had designated so ambiguously.

As we know from what has already been said, Marx deliberately took the concrete individual as the point of departure for his analysis. But he also insisted on the latter's relationship with society—and this was one of the reasons why he asserted that man is a species being. What then did he understand by such notions as "species" or "society"? If taken in isolation from individuals who make up society or species, he considered them a hypostasis of language, and, fully aware of this, warned against excessive use of similar expressions.

In criticism of the so-called "true socialism," Marx and Engels in 1846 wrote a *Circular against Kriege* in which they expressly protested against such hypostatizing. Commenting on Kriege's claim that communist man sets himself targets that conform with the targets of the species, they add in parenthesis "as if the species were a person who can have targets." [31] And on another page, referring to Kriege's platitudes about humanity, they talk about servility "to an abstract and impersonal 'humanity' which as such is a metaphysical, and (in Kriege) even a religious fiction." [32]

This attitude had its sharpest reflection in Marx's criticism of Proudhon:

> To prove that all labour must leave a surplus, M. Proudhon personifies society; he turns it into a *person, Society*—a society which is not by any means a society of persons, since it has its laws apart, which have nothing in common with the persons of which society is composed, and its "own intelligence" which is not the intelligence of the common herd but an intelligence devoid of common sense. M. Proudhon reproaches the economists with not having understood the personality of this collective being. We have pleasure in confronting him with the following passage from an American economist who accuses the economists of just the opposite: "The moral entity, the grammatical being known as society, has been invested with attributes which have no real existence except in the imagination of those who turn a word into a thing. . . . This has given rise to many difficulties and to some deplorable misunderstandings in political economy." [33]

What is significant here is the approving quotation from Cooper. Pervaded by a nominalist spirit, it leaves no doubt—especially when compared with Marx's other statements—of his dislike of language hypostases; and it is obvious that he was fully aware of their role in human thinking.

Following these remarks, we can with greater safety move on to the slippery ground of the doctrine of "species-essence" and its meaning. Let me repeat: it is not our intention to supply a detailed reconstruction of Marx's early doctrines (here again we refer to

Marek Fritzhand's "Man–Humanism–Morality"). I merely want to elicit those elements of Marx's theory of "species-essence" which can shed some more light on his concept of the individual.

As Marx himself admitted in later years, "species-being" was part of the current philosophical phraseology of the age. He had taken it from Feuerbach. As I have already pointed out, this is not an essay to search for influences; I am interested in the shape of Marxist thinking on the individual, as it emerged in the course of Marx's intellectual development or as it could be deduced from his theory whenever he himself did not draw all the conclusions of his thoughts. But in some cases an exception must be made, notably when a study of the influences on Marx's thought can make for better understanding. This is particularly true of the "phraseology" (as he called it) that he took over from the current philosophical vocabulary—not necessarily lock, stock, and barrel but at any rate with much of its semantic paraphernalia: without appreciating these liabilities, much, and sometimes all, of the sense of the problem is lost.

To Feuerbach—as to Marx after him—the question of human essence was inseparable from man's relationship with other men, his membership of the species *Homo sapiens*—and consequently inseparable from the fact that man is, as the jargon of the time put it, a species being.

The human essence, that is, the set of features characteristic of man, lies, according to Feuerbach, not with the individual as such, but in the unity of man with other men. Today we would say that it is linked with the *social* individual, but Feuerbach—and he was taken to task for this by Marx—did not yet apprehend society in the proper sense of the word, but only the I–Thou relationship in the sphere of love and friendship. Even so, the meaning of his doctrine is not only quite clear but also—apart from its limited character—fully acceptable to Marx.

> The human individual as such [*für sich*] does not contain the essence of man either in itself as a moral being or as a thinking being. The essence of man is only contained in the community, the unity of man with man—but in a

unity which is at the same time based on the real difference between I and Thou.[34]

Feuerbach, as Marx later pointed out in his *Theses on Feuerbach,* conceives the human essence as an abstraction inherent in each individual, since he interprets it merely as a natural bond, a "species," not as a function of social relations—and thus not historically. But Feuerbach is aware that what he calls human essence is not linked with any particular individual, since what is involved is a set of features characteristic of a *whole* class, and not any of its elements. It is this that leads Feuerbach, despite the shakiness of his conceptual apparatus and the limited nature of his doctrine, to protest against subjectivist individualism in the manner of Stirner and to defend the idea of a social individual. He emphasized this himself in his criticism of Stirner on the matter of "species:

> In Feuerbach, the species does not designate an abstraction, but merely some Thou opposed to a particular, self-established I, some other human individuals, existing generally, outside myself. Thus when we read in Feuerbach: "the individual is limited, the species is limitless" —this only means that the limitations of this particular individual are not necessary limitations of others, and so the limitations of men today are not limitations of future men.[35]

Thus "species" here means simply "other individuals existing apart from me." Or, to put it differently, when I say "species-essence" I want to indicate that the meaning of "being human" cannot be explained by the example of any single individual, since his limitation is not necessarily the limitation of others. Perfection is an attribute of a multitude of individuals, and so of a species conceived in space and time. Hence the meaning of the model of "man" or the ideal type of "being human" can only be referred to the species—that is, to a class of individuals taken synchronically and diachronically, never to some concrete individual. Perfection is only attainable as a process of fulfillment of what is possible from the point of view of the species. This is Feuerbach's position.

What does it mean to "realize the species"? To realize some disposition, some ability, in general some feature of the human nature. The caterpillar is an insect, but not yet the whole insect. . . . Only the butterfly is the fulfilled insect, fully realized. Similar metamorphoses occur both in the life of mankind and in the life of a single individual.[36]

It is only by grasping the meaning of the notion "species" in Feuerbach's writings that we can fully understand Marx's "species-essence."

How Marx interpreted Feuerbach's thinking is authoritatively clear from his own letter to Feuerbach of August, 1844, the period of his work on the *Manuscripts.* Commenting on Feuerbach's *Philosophy of the Future and Essence of Religion,* Marx wrote:

In these studies you have created—I do not know whether this was your purpose—the philosophical foundation of socialism, and this is how the communists have immediately understood your works. Men's unity with men, based on their actual differences, the notion of the human species brought from the heaven of abstraction to the earth of reality—what else is this if not the notion of *society!* [37]

This is an instance of what a jurist would call authentic interpretation, and it testifies that when Marx refers to "species" in connection with man, he means "society" and when he speaks of man as a "species being," he means a "social individual." These words, written as they were in the summer of 1844, are an important clue to Marx's early writings.

It was in those years that Marx analyzed the duality of man in bourgeois society: by this he meant the duality, or even inner conflict, of man as an individual motivated by selfish private interests —that is a citizen (*bourgeois*), a member of a civil society—and of man as a member (*citoyen*) of a political community that pursues common interests. In this connection the meaning of the phrase "species essence" becomes particularly clear.[38]

"Species-being" (*Gattungswesen*) also has other meanings in Marx's writings:

1. ". . . man is only individualized through the process of history, he originally appears as a *generic being*, a *tribal being*, . . ." [39]

2. a being engaged in a conscious life activity. ("Conscious life activity distinguishes man from the life activity of animals. Only for this reason is he a species-being. Or rather he is only a self-conscious being, i.e., his own life is an object for him, because he is a species-being" [40]

3. a being who treats his species as his own being (incidentally, the word "being"—*Wesen*—is used here twice in two different meanings)

4. further, ". . . *manipulation* of inorganic nature is the confirmation of man as a conscious species-being, i.e., a being who treats the species as his own being or himself as a species-being") [41]

Thus the phrase "species-being" or "species-essence" is used by Marx in at least four different meanings, notably as a synonym for

1. "social being" (see the above letter to Feuerbach and also the quotation from Marx's essay *On the Jewish Question*, note 38 above)

2. "a being constituting a specimen of the species" or a "herd being" (see the quotation from *Grundrisse der Kritik der politischen Ökonomie,* note 39)

3. "a being engaged in a conscious life activity" (see the quotations from the *Manuscripts*)

4. a "being which corresponds to the model of man" (*ibid.*)

What matters here above all is to draw a line between two meanings of the phrase "species-being": First, one stresses that man belongs to a biological species as a specimen sharing some general characteristics with all other specimens of this species; and Second, one emphasizes that man possesses a certain model of what man should be like, which is a result of his own reflection on the properties and tasks of his own species—a model which is a source of the norms of human conduct as a "species-being," that is a being which fits in with a certain model or stereotype of man (the "essence" of man).

The point in the first case is *membership* in *the species,* while what is involved in the second is *compliance with a certain model.* The latter sense is particularly interesting in this context, for it is connected with other categories of Marxist anthropology—those of "human essence" and of "true" and "real" man ("human essence" is what constitutes the model of man, and man is only "true" if he complies with his model).

I have devoted so much space to this question only to indicate that the young Marx was no stickler for accuracy and semantic precision in his vocabulary. If it is remembered that after a few years he himself ridiculed these mannerisms and repudiated this terminology, this should be sufficient warning to be wary in the interpretation of similar texts—or at any rate to think twice before using them as a basis for constructing ingenious theories in the name of Marxism. Certainly they contain much that is stimulating, and they illuminate Marxian humanism—and this is a great deal. But one should not try to "find" in them what is not there.

From the point of view of Marx's concept of the individual, analysis of the "species-being" sheds additional light on the evolution of the notion of the *social* individual in Marxian anthropology. The human individual was the point of departure, but he was from the outset seen in his relationship with other individuals, and thus socially. But Marx's appreciation of the individual's social nature grew as he moved away from Feuerbachian materialism, and his final break was accompanied by the disappearance of the "philosophical phraseology" of the species-being; this was replaced by the social individual interpreted in terms of the whole of social relations. "Human essence," that is, the set of attributes characterizing the class of objects designated by the term "man," was at first seen by Marx as connected with the species of which each "species-being" is a specimen; then it became quite clearly related to society which, while absorbing the characteristics of the biological species, adds specifically social features to purely biological ones and thus allows a fuller understanding of the "human essence." In this context the concept of the "species-being"—and its importance for Marx's intellectual development—becomes much more lucid, but it also brings out its limitations when viewed in the light of his mature concept of the individual.

Another category that occurs in Marx's writings and so, if only for this reason, requires interpretation and consideration of its implications for the concept of the individual, is that of "human nature."

According to Marx himself, this was also part of the "philosophical phraseology" current in the circles of his youth. Its tradition goes back to the Age of Enlightenment with its belief in the existence of something like an unchanging human nature. Such a doctrine is so clearly incompatible with the Marxian historical understanding that obviously it could have no place in Marx's own system. Yet he did not avoid the phrase and in his early writings often referred to "human nature." It is sometimes asserted that he interpreted it historically, as a set of characteristics that vary according to conditions, while "human essence" was to him the set of general and universal features undergoing no change during the whole course of the development of the species *Homo sapiens.* This view can be easily refuted if only by pointing to the famous sixth *Thesis on Feuerbach,* which describes human essence as an *ensemble* of social relations and so apprehends it in historical terms, stressing the variability of the human individual in accordance with social relations. It seems to me to be an attempt to provide a rational explanation of Marx's early vocabulary, which was neither consistent nor precise.

The problem remains, however, and whether it actually was taken up by the young Marx or not, it is worth analyzing in the context of our reflections on the Marxist concept of the individual.

There are two antithetical ways in which the problem of "human nature" can be solved. One of them is implied by the philosophy of the Enlightenment, Age of Reason, when an unchanging, naturally given "essence" or "nature" of man was taken for granted. The opposite way is the relativist idea of man as a product and function of conditions.

Marx rejects the idea of an unchanging "human nature" as incompatible with experience—and with that historical understanding, which is the theoretical generalization of this experience. Does this mean that he accepts relativism, thus rejecting any constant elements that are more or less stabilized, not only in the anatomic and physiological, but also in the psychological structure of man? Certainly not. This can be even proved by Marx's later words.

In his criticism of Bentham in the first volume of *Capital,* Marx wrote:

> The principle of utility was no discovery of Bentham. He simply reproduced in his dull way what Helvetius and other Frenchmen had said with esprit in the 18th century. To know what is useful for a dog, one must study dog-nature. The nature itself is not to be deduced from the principle of utility. Applying this to man, he that would criticise all human acts, movements, relations, etc., by the principle of utility, *must first deal with human nature in general, and then with human nature as modified in each historical epoch.*[42]

In this passage—and it certainly cannot be called a "youthful aberration"—Marx refers to human nature "in general" or "historically modified." While there is no doubt that he is clearly dissociating himself from relativism, exactly what he means by "human nature in general" is more difficult to clarify. On this point, for that matter, Marx's position does not seem conclusive and more than one interpretation is possible. Let me point to the problems implied.

Erich Fromm, who deals with this question in several of his books, poses what I think is an interesting question:

> That all men share the same basic anatomical and physiological features is common knowledge, and no physician would think he could not treat every man, regardless of race and colour, with the same methods he has applied to men of his own race. But does man have also in common the same psychic organization: do all men have in common the same human nature? Is there such an entity as "human nature"?[43]

And he answers:

"The whole concept of humanity and of humanism is based on the idea of a human nature in which all men share." [44]

Let me begin with a negative argument: a defense of relativism in this case would be tantamount to a defense of racism. For if we agree that different conditions breed different human types, then, even if we restrict the scope of this principle to human psychic organization, we give the racist an argument to use: if there are human types at higher and lower levels of organization (psychically, if not physically), a doctrine of superior and inferior races becomes tenable.

This, however, is a wild shot in the dark, not an argument; for if facts can be cited in support of relativism, it cannot simply be rejected because we are afraid of its implications. Let me then tackle the positive argument.

As Fromm points out in the passage just quoted, no doctor would dream of denying the identity of the anatomy and physiology of all men regardless of their color or other distinctive physical traits—and therefore the similarity of diagnosis and treatment in all cases. But what is the position regarding the psychic structure of men?

Can we assume that this structure is fully dependent on conditions and therefore has no stable elements, that it varies in space and time? If this were true, we would be unable to understand the attitudes and views of people from distant historical periods; indeed we could not understand those of our own time who live in different conditions and have other historical traditions.

That this is not the case is proved by the fiasco of the two most extensive attempts in the twentieth century to justify psychic relativism: Lévy-Bruhl's theory of prelogism and the so-called Sapir-Whorf hypothesis of linguistic relativism. Without going into the detail, we recall only that according to both these theories the so-called primitive peoples have, because of completely different living conditions, a psychic organization quite different from ours; this is based on a different logic, as was maintained by prelogism (before his death, Lévy-Bruhl admitted this was a fallacy), or on a different articulation of the word, as is asserted by the radical ver-

sion of the Sapir-Whorf hypothesis, although in this form it is uni-
versally rejected.

It is a fact that men, regardless of differences in their history,
civilization, culture, or race, not only can understand each other,
but can experience similar states of mind, particularly emotions. It
is due, at a minimum, to their common phylogenesis, which has produced an identical anatomical and physiological structure in all
groups belonging to the species *Homo sapiens*. This phylogenesis
and the resultant physical organization makes for analogous, if not
identical, intellectual, emotional, and volitional reactions in the
fundamental situations of human life. What matters here is not only
behavior, but also various kinds of psychic processes inseparably
linked with these reactions. It is not necessary to follow the Freud-
ians in their emphasis on the role of the different instincts (although, however we may interpret them, instincts certainly play a
role in this respect) to ascertain a certain homogeneity of the
human psyche—and this is by definition necessary to recognize a
given being as a specimen of the species "man."

How shall we therefore deal with the evident differences between
various human groups that have been formed under different conditions and are at various stages of development of intellectual life,
customs and manners, emotional response, etc.? Surely in the same
way as linguists do when refuting the Sapir-Whorf hypothesis that
various systems of language determine various ways of perceiving
the world. First, the differences are insignificant compared with
what unites all languages and the systems of thought based on them
(it is these links that make it possible to translate one language into
another, remote as they may be culturally); second, each language
can be suitably adapted to become a correlate of another, since it is
potentially capable of recording the objective reality in more than
one way.

Feuerbach—in the passage quoted above—understood "species"
as a definite possibility, a disposition to development; he said that
to "realize the species" means to transform these dispositions into
reality (as the caterpillar turns into a butterfly). Should we, therefore, identify what is common to all men—which is described in
"philosophical phraseology" as their nature—with those potenti-

alities of psychic development that are connected with the anatomical and physiological structure of the species *Homo sapiens* as
given in phylogenesis? This does not mean that we should ignore
the specific variety of ethnic groups—even in the sphere of their
psychic structure. There certainly exists something like a specific
national psychology, a specific temperament, etc. But it is also
certain that there is a set of traits that, at least potentially, are characteristic of *all* normal specimens of the species "man" and that—
although they too have been historically formed—change very
slowly and over relatively long development periods; it is due to
them that a living being can be classified as man. Is this not remi-
niscent of the Marxian distinction between human nature "in general" and its "historically modified," concrete forms in various ages
and societies? On this point, Fromm seems to be right:

> Marx was opposed to two positions: the unhistorical
> one that the nature of man is a substance present from the
> very beginning of history, and the relativistic position
> that man's nature has no inherent quality whatsoever and
> is nothing but the reflex of social conditions. But he never
> arrived at the full development of his own theory con-
> cerning the nature of man, transcending both the unhis-
> torical and the relativistic positions; hence he left himself
> open to various and contradictory interpretations.[45]

Closely related to this question is the distinction between the
"real" and the "true" man, which, although couched in the "philosophical phraseology" of the age, is extremely interesting in its
implications. This distinction between existence and essence, so
beloved of the existentialists, and as can be seen, known long before their time, was bound to appeal to certain circles, doubtless
enhancing the popularity of the young Marx. While the fact in itself is hardly deserving of historical note, the implications of the
problem for the concept of the individual are of considerable
importance.

What semantic connotations can be traced behind the distinction
between "real" and "true" man? Without going into all the subtle-
ties and nuances of these expressions, I think that the question can

be reduced essentially to the following argument: at the present time, there exist concrete human individuals who live in a world of alienation that deforms them and limits their development. These are real individuals, who *really exist* in the world around us. But over and above this, there is an *ideal* of man, his *ideal type,* as we would say today, corresponding to a vision of his potential development (the "nature," "essence" of man) were it not limited and deformed. This is the *true* man in the sense of an ideal, as distinct from the *real* man in the sense of his actual condition.

The *ideal type* of man, the image of *true* man, is at the basis of all aspirations in the human world—in efforts to "make man human" (as Marx wrote to Ruge), in resistance to the *"non-human"* world. Therein lies its importance—a point to which we shall return when discussing Marxist humanism and the struggle against alienation. It is clear that this vision is based on a certain system of values—and it is our choice of this system that is responsible for what we recognize as "human nature" and for our vision of the "true man" in a given age under given conditions. It is also easy to understand the links that connect Marx's distinction between the "true" and the "real" man with his acceptance of the idea that there exists something that he calls the "essence of man" and his "nature."

The concept of the "true" man as a "species-being," as distinct from "real" individuals, was taken directly from Feuerbach—who, however, as stressed above, saw human essence only in the community.

Marx, referring to Hegel and Feuerbach, developed his concept of the "true man" in close association with his analysis of political alienation and of the duality of man both as a selfish individual living in conditions of economic alienation (the individual as a member of a middle class civil society—a *bourgeois*) and as an individual belonging to society (the individual as a member of the "political community"—a *citoyen*). The "real" man is the bourgeois who, however, comes into conflict with the essence of man, with the "true" man. Hence the postulate that this duality must be overcome—which later led Marx gradually towards communism.

"The *real* man is the *private* man of the modern state system,"

Marx wrote in *A Contribution to the Critique of Hegel's Philosophy of Right.*[46] His essay *On the Jewish Question* contains a logical elaboration of this argument:

> The perfected political state is, by its nature, the *species-life* of man as *opposed* to his material life. All the presuppositions of this egoistic life continue to exist in *civil society outside* the political sphere, as qualities of civil society. Where the political state has attained its full development, man leads, not only in thought, in consciousness, but in *reality,* in *life,* a double existence —celestial and terrestrial. He lives in the *political community,* in which he regards himself as a *communal being,* and in *civil society* in which he acts simply as a *private individual.* . . . Man, in his *most intimate* reality, in civil society, is a profane being. Here, where he appears both to himself and to others as a real individual, he is an *illusory* phenomenon. In the state, on the contrary where he is regarded as a species-being, man is the imaginary member of an imaginary sovereignty, divested of his real, individual life, and infused with an unreal universality.[47]

The category of "true man" is closely associated with that of "whole man" (*totaler Mensch*) and becomes fully clear only in its light.

Just as the category of "true man" can only be understood when contrasted with that of "real man," so the meaning of the "whole man" (the "universal man") only emerges in contradistinction to the "alienated" and thus curtailed crippled man. I shall revert to these questions in my discussion of alienation and of communism as a social order which makes possible a full development of human personality. Here we shall deal with this subject only to the extent that clarification of certain categories and attitudes can enhance our knowledge of Marx's concept of the individual.

The universal man is the ideal individual who fully realizes the features that make up the "essence" of man or his "nature." He is a man of all-round accomplishments whose full development is not hampered by the prevailing social relations with their various forms of alienation. Above all, these include economic alienation (relations based on the private ownership of the means of production), political alienation (state, bureaucracy), ideological alienation, and others. We abstract here from the utopian element in the young Marx's views on the universality of the individual (particularly in *The German Ideology* with its glowing vision of an individual of all the talents who is, as the fancy takes him, by turns hunter, workman, artist, thinker, etc.). What matters now is to grasp the heart of this idea and the stimulating perspectives it offers.

The system of private property, with its characteristic division of labor, maims the individual, prevents the fulfillment of his personality. Only the "real" man can be found in this system—not the "true" man, who remains merely an ideal. On the other hand, it is only the true man who can be universal, whole as distinct from the crippled real man within the capitalist system. Actually, "true man" and "whole man" form a tautology, for the two notions are only semantically different aspects of the same thing. In this way, the categories of "human essence," "true man," and "whole man" are inseparably linked with each other. A "true" or "whole" man is a man in whom the "nature of man" is fulfilled. Apart from this logical connection, these categories have a practical link, for the realization of each of them depends on the elimination of alienation in social life—which is supposed to lead to the transformation of the individual into a species-being. The practical implications of this situation for Marxian communism, and the problem of its confrontation with practice, will be dealt with below. But it should be pointed out at once that no matter how one feels about the "philosophical phraseology" in which these questions are stated, there is no getting away from their real meaning and import.

Apart from the connection between the development of human personality and communism, the question of the "whole man," as it appears in Marx's early writings, has certain more general implications for the conception of the humanization of the world and for the links between humanism and naturalism. These are somewhat obscure, and misunderstandings have accumulated about them. A closer analysis will, therefore, be in order.

In the *Manuscripts* Marx wrote:

> Man appropriates his manifold being in an all-inclusive way, and thus as a whole man. All his *human* relations to the world—seeing, hearing, smelling, tasting, touching, thinking, observing, feeling, desiring, acting, loving —in short all the organs of his individuality, like the organs which are directly communal in form, are in their objective action (*their action in relation to the object*) the appropriation of this object, the appropriation of human reality. The way in which they react to the object is the confirmation of *human reality*.[48]

Marx goes on to argue that it is only in social practice that man's senses have become human senses, that man appropriates the objective reality as human reality. This leads him to the conclusion that consistent naturalism is equal to humanism, and vice versa. The whole argument, expressed as it is in the "philosophical phraseology" of his time, becomes intelligible only in the light of Marx's concept of *praxis* and only when reality is interpreted not passively but as a product of *activity*.

Such an approach involves two related questions.

One of them is connected with the concept of the "whole" man. He is an all-round man, for he is free from alienation and from the limitations it creates. But this is precisely why the objective world appears to him not merely as outward reality, which can only be contemplated, but also as a *product* of human activity. Objects are therefore objectified and reified human activity; in them man discovers himself and others, and in them he demonstrates himself to others, for—directly or indirectly—they are products of human activity. This world is human, and in appropriating it —and this can only be done by a man who is free of alienation—a man grows spiritually richer and enhances his talents. It is in this sense that the humanization of the world is linked to the concept of the whole man.

But there is another problem: does this approach entail the negation of objective reality, and so a rejection of materialism in favor of subjectivism?

We have already seen how groundless this is. In the *Manuscripts* Marx speaks clearly (we quoted the relevant passage) of reality existing independently of man, and this is by no means incompatible with his humanism. The point is that his idea of the humanization of the world through *praxis* is wholly compatible with materialism, although it has a certain form of particular importance for a specific treatment of this materialism.

When we say that the world is a product of human activity, we only mean that a given reality, as perceived by men acting socially, is transformed by them; it is also created by them in the sense that man perceives this reality on the basis of his social experience, that his perception and its organs—the senses—are a product of phylogenesis and so forth. None of this bears the slightest hint of idealism, and it is fully compatible with the doctrine of a material world that in a sense exists outside man and independent of him, a world that is not a product of men's consciousness, although a product of their work. There are no grounds whatsoever for the kind of speculation that tries to draw subjective—or idealist conclusions from these statements which paved the way to materialism. Such attempts cannot be blamed on the young Marx.

On the other hand, the doctrine of the humanization of nature and the objective world—in the sense of their being transformed and perceived by human activity and practice—contains something that is essential for our concept of the human individual and for our world-outlook in general. What is involved, in fact, is the dividing line between contemplative materialism, which segregates the world from man and interprets human perception in a purely passive way, and dialectical materialism, which is aware of the reciprocal dependence of the objective world and man—and the effects of that dependence in human perception.

In *Geschichte und Klassenbewusstsein,* Georg Lukács made the extremely crucial points that economic fatalism entails "ethical socialism," since so limited a view does not supply the justification for revolution; and, more generally, that a philosophical interpretation of the world as divorced from man leads to a concept of a human world divorced from nature. It is a commonplace that in the struggle between materialism and idealism each side seizes on the other's extravagances, which by militating against a full vision of the world, offer a target for attack.

A consistent materialist conception must recognize the objectivity of both nature and society. But this conception is organically bound to an acknowledgement of the role of practice, the activity of social man who transforms the world. Anyone who fails to grasp this truth can see with only half an eye. But once he has done so, he must take into account the interaction betwen nature and social man and appreciate their inseparability. In this sense materialism is integrally linked with man and his activity, and so with humanism in a special sense of the word. Behind the language of the young Marx, bizarre and imprecise as it may seem today, lie problems that are not only real, but also important. It is worth noting them, therefore, as spurs to thought and with projecting them onto the ground of Marx's mature inquiry.

Does the Marxian concept of the individual also embrace the *problem* of personality? Certainly. But does it contain a developed *theory* of personality? To this question no simple yes-or-no answer can be given: the Marxian treatment of the individual assuredly contains some of the strands for such a theory but not in a fully developed form.

Marx was familiar with the notions of personality and individuality and employed the appropriate terms. From his early youth he also had a clear idea of the ontological status of personality, thus creating the foundations of his own theory of personality: it was the defining factor of a real individual, peculiar to the individual. Individual and person cannot thus be separated, for they are merely two different names for the same real object. This statement —and it is of essential importance for a theory of personality based on materialism—follows from Marx's critique of Hegelian idealism, but its significance is much wider, extending as it does to other idealist theories of personality—particularly to Christian personalism.

But genuine subjectivity [says Hegel] exists only as a *subject,* personality only as a *person.* This too is a mystification. Subjectivity is a determination of the subject, personality a determination of the person. Instead of grasping them as predicates of their subjects, Hegel makes the predicates self-sufficient and in a mystical way has them later transformed into their subjects.

The existence of the predicates is the subject: thus the subject is the existence of subjectivity, etc. Hegel makes the predicates, the objects, self-sufficient but separated from their actual self-sufficiency, from their subject. . . . Hence the mystical substance turns into the actual subject and the real subject appears as something else, as a moment of mystical substance.[49]

This may be written in the ponderous, abstruse language of "philosophical phraseology," but the meaning is quite clear: there is an actual human individual who should be the starting point of analysis. He is a complex physico-spiritual unity and thus as a species can be examined in the light of his various properties and characteristics. A certain set of these, namely the spiritual, or mental properties, is called the personality of the given individual, the complex of his views, attitudes, and dispositions. Though this still leaves the problem of the individual somewhat obscure and imprecise, and in need of scientific elaboration (particularly by psychologists and anthropologists), we have at least recognized the essential issue: there is no person as a spiritual unity who can be distinguished from the individual as a real being. Personality is merely a special description of the individual, an attribute in the same way as his physical appearance. Thus, to hypostatize personality into "person" and separate it from the individual is as much a mystification as it would be to dissociate the individual from his physical appearance or his shadow and to endow them (as in Chamisso's strange story of *Peter Schlemihl*) with an independent existence.

Personality can be discussed tortuously and at length—all the more easily since no scientific school of thought has so far succeeded in saying anything precise on the subject. But common to all is the idea that the central issue of the theory of personality is dependent on the solution to the problem of the individual's onto-logical status, and the choice is relatively simple: *either* personality is conceived as a set of certain properties of a real subject—which thus becomes the natural point of departure for further analysis—*or* it is treated autonomously as a *spiritual person*—which implies an idealist approach not only to personality but also to the indi-vidual in general.

Thus the Marxist approach to the problem of personality is closely connected with its materialist answer to the question of the individual's ontological status. Recognition of the individual's social character and treatment of him as the totality of social rela-tions imply another conclusion: the personality of the individual is formed socially, it has a *social character*.

> The functions and spheres of state activity are linked to the individual (the state only acts through individ-uals); not, however, with the individual as a *physical* individual, but as a *member of the state*. They are con-nected with the *character* of an individual as a member of a state. Thus it is ridiculous for Hegel to say that "they are linked to the individual personality as such *in an external and accidental way*.". . . The state's func-tions and spheres are conceived by Hegel abstractly, in themselves, and the particular individuality as their con-tradiction; but he forgets that the particular individuality is human and that the state's functions and spheres of ac-tivity are human functions; he forgets that what consti-tutes the essence of a "particular individuality" is not beard, blood, abstract physical nature, but *social charac-ter*. . . .[50]

This is another blow at the idealist (personalist) concept of the *person:* personality is not some independent or autonomous spir-itual being (autonomous, that is, with regard to the material world, and so the world of concrete individuals as well)—but it is a *social product,* a function of social relations between concrete individuals.

Human personality thus changes in the course of history, just as the conditions that shape it.

And finally, the third inference from the Marxist concept of the individual: precisely because of its social character, human personality is not given but is *made;* it is a *process;* it is not a product of some ultrahuman forces, but *social* man's own product, a product of human *self-creation.* Here is another connection between the Marxist theory of personality and the general Marxist concept of the individual—and yet another blow to idealist whimsies with the weapons of consistent anthropocentrism.

One more remark on the problem of personality in Marxist theory: the category of personality is inseparably related to that of individuality—conceived as uniqueness, non-repeatability. Marxists, it is true, hold the view that personality is a social product and has social character, but this is only an interpretation of its *origins.* Human personality is socially conditioned, a kind of intersection of social determinants but, if only because of its complexity, it is—as an entity—not repeatable and in this sense individual.[51]

It is in fact as an *integral* structure, and so as a psycho-physical structure, that non-repeatability is an attribute of the individual. Consequently, it primarily concerns the human character of man's attitudes, dispositions, views, volition, preferences, and choices, etc. It is in this sense that Marxism, while repudiating personalism's metaphysical approach to the human person, presents a full theory of the human person as individuality—or at least its anthropological system has room for such a theory. The controversy concerns the interpretation of the phenomenon, but not the phenomenon itself.

This entails a conclusion that, although not expressly stated by Marxist theorists, is fully authorized: as a non-repeatable, structural entity the individual constitutes a certain value that is unique and only disappears with the individual's death. In a sense, therefore, the individual, although not a monad—on the contrary, he is tied to society in a myriad of ways and is a product of this society—represents, as a non-repeatable whole, a world in himself that disappears with his death. Here again, while rejecting the metaphysics of existentialism, Marxism does not deny an obvious fact in existentialist doctrine; once more the controversy is over interpretation, not over the existence of the phenomenon. This entails fundamental consequences, both for the theory of morals and for human actions that affect the lives of others.

These then are the general outlines of the theory of personality in accord with the Marxist concept of the individual—and to this extent it is possible to maintain that such a theory exists in Marxism or at any rate is deducible from its assumptions. But this does not mean it has actually been developed in Marxism; this is certainly not the case and the problem still remains open—all the more so since what is involved is not philosophical speculation but the general inference to be drawn from research into such specialized fields of the science of man as psychology, social anthropology, sociology, etc.

This particular area has been patently neglected in Marxism—as has everything that concerns individual and social psychology. The sociology of knowledge helps explain this omission: when Marxism lost sight of the problems of the individual and emphasis was shifted to the study of mass movements, neglect of everything connected with the individual was a natural result. No wonder that a Marxist broaching the problem of personality today comes up against a host of notions, which were usually formulated on the basis of idealist premises, and he has little to offer in their place apart from his methodology. This is why Marxism here must be destructive, refuting erroneous views and propositions about personality, although naturally without foregoing its own construction. Negation also leads to affirmation. A useful effort in this direction has been made in Leszek Kołakowski's essay "Cogito, Historical Materialism, the Expressive Theory of Individuality," in which the personalist conceptions of individuality are critically analyzed from a Marxist point of view.[52]

The constructive side of this work still remains to be done. If for no other reason, this is necessary to obtain a full picture of our view of the nature of the individual. As a working proposition I might revert to Fromm's suggestion—which I have already mentioned in my introductory remarks—that human *character* should be studied as a system of filters, through which the stimuli of the base are selected and guided to the superstructure. This suggestion offers a valuable pointer toward research into the problem of personality—at least in the sense that the full recognition of the social character of personality, as far as the genetic aspect is concerned, involves the necessity of studying its concrete psychological content, including the subconscious. When human personality is investigated, allowance must also be made for the irrational factor if it shows itself in human behavior, and where feasible a rational interpretation should be attempted of the genesis of any such irrational factor. This is certainly not an easy task and it will force Marxists to revise many a preconception and repudiate many a taboo. But the effort must be made if we want consistently to develop our own conception of the individual and to confront the rival theories successfully.

The concept of the individual is, in my view, the crux of any philosophical anthropology—if only because it must solve the problem of the individual's ontological status and thereby provide a link between anthropology and the whole view of the world. For philosophical anthropology—despite all appearances to the contrary and the often very fierce disclaimers of its proponents—is tied by a thousand threads to a view of the world; what is more, these bonds act both ways: in a coherent system the world-view entails certain inescapable choices in the field of anthropology, and vice versa.

How an anthropological system should be expounded is debatable. In my opinion, the best and most convenient way is to begin with the concept of the human individual, since the whole argument can then be arranged into a deductive system. But in the actual process of inquiry and reflection, the concept of the individual is not a point of departure but a goal. It is only on a solution of the various problems of individual life that a complete theory of the individual can be constructed. And this is precisely why the system can be presented in reverse—beginning with the *result* of the investigation, the concept of the individual.

At any rate, it is around the concept of the individual, particularly his ontological status, that the chief differences among the various anthropological schools revolve; and that is why this conception can serve as a basis for a typology of these schools.

The individual's ontological status is clearly defined within the framework of the Marxist doctrine: the individual is part of nature and society, and this determines his ontological status. He is that part of nature which thinks and consciously transforms the world, and as such he is part of society. As a natural-social entity he can be apprehended with no additional factors, apart from objective reality. Such an approach to the individual's ontological status—based as it is on the whole Marxist view of the world—makes it possible to construct a consistently *man-centered* philosophical anthropology, which is thus *autonomous* in a specific sense.

Whatever its outward appearances, the anthropological conception depends on what it takes as point of departure: either the concrete individual with his social involvement or the ultrahuman world.

In the former case, it is possible to construct a consistently man-centered anthropology that needs no ultrahuman adjuncts, that approaches the world of man as his product. This and only this anthropology can be coherently united with the materialist view of the world: on the one hand, it can be considered as its logical outcome—Engels once spoke of materialism as an approach to reality without additions from outside the sphere of reality—and, on the other, as a position that leads to such a view of the world.

Such an anthropology—man-centered and thus materialist—is also autonomous; that is, the human world is conceived as *independent* of any forces beyond it (nature and society), as a product of man. Autonomy must be always *relative to something*—in this case, to some supernatural, ultrahuman forces that might affect human destiny and govern man's conduct. This sense of the term "autonomous anthropology" must not be forgotten, and it must not be confused with "autonomy" as interpreted by personalism whose anthropology is based on the notion of the human person as a spiritual unity. In such a view, the soul is regarded as autonomous with regard to the actual world—a relationship diametrically opposed to what we mean when speaking of "autonomous anthropology." Any confusion of these meanings may lead to basic misconceptions—even to a denial of the autonomous character of Marxist anthropology.

In the latter case, that is, when anthropology starts from an ultra-human world—God, supernatural forces, the Absolute Idea, a world of objective values, etc.—man is not its point of departure but a point of arrival. It then has a *theocentric* character when (as is usually the case in traditional anthropologies) it is based on religious faith, or, more broadly, a *heteronomous* one when what is implied is the influence of an ultrahuman factor that is not necessarily supernatural in the traditional sense of the word. "Heteronomy" is thus a broader notion than "theocentrism." Theocentric anthropology (for example, Christian personalism) is heteronomous, since it is based on the idea of God's superior and governing role with regard to the human world; but Hegelian anthropology, although heteronomous, is not theocentric, for it is the Absolute Idea that is credited with a role similar to that of supernatural force in religious systems.

Anthropology's point of departure is not, of course, fortuitous; it is closely linked to the whole world outlook within which the theory of man has been developed. It is an illusion to think that an anthropological theory can be expounded without reference to a world-view, "without philosophical foundations." Unless he is prepared to contradict even to explode his own system of thinking, a materialist cannot accept the concept of a person in the sense in which it is interpreted by Christian personalism; and vice versa, an existentialist or personalist cannot—at the risk of similar consequences—accept the theses of materialism (as illustrated by the unhappy marriage of existentialism and historical materialism in the most recent stage of Sartre's evolution).

When an anthropology has chosen its point of departure, this choice determines not only its general character, but its treatment of many specific questions. Thus, for example, the problem of moral responsibility is viewed in one way by an anthropology which presupposes the existence of supernatural forces and an act of creation, and in another by an autonomous anthropology which combines materialism with the doctrine of man's self-creation. This is one reason why philosophical anthropology has a clearly ideological nature.

Among the many customary meanings of the word "ideology," we are here primarily interested in the sense in which it appears in such phrases as "socialist ideology," "bourgeois ideology," etc. What is implied are the views and attitudes that affect people's social behavior in relation to an accepted objective of social development and to a system of values that makes them choose this objective. "Ideology" so defined will also include philosophical anthropology. This does not mean that given practical, above all political, conclusions are directly postulated by anthropology, but there is certainly an indirect connection. For this reason philosophical anthropology is an area of ideological battle, an arena for struggle among various schools and trends. The concept of the individual, for example, is, from a certain point of view, a highly *abstract* problem, and yet it provokes bitter controversies whose nature and repercussions can only be grasped when their *ideological* significance is taken into account, that is, their influence, even though indirect, on the formation of man's social ideal, and thereby his conduct and actions. *Directly,* no practical conclusions can be drawn from adherence to one or another theory of the individual; indirectly, however, such conclusions are very significant. Here, in the final analysis, lies the social importance not only of the concept of the individual but of philosophical anthropology in general.

Chapter 2
The Individual
and His Products

(The Problem of Alienation)

Individuals have always taken themselves as the point of departure, they always set out from themselves. Their relations are those of the actual process of their life. *How is it that their relations become independent of them? that the forces of their own life acquire power over them?* [1]

In these plain words we are brought to the very heart of the problem known aptly, if a little rhetorically, as "alienation," "estrangement." In *The German Ideology,* Marx gives a more detailed definition of this relationship:

> This crystallization of social activity, . . . this consolidation of what we ourselves produce into an objective power above us, growing out of our control, thwarting our expectations, bringing to naught our calculations, is one of the chief factors in historical development up till now. . . .
>
> This "estrangement" (to use a term which will be comprehensible to the philosophers) can, of course, only be abolished given two *practical* premises. For it to become an "intolerable" power, i.e., a power against which men make a revolution, it must necessarily have rendered the great mass of humanity "propertyless," and produced, at the same time, the contradiction of an existing world of wealth and culture, both of which conditions presuppose a great increase in productive power, a high degree of its development.[2]

The problem of "alienation" is a real gold mine for the philosopher, and particularly for the historian of philosophy. Its longevity, showing as it does that students of social life have long realized that man's products may become autonomous and even dominate him (according to Fromm, the problem can be traced back to idol worship, and thus to the Bible); the complex, interwoven influences of the filiation of ideas; the immensely completed intellectual background of the problem in Marx—all this has already stimulated hundreds of scholarly studies on the subject. This is one reason why we can forgo any further exploration of this rich field of "influence" hunting. No matter how much Marx owes in this respect, and to whom, his own concept is different, if only because he got rid of the whole ballast of idealist metaphysics and sharply delineated its distinctions. Significantly, Marx hastened to repudiate the current terminology (elsewhere in the same passage from *The German Ideology* he spoke sarcastically of the philosophical language of alienation and always put this word between quotation marks) in order to be free from an embarrassing tradition and its antecedents, Hegel above all. On the other hand, he never discarded the problem itself (nor could he have done so without abandoning the very foundations of his position); and later, when the danger of confusion had clearly decreased when (as he said in *Capital*) Hegel began to be treated as a "dead dog" he did, in fact, return to the word "alienation" (*Entfremdung*) although sparingly.

Before we go any further, let me make a brief comment on terminology. In these pages, I have decided to use "alienation" (whose meaning I shall try to make more precise below) simply because I cannot think of any better word which would more adequately express what is involved. It is true that this term is loaded down with a long and ambiguous tradition; that it is open to use by various doctrines, some of them even bordering on mysticism; that it has been associated with an ahistorical, and thereby abstract, conception of the "human essence" or "human nature"; that it is alienated; and that this was precisely why Marx dropped a term of which he was once so fond. But it is also true that "alienation" denotes certain real social relations and it is connected with real problems for which no one yet has thought of a better name. (The suggestion that "fetishism" is identical with "alienation" in meaning and scope, is muddleheaded.) Since, in addition, the hazards of using a word which is, as it were, tainted by alien schools of thought are now infinitesimal (who, apart from the specialists, knows anything about alienation in the doctrines of Hegel, Rousseau, or any other thinkers before Marx?), I see no objection to returning to a term which fits the problem so well and which can now be given a clearcut meaning.

The problem of alienation concerns the relations of the individual with society and with the manifold *products* of man as a social man. The point of departure, as we have said, is the human individual—but a real, concrete individual, who is involved in a variety of ways within society. Seen thus, the individual, is "the ensemble of social relations," not only genetically, i.e., as a product and function of social relations, but also *here and now*—i.e., from the viewpoint of his relations with society in his day-to-day activity. This applies both to the process of production of material goods with its dominant division of labor, and also to man's social life within a state organization, within a given system of values, and so forth. In each such case, we are dealing with *men acting within society,* and therefore with relations between men, in part direct, in part those which arise through the mediation of things which are the products of man. In this sphere, there unfolds a process in the course of which, through the objectification and reification of human activity and under certain conditions, the creation of men become independent of their creators, and then fully autonomous in their functioning; and so, they subordinate man to things, and lead to the phenomenon of *alienation.*

Starting with men's social activities and social relationships, we must proceed to distinguish following Marx, the phenomenon of objectification (reification) of human activity, from the phenomenon of alienation of the products of that activity, its consequences for human action, and, ultimately, for man as man (self-alienation).

". . . *object* as *being for man,* as the *objectified being of man,* is at the same time the *existence of man for other men,* his *human relation to other men, the social relation of man to man.*" [3]

Man acting in society reveals his self in forms that have been objectified so that he can be comprehended by others: first of all, in the form of *things* he creates (reification), but also in the form of transformed human relationships and materialized spiritual values, perhaps in written or spoken words. This objectification of activity, particularly the activity of human spirit, is of enormous social import. For man, an object is "being for man"; i.e., it is intellectually perceivable, and serves, in addition to all other purposes, as a sign of s*omething else*—particularly as a sign of his intentions, purposes, capabilities, of his character, as man-the-creator of values. Man thereby becomes an "existence of man for other men;" he becomes the "social relation of man to man," etc.

The objectification and reification of human activity is thus the basis of men's worldly existence, and so a fundamental anthropological category. Rid of the dark shadows that it is given by Hegelian ontology and turned "upright on its feet," objectification becomes a rational category.

It is only in certain conditions that the objectification and reification of human activity lead to alienation: namely when man's products acquire an existence that is independent of him and autonomous, and when man is unable to resist, in a conscious way, the spontaneous functioning of his own products, which subordinate him to their laws and can even threaten his life. Subjection to a reality that has slipped out of his control—and thus is nonhuman —robs man of his humanity, circumscribes the development of his personality, and makes him an appendage to the world of things: machines, the state bureaucracy, etc. Thus alienation is at the same time the self-alienation of man—the maker of the world of things who is lost in this impersonal, nonhuman world that has subordinated him. Not only are the products of man estranged from him, "alienated"; he also alienates himself, becoming as strange to himself as an object. Man begins to feel himself as a thing that is part of the surrounding world of things, to respond to himself through the intermediary of these things.

It was in reference to this complex phenomenon that Marx posed the question of its source quoted from *Capital* at the beginning of this chapter: How is it that man's products acquire an existence that is independent of him, a power over him? Marx hoped that an answer to this question would clarify how to overcome alienation in a capitalist society, how to create conditions for a full and unrestricted development of human personality, how to fulfill the "essence" of man in practice. And this is the essential meaning of communism *as a movement,* of communism which proceeds from the problem of individual happiness and makes it its supreme purpose.

Marx's question confronts us today in a different but no less important form: to the problem of alienation under capitalism is added the problem of alienation under socialism.

To Marx it was an axiom that, since economic alienation is the basis of all other forms of alienation, its elimination—by the abolition of private ownership of the means of production—would automatically put an end to every other kind of alienation. But is this the case? Is alienation impossible under socialism? Or can it perhaps arise from other sources than private property? This is the question that makes alienation an outstanding problem not only in the context of capitalism, but also of socialism.

When we say that alienation is the domination of man by his products, we mean an elemental social development in which the turnover of goods on the market, the arms race between countries, nationalism, racial hatred, religious intolerance, etc., are no longer submitted to the will and control of human individuals, but instead they subjugate the individual, threaten his existence, and limit his freedom. The struggle against alienation is, therefore, an effort to replace an elemental development of forces by one planned by man and subordinated to his will. In other words, it is a struggle for human freedom, but a real, not apparent freedom, in which man consciously forges his destiny. Engels said that the transition to socialism is a leap from the realm of necessity to the realm of freedom. Today, when trying to reconstruct Marx's thinking about socialism to grasp its humanist core, we must follow his notion of alienation in the capitalist system. It is only then that the meaning of Marx's socialism can fully be understood. But when faced with the broader issue of Marxism's approach to the human individual, we must—in the presence of experiences unknown to Marx—restate this problem

as follows: is it true that private property is at the basis of all alienation? And, consequently, does the end of capitalism mean the end
of all alienation? Is alienation impossible under socialism?

In our further analysis of the various forms of alienation, from
which we hope to draw some general conclusions, we shall try to
examine this question not only as it appears in a system of property
but also in relation to the thesis about the end of alienation under
socialism.

Chronologically, the question of alienation first appeared in
Marx's work as the problem of religious alienation. This is only
natural if we bear in mind the atmosphere of the times and the
issues dominant in the Young Hegelian circles in which both Marx
and Engels originated. They could not stand aside from the great
debates of the day or be unmoved by the great questions absorbing
their milieu. This is specially evident if we remember the revolu-
tionizing influence of Feuerbach's theory of man with its leitmotif
of consistent struggle against religious alienation.

What is more, this was a *crucial* struggle in the ideological up-
heaval that took place in men's minds. Engels wrote much later
that what the French had accomplished in practice—a revolution
—the Germans were content to pursue in the abstract sphere of
the mind; and if this was the bitter sarcasm of a man of action, dis-
gusted and disenchanted by his countrymen's lethargy and lack of
revolutionary activity, it also contained an important positive truth.
The Germans, backward though they were in economic and political development, were far ahead of other peoples in ideological
progress, and their revolutionary achievements in this field—particularly in philosophy—had significance far beyond Germany.

It is interesting and characteristic that the people waging this
ideological campaign were thoroughly aware of its revolutionary,
practical implications. This is important, because it is evidence that
the temper of this struggle was consciously revolutionary in a country prevented by circumstances from taking to arms like the French
in 1789, the battle was fought out on a ground where it was par-

ticularly favored by tradition but in the full awareness that the way was thus being paved for revolutionary practice. This throws sharp light on the fierce assaults mounted against religious alienation.

In 1842—when he was twenty-four and still far from materialism and communism—Marx wrote some beautiful and little-known lines in an article for the *Rheinische Zeitung:*

> We are firmly convinced that it is not the *practical effort* but rather the *theoretical explication* of communistic ideals which is the real *danger*. Dangerous practical *attempts,* even *those on a large scale,* can be answered with *cannon,* but the *ideas,* won by our intelligence, embodied in our outlook and forged in our conscience are chains from which we cannot tear ourselves away without breaking our hearts; they are demons we can overcome only by submitting to them.[4]

It was only an awareness of the *practical* significance of ideology that could give as clear-headed an insight into the goals of the struggle against religious alienation as that possessed by the young Marx:

> The weapon of criticism obviously cannot replace the criticism of weapons. Material force must be overthrown by material force. But theory also becomes a material force once it has gripped the masses. Theory is capable of gripping the masses when it demonstrates *ad hominem,* and it demonstrates *ad hominem* when it becomes radical. To be radical is to grasp things by the root. But for man the root is man himself. The clear proof of the radicalism of German theory and hence of its political energy is that it proceeds from the decisive *positive* transcendence of religion. The criticism of religion ends with the doctrine that man is the *highest being for man,* hence with the *categorical imperative to overthrow all conditions* in which man is a degraded, enslaved, neglected, contemptible being—conditions that cannot be better

described than by the exclamation of a Frenchman on
the occasion of a proposed dog tax: Poor dogs! They
want to treat you like human beings! [5]

Until recently, that part of Marxological literature which was
regarded as orthodox clung to a certain stereotype that can be
partly blamed on some words of Engels: the Germans, incapable of
revolutionary *action,* concentrated their effort on the criticism of
religion, since this was less dangerous in its consequences; in other
words their attacks were dictated by opportunism. I cannot discuss
here the opportunism of the radical German intelligentsia in the
nineteenth century, but I think it essential to correct the mistaken
view, based on a misinterpretation of the ideological struggles of
the time, that the critique of religion was just a subterfuge for intellectual opportunism, of little import compared with political
issues. The truth is that in the field of ideology this criticism was of
prime importance; without it the decisive road to communism was
blocked. For what was at stake was the victory of consistent anthropocentricism, and thus of the contention that for man the most
important being, the highest good, *is man.* The implications of this
argument were decisive for the evolution of German radicalism in
those days and for its grip upon the masses. Marx knew this well, as
the passage quoted from his *Contribution to a Critique of Hegel's
Philosophy of Right* indicates, and so did many of his contemporaries with whom he was then allied. No better proof could be found
than the moving words with which Ludwig Feuerbach concluded
his *Vorlesungen über das Wesen der Religion* (*Lectures on the Essence of Religion*):

> When we cease to *believe* in a better life and begin to
> *crave* it, not individually but in concert, then we shall
> succeed in *creating* it, in removing at least the most glar-
> ing, the most hideous, the most heartrending evils and
> injustices which have oppressed mankind. But to crave
> and achieve this we must recognize love of man instead
> of love of God as the only true religion, and instead of
> faith in God propagate man's faith in himself, in his pow-
> ers, a faith that the destiny of mankind does not depend

on a Being beyond or above it, but depends on itself, that man's only devil is man himself—primitive, superstitious, selfish and evil man—but also that man is man's only God.[6]

Can there be a more striking and at the same time more beautiful commentary on the division of theories of human nature into man- and God-centered, autonomous and heteronomous? It is embarrassing to contrast the clarity of thought and intellectual breadth of this pre-Marxian philosopher with the opinions of some people today who, in the name of Marxism, deny the ideological significance of religious belief and of the struggle against it as a form of alienation. One may be a believer or a non-believer; this is a question of individual choice that is certainly the right of each individual. But no one, least of all an intellectual, may obscure something that is perfectly clear. Acceptance of religion—and with it of theocentricism (which, like it or not, is the inevitable consequence)— is a matter not only of the "Beyond" but also of "this world." On it are constructed political programs that are guides to human action in the most mundane matters. It represents an ideology (in the sense of views and attitudes forming men's social activity according to an accepted goal of social development) that is connected with a straight choice between two alternatives: either God or man is the supreme being for man. If this were not so, if the God-centered option did not entail consequences in the field of ideology and the conflicts of this world, these issues would not provoke such bitter struggles. If such struggles occur, it is because people—at least those who direct the struggles and seek to sway the masses—are aware of their ideological implications and significance.

Feuerbach can be credited with the discovery, or at least the radical formulation of the truth, that it was not God who created man, but man who created God, after his own likeness. God, a supernatural being, is simply a projection and absolutization of man's attributes, made absolute in an idealized form, that is in the shape of an ideal type. Hence the image of God—even in racial features—varies according to the society and epoch when it comes into being. But for the same reason there are some traits that are unchanging, because they reflect those enduring human qualities and relations that can be found in every society. In each case, God, a supernatural being, is a creature of man, an externalization and objectification of his own characteristics and attributes. This impoverishes man, because it robs him of his own features and content in favor of a projection, a product of his mind, which acquires the guise of a social belief—and so, by making its existence independent of its maker, becomes an alien and often hostile force, *gradually coming to rule over man*. Once created, and socially objectified, religious beliefs become a force that is not only alien to man but also rules him and its grip, dangerous and destructive as it often is, he is unable to shake off. This domination of man's products over man, Marx considered to be the crux of religious alienation and while he only unwillingly used the expression later, the author of *Capital* did not forget: "As, in religion, man is governed by the products of his own brain, so in capitalistic production, he is governed by the products of his own hand." [7] But he had already perceived this in his doctoral dissertation where, though still using the language of idealist philosophy, he propounded his basic ideas about religious alienation, characteristically urging a struggle against religion in order to achieve a transformation of the world in harmony with human requirements. Marx's youthful appeal for the liberation of man from religious bondage ends with these words:

> Philosophy hides nothing. Prometheus' admission: "In truth I hate all gods" is its own creed, its own motto against all gods heavenly and earthly, who do not acknowledge the consciousness of man, as the supreme divinity. No good may be raised to the same level. [8]

It is obvious that the struggle against alienation in those days was also a struggle for a consistent humanism, attainable only from a man-centered viewpoint. It is equally evident that, as far as the self-knowledge of the age was concerned, this was a struggle over *fundamental* issues, and not just an opportunist evasion; unless the battle for anthropocentricism were won, there could be no sustained and consistent development of the humanism that leads to communism. This idea was clearly stated by the young Engels in his criticism of Thomas Carlyle—and his words are all the more valuable since they bring out the completeness of the agreement between him and Marx as members of the same intellectual circles. They are, therefore, particularly characteristic of the ideological attitude of the milieu from which they both originated.

Declaring on its behalf, that an end will be put to atheism as described by Carlyle, Engels wrote:

> . . . we give man the substance which he has lost through religion; not as a divine but as a human content, and the whole restitution consists simply in the awakening of self-consciousness. We wish to get everything out of the way which offers itself as supernatural and superhuman and thereby remove untruthfulness; for the pretense of the human and natural to desire to be regarded superhuman, supernatural, is the root of all untruth and falsehood.[9]

Continuing his humanist manifesto Engels writes:

> The question has always been, hitherto, What is God? and German philosophy has solved the question: God is man. Man has only to know himself, to measure all conditions of life against himself, to judge according to his being, to arrange the world in a truly human way according to the needs of his nature—then he has solved the riddle of our time. Not in distant regions that do not exist; not out beyond time and space; not through a "God" immanent in the world or set over against it, is truth to be found, but much nearer, in the human being's own breast. The human being's own nature is much more glorious and sublime than the imaginary nature of all possible "Gods," which are after all only the more or less unclear and distorted image of the human being himself. . . . Man has in religion lost his own existence, he has renounced his humanity, and now is aware (since through the progress of history, religion has begun to totter) of its

emptiness and lack of content. But there is no other salvation for him, he can once more win his humanity, his
essence, only through a basic overcoming of all religious
assumptions and a decisive, honest return not to "God,"
but to himself.[10]

Here with his typical clarity and trenchancy, free of excessive
"philosophical phraseology," we have a statement of the humanist
meaning of the campaign against religious alienation.

Whatever we think of the efficacy, even in its radical form, of
this demand that religion die out, it is a program that has lost none
of its relevance to this day and explains why these particular issues
so engrossed that age. Without overcoming theocentricism, without
laying solid foundations for a consistent anthropocentricism in
philosophical anthropology, no headway could be made towards
the kind of radicalism that, in Marx's words, saw the root of the
problem in man himself.

Thus this was an ideological battle of crucial importance that
had to be the *first* point of attack. But it was a campaign that, resolutely pursued, could not be considered the *end* of the war. Accordingly, it led Marx forward—to the problems of political alienation.
As he himself said (in the quoted passage from the Introduction to
his *A Contribution to the Critique of Hegel's Philosophy of Right*)
the critique of religion ends with the affirmation that man is the
supreme being for man, and from this flows an obligation to *overthrow* all relations in which man is a humiliated, servile, and contemptible being. Consistent humanism consequently becomes a
stimulus to critical analysis of political relations, and, above all,
the state.

Man becomes servile, degraded, and in a sense contemptible
when he falls under the sway of forces that are independent of him
and when these forces, even though they are his own products,
prescribe his way of life. The fight against this situation, if it is to
be successful, must, therefore, be a struggle against alienation; and
indeed not only against religious alienation.

The "self-estrangement" of man's products, which include the things of the spirit and interpersonal relations as well as material goods, occurs in the ideological, socio-political, and economic spheres.

In the first of these lies religion, but it is not the only nor always the chief, actor present. We have already explained why the young Marx, like his contemporaries, began with religious alienation, since it was here that the battle for a truly man-centered view of the world was being waged, and its outcome was decisive to the philosophical self-knowledge of his generation. But Marx was perfectly aware of the meaning of ideological alienation in general, and of alienation in philosophy in particular. This awareness is at the foundation of his theory of ideology.

Ideology is a part of social consciousness, distinguished by the fact that the views and attitudes of which it consists largely control action undertaken in pursuance of a chosen objective of social development. It is, therefore, indissolubly bound up with a definite system of values whose choice depends on men's social interests; and in a class society the choice necessarily has a class character. In this sense, ideology is identical with the superstructure whose movements and changes are in the final resort (and by this, I mean to emphasize that in the interaction between the base and the superstructure of society, the former is the determining factor *over longer periods of development*) determined by changes in the productive base, that is, the mode of production of the given society. As in the case of social consciousness in general, ideology is a "reflection" (in a special philosophic sense of the word) of objective reality in human minds. But since men's interests affect the way in which they view and represent this reality, the reflected image is socially determined; and therefore, it is distorted as the particular interest of a given class or group demands. This also accounts for the differences in the judgment of identical or similar phenomena at different periods, or in different social milieus. But once an ideology has been created, it begins to live a life of its own, and to acquire a relative autonomy, as shown by its repercussions on the base of society. Ideology may shape human behavior, the further evolution of ideology itself through a filiation of ideas, and by conservatism perseverance that enables it to resist transformations of the base.

Let us briefly recapitulate some of what Marx said about the theory of ideology, and some conclusions consistent with his system, that may be drawn from them.

Ideology, Marx wrote, becomes a material force when it rallies the masses. This is where it draws its strength whether constructive or destructive. But it is also a potential danger of its alienation.

In ideology in general, and particularly in philosophy, it is not always the intention of the author of a theory that really counts, but the function to which it is actually put. History offers many examples, the noblest ideals of brotherly love served to send thousands of victims to the stake in a spirit of the most bitter hate. And it is not only in response to religious doctrines that this has happened.

In *The German Ideology* there is a fine passage on the alienation of philosophy; it is also worth quoting because of its wider implications:

> For philosophers, one of the most difficult tasks is to descend from the world of thought to the actual world. *Language* is the immediate actuality of thought. Just as philosophers have given thought an independent existence so they had to make language into an independent realm. This is the secret of philosophical language, in which thoughts in the form of words have their own content. The problem of descending from the world of thoughts to the actual world is turned into the problem of descending from language to life.
>
> We have shown thoughts and ideas acquire an independent existence in consequence of the personal circumstances and relations of individuals acquiring independent existence. We have shown that exclusive, systematic occupation with these thoughts on the part of ideologists and philosophers, and hence the systematization of these thoughts, is a consequence of division of labour, and that, in particular German philosophy is a consequence of German petty-bourgeois conditions. The philosophers would only have to dissolve their language into the ordi-

nary language, from which it is abstracted, to recognise it as the distorted language of the actual world, and to realise that neither thoughts nor language in themselves form a realm of their own, that they are only *manifestations* of actual life.[11]

Two general conclusions can be drawn from these words of Marx.

First, that every ideology should be seen as a *manifestation* of real life, of real relations between men, and that it is necessary to "translate" it into the language of this reality.

Second, that the independence of human thoughts and ideas, and thus also of ideology, is the result of the independence (Marx here guards against the word "alienation") of relationships between men and of a specific division of labor.

The first precept is important in countering idealist mystification, particularly in the "world of values," "world of norms," and the like, which are often credited with an existence independent of man, and so, because of thir heteronomy, made divine. What is involved here, after all, are the thoughts and ideas of men, that are manifestations of actual human relations. Their "externalization" or "objectification" (to use "philosophical phraseology") are essential for their communication in speech or writing, and are therefore indispensable conditions for their existence, not only for others but for myself too. Their alienation, however, is the result of a hypostasis that has its own social background. For people are not always and not everywhere ready to accept such principles.

Here we come to the second precept: to overcome the alienation of ideology, we must attack the relations which made it possible. These are class relations, and the property relations that determine them. In this way, reflection on ideological alienation leads us on to the problems of socio-political alienation, and to their basic foundations: economic alienation.

The young Marx treated the questions of socio-political alienation in a way that is characteristic of the intellectual controversies and the consciousness of his age. But though the form is a little odd and heavy for the modern reader, the content is rational and straightforward. Today we are familiar with it as formulated and stated by the mature Marx, but in this case, too, there is continuity —at least of the problems—in Marx's intellectual evolution.

The question that absorbed the young Marx—like the whole milieu influenced by Hegel—was the disruption of man who appears in two roles although in one and the same person: as a member of the "civil society" (*bourgeois*) and of the "political community" (*citoyen*). In the former case, we have to deal with economic individuals—products of bourgeois society, and therefore real people, the "real man"; in the latter, with members of a political community, the State, who share in the ideal, of "true man." This duality of roles leads to inner conflicts, and to that "unhappy consciousness" which shows evidence that in the world of his alienated products man himself feels strange since he is estranged from his "essence."

> The civil society and the State are separated from each other. Consequently, the citizen of the state is also separated from the citizen who is member of the civil society. Man must therefore himself succumb to an essential split. As a real citizen he finds himself with a dual organization: the bureaucratic—it constitutes the external, formal definition of the State being something that is outside it, the ruling authority which has no points of contact with the citizen or his independent reality—and the social, within the organization of civil society. But in the latter he finds himself as a private man outside the State, this organization having no points of contact with the political state as such.[12]

Marx not only states that man is split as a result of alienation; he also draws the conclusions that became the foundation of his program of action in those days, and later led him to communism.

> Only when the actual, individual man has taken back into himself the abstract citizen and in his everyday life,

his individual work, and his individual relationships has become a *species-being*, only when he has recognized and organized his own powers as *social* powers, so that social force is no longer separate from him as *political* power, only then is human emancipation complete.[13]

The language is strange, and so, too, for the reader today, is the way in which the problems are posed. But the issue itself is wholly comprehensible and contemporary.

In their social life, men enter various relationships which arrange themselves in permanent structures, most often in the form of institutions: the state and its bureaucratic apparatus, political parties, nations, social classes, professional groups, family, and so on. I have deliberately listed different types of human relations, with their different structures and institutions. All of them, however, have something in common. Once they are constituted as an institution (state, party, family, etc.) or as a permanent form of social organization (people, class, professional group, etc.) they begin to live an autonomous life, independent of the will and choice of the individuals who are born into these institutions and forms of social organization and absorbed by them. This subordination of the individual to the autonomous products of man may vary in character according to the type of social relations represented by a given institution or organizational pattern—but it is always unconditional and irrevocable. In some cases, particularly when the *state* is involved, the estrangement of the human product is exceptionally harsh, painful, or even destructive of the individual.

According to Marxism, the state is an organization of the ruling class which maintains its economic and political rule by means of physical force; but it is also an organization that administers the complex business of social life. In a sense, the state can be likened to assemblies of armed men (the army, police, etc.). The greater its power, the more dangerous its alienation as it grows into an autonomous force and slips out of the control of the individual. What is involved is no longer the Hegelian cleavage of the individual consciousness, both *bourgeois* and *citizen,* but the sinister reality of the machinery of coercion which crushes a rebellious individual. To a growing degree—a point to which we shall return when discussing the possibility of alienation under socialism—it is also the reality of an estranged machinery of administering things that cannot, despite the illusions once entertained, be kept separate from the administration of human beings; and although in a different way, can become no less dangerous for the individual than the instruments of physical coercion.

The alienation of the state poses the problem that uniquely focuses all questions of socio-political alienation. For it is inseparably linked with the question of social classes and their struggle, and this, in turn, is closely bound to problems of economics and production. It is natural, therefore, that the founders of Marxism considered the central issue in their socio-political analysis to be the alienation of the state, not only under capitalism, but also in their image of future socialist society.

Many years later, when the language of "alienation" was no longer used, Engels wrote in his *Ludwig Feuerbach,* which was also a retrospective appraisal of his early days:

> Society creates for itself an organ for the safeguarding of its general interests against internal and external attacks. This organ is the state power. Hardly has it come into being, than this organ makes itself independent in regard to society; and, indeed, the more it does so, the more it becomes the organ of a particular class, the more it directly enforces the supremacy of this class. The fight of the oppressed class against the ruling class becomes necessarily a political fight of all against the political dominance of this class.[14]

It was these theoretical standpoints which linked Marx' and Engels' struggle against alienation under capitalism with their doctrine of the "withering away" of the state under socialism—which, as Engels put it in *The Origin of the Family, Private Property and the State,* would one day be placed in a museum of antiquities, together with the spinning wheel and the bronze axe. For both of them, communism was, by definition, a stateless system (the state being understood as a machinery of coercion, not of administration), nor was this denied by Lenin in *State and Revolution.* Stalin's later modification of this thesis was purest revisionism, undermining one of the pillars of the revolutionary content of Marxism.

It is significant that in this respect the position of Marx and Engels remained unshakeable during the whole course of their intellectual evolution. The doctrine of the shattering of the bourgeois state machinery, of the "withering away" of the state, and of communism as a stateless system, (which is found in *Anti-Dühring,* in the *Critique of the Gotha Programme,* in the *Critique of the Erfurt Programme* and in Lenin's *State and Revolution,*) was already formulated in 1846 by Marx in *The Poverty of Philosophy:*

"The working class, in the course of its development, will substitute for the old civil society an association which will exclude classes and their antagonism, and there will no longer be any political power, properly so-called, since political power is precisely the official expression of the antagonism in civil society." [15]

The same idea is conveyed even more pointedly and cogently in *The Communist Manifesto.*[16]

Though fully aware of the nature of political power, Marx perceived the connection between the state and the class interests of its members, between the state and the "civil society." It is not the state that conditions the existence of the private individuals who pursue their own interests, but on the contrary, the "civil society" conditions the state.

> It is therefore not the *State* that holds the *atoms* of civil society together, but the fact that they are atoms only in *imagination,* in the *heaven* of their fancy, but in *reality* beings tremendously different from atoms, in other words not *divine egotists* but *egotistic human beings.* Only *political superstition* today imagines that social life must be held together by the state, whereas in reality the state is held together by civil life.[17]

Though still expressed a bit strangely, this is the core of Marx's thought; from here he moved logically to communist conclusions, at the same time turning towards economics: for the root of all alienation in capitalist society is economic alienation. It is the ground of socio-political alienation and it conditions ideological alienation. Consequently, it is on this phenomenon that major attention should be concentrated, both in theory, since this is where the secret of alienation in class society lies, and in practice, because it is here that the attack should be directed if alienation is to be overcome and man is to be liberated from conditions that oppress and debase him.

The problem of alienation is also discussed in Marx's mature works. It recurs continually in *Capital,* either explicitly or in the form of commodity fetishism. But a detailed exposition of his thinking is contained in Marx's early writings, particularly in the *Manuscripts,* which, on this point, are certainly the key to his later writings and explain his turn toward economic studies. Thus it is on the *Manuscripts* that our own argument must primarily be based.

The point of departure for the theory of alienation was observation of market relations in the developing capitalist society. It was the indubitable merit of capitalism that it lay bare the mysterious economic relations of the feudal age by brutally revealing the modes of the subjugation and exploitation of man by man. It also disclosed with ruthless clarity the estrangement of man's products from their maker, products which as commodities lead an independent existence in the market. This phenomenon, and its economic and social effects, could hardly escape the economists; it was from them that the idea of alienation was taken over by Hegel, who handed it on in the mystifying disguise of his idealism. So Marx had sources to stimulate creative attention to this fascinating social phenomenon. In standing Hegel "right side up," he turned back to real economic phenomena, and analyzed them, and although his analysis was still couched in the language of "philosophical phraseology," it pushed him consistently to revolutionary communist conclusions.

Above all, observation forced him to the conclusion about *the alienation of the product of human labor:* this product is transformed into a commodity, that is, into a bearer of abstract value that can be exchanged on the market. Working under these circumstances, man does not produce goods that serve to satisfy his needs, but commodities that acquire an independent existence on the market and contribute to the impoverishment of their producer, the worker. The product of labor is the objectification of labor, but for the worker it means alienation—the loss of the object.

> . . . the worker is related to the *product of his labour* as to an *alien* object. For it is clear on this presupposition that the more the worker expends himself in work the more powerful becomes the world of objects which he creates in face of himself, the poorer he becomes in his inner life, and the less he belongs to himself. It is just the same as in religion. The more of himself man attributes to God the less he has left in himself. The worker puts his life into the object, and his life then belongs no longer to himself but to the object. The greater his activity, therefore, the less he possesses. What is embodied in the product of his labour is no longer his own. The greater this product is, therefore, the more he is diminished. The *alienation* of the worker in his product means not only that his labour becomes an object, assumes an *external* existence, but that it exists independently, *outside himself*, and alien to him, and that it stands opposed to him as an autonomous power. The life which he has given to the object sets itself against him as an alien and hostile force.[18]

Marx abided by this concept of the alienation of the product of labor throughout his writings, *Capital* included, though the word itself was very sparingly and infrequently used in his later work; in *Capital*, we have the notion of "commodity fetishism," which denotes a relationship, apparently between *things* (commodities that are exchanged on the market), but in fact between *men* as producers.

The relation of fetishism, which can be extended to all reified products of human labor, is closely connected with alienation, but the two notions are not identical and "fetishism" cannot be simply replace "alienation." For it is only when the product of man is estranged from its maker and becomes independent of him that the mystifying situation arises in which relations between men appear, on the surface, as relations between things (similarly, relations between values, meanings and similar "spiritual goods," which seem to exist independently of their human makers, obscure the actual relationship, which is between men). But if alienation is a condition for the occurrence of fetishism, and if commodity (or another) fetishism is a specific effect of alienation, then alienation is a wider and richer notion, which cannot be reduced to fetishism.[19]

It is not only the product but the very *process of labor* that is subject to alienation.

The point is that the worker experiences his labor as a compulsion, not as a means of satisfying the *need to work,* but as a *means* of meeting other necessities. This is why man avoids work whenever he can, why he is unhappy when working, and why he feels at ease only away from work. Since, in addition, the worker's labor does not belong to him but to someone else, man comes to regard his animal (biological) functions as free of any compulsion, and his specifically human function—labor—as inhuman.

This theme runs through the whole of Marx: it returns in an almost unchanged and in a sense even more acute form (since its validity is extended to all systems) in the third volume of *Capital.*

> In fact, the realm of freedom does not commence until the point is passed where labour under the compulsion of necessity and of external utility is required. In the very nature of things, it lies beyond the sphere of material production in the strictest meaning of the term. Just as the savage must wrestle with nature, in order to satisfy his wants, in order to maintain his life and reproduce it, so civilized man has to do it, and he must do it in all forms of society and under all possible modes of production. With his development the realm of natural necessity expands, because his wants increase; but at the same time the forces of production increase, by which these wants are satisfied. The freedom in this field cannot consist of

anything else but of the fact that socialized man, the associated producers, regulate their interchange with nature rationally, bring it under their common control, instead of being ruled by it as by some blind power; that they accomplish their task with the least expenditure of energy and under conditions most adequate to their human nature and most worthy of it. *But it always remains a realm of necessity. Beyond it begins that development of human power, which is its own end, the true realm of freedom,* which, however, can flourish only upon that realm of necessity as its basis. The shortening of the working day is its fundamental premise.[20]

In the light of this statement, we should be very cautious before heaping sarcasm (as Marxist literature on this subject frequently has done) on authors who suggest that Marx did not confine the phenomenon of alienation to the capitalist system.

Marx further distinguishes between alienation of the process of labor and alienation of labor as a specific activity of man. To appreciate this distinction, we must go back to what was said in the previous chapter on the "essence" of man.

According to Marx, man differs from the animal world in that he is a being who *consciously produces* the means of satisfying his needs. If man's labor is estranged, he loses his unique attribute, his humanity. In this way, he estranges himself, becomes self-alienated.

. . . labour, *life activity, productive life,* now appear to man only as *means* for the satisfaction of a need, the need to maintain his physical existence. Productive life is, however, species-life. It is life creating life. In the type of life activity resides the whole character of a species, its *species*-character; and free, conscious activity is the species-character of human beings. Life itself appears only as a *means of life.*[21]

As a logical consequence of this view of alienated labor, Marx postulates the disappearance of labor under communism and its replacement by frequently chosen activity.[22] This, however, must have been a "youthful folly," for as we can see from the above passage in *Capital,* Marx later recognized that labor was necessary in all social systems.

Alienated labor cripples the human personality, subordinates him to the division of labor, and even turns him into an appendage of the machine. (This idea frequently recurs in *Capital.*) Robbed of the object of his labor and of the possibility of free activity, and crippled in his personality, man loses and alienates himself, just as others alienate themselves from him.

Tracking down the source of dehumanization, we find alienated labor, which is the result of private property and at the same time—through mutual interaction—its cause. From this derives the consistent conclusion that leads directly to communism: to eliminate alienation—and thereby to eliminate the dehumanization of life, it necessary to abolish private property.

> The positive supersession of *private property*, as the appropriation of human life, is, therefore, the positive supersession of all alienation, and the return of man from religion, the family, the state, etc., to his *human,* i.e., *social* life.[23]

About the same time a vision of the alienated world was cogently presented by Engels:

> The liquidation of feudal bondage made "cash payment" mankind's only tie. Property . . . is thus raised to the throne and, in the end, to make alienation complete, money, that alienated, empty abstraction of freedom, becomes the master of the world. Man has ceased to be the slave of man and has become the slave of things; human relations have been turned completely upside down.[24]

The conclusion? Such a situation must lead to a breakdown: the state will disappear and so will the atomization of society; "intelligent order" will triumph, and ". . . the alienation of man, as reflected in the domination of money, constitutes the inevitable transition to the now imminent hour when man once again finds himself." [25]

Following the intellectual evolution of Marx and Engels, we cannot fail to see that observation and theoretical analysis of the phenomena known under the general name of "alienation" led them, step by step, to awareness of the fundamental role of economic alienation in the whole life of bourgeois society, and on from there to communism.

Abolition of private ownership of the means of production is the prerequisite for the elimination of alienation in capitalist society and its attendant "human condition." This unimpeachable conclusion had already been reached by Marx and Engels in their youthful writings. But is it permitted to argue from this that the overthrow of private property would automatically put an *end* to all alienation? (In their later works Marx and Engels do not commit themselves categorically on this.) Was it a conclusion that could validly be drawn from the premises they employed? Must alienation inevitably disappear in a socialist society? These are the burning questions indeed from the point of view of this, our socialist society.

Logically speaking, it cannot be deduced from the the fact that economic alienation is at the basis of all other forms of alienation in bourgeois society, that the abolition of private property automatically ends all alienation in any form of social life. For even if, in capitalism, economic alienation, of which private property is an expression, determines all other forms of alienation, this does not mean that no other causes exist, which, in different conditions, might not cause some other forms of alienation. *This* can only be ascertained empirically, concretely. And what is the lesson of experience in this respect?

Here we should clearly distinguish two sets of problems:

First, the question of alienation in a society like ours, which is building socialism.

Second, the inferences that can be drawn about the future communist society from our current experience of alienation in a socialist society.

With regard to the first problem, the situation is clear: in all the socialist societies that have so far existed, various forms of alienation have appeared. In other words, there is no automatic process whereby abolition of private ownership of the means of production eliminates alienation—if only because of the continued existence of the state as a coercive machinery.

From the point of view of Marxist theory, there is nothing irregular in the fact that various forms of alienation survive the demise of private property: Marxism after all, speaks of a period of transition, to allow both for a gradual elimination of class organization of society and for the conservative nature of social consciousness. Therefore, the distinction between socialism and communism as two phases of development of socialist society should be treated not in a purely formal way, that is, only in terms of the abolition of private ownership of the means of production, but realistically, that is with consideration of the *whole pattern of relations* characteristic of the constructed socialist system and the transition to communism. (And this includes the withering away of the state and the removal of other forms of alienation, together with a different class consciousness which lasts longer than its material basis.) Then it might safely be assumed that the period of transition is—and in fact must be—a whole historical epoch, during which the existence of various forms of alienation is quite understandable.

One more point must be made: since socialism has not triumphed throughout the world simultaneously, nor in countries of the most advanced capitalism and the longest tradition of bourgeois democracy, an additional factor comes into play, prolonging the effective life of alienation. This operates both externally (the state as an apparatus of defense against armed attack or subversion) and internally (difficulties in the liquidation of the class structure of society due to economic causes, and the influence of alien ideology on people's minds).

It is possible, therefore, to explain the persistence of alienation in socialist countries. But it is unconvincing, or at any rate ill-advised, to deny its existence, as, unfortunately, is often done even in books which claim to be scientific. It is disingenuous to imagine that men's consciousness, attitudes, and social institutions can be changed overnight simply as a result of the abolition of private ownership of the means of production. This has never been claimed by Marxism, and the kind of propaganda that is more concerned with national or political "pride" than with historical truth is bound to backfire.

The difficulties begin when we come to the second problem, when we try to visualize the outlines of the future communist society on the basis of current experience. This, of course, is not a matter of speculation nor of elaborating on features that are given *ex definitione*. That was feasible a hundred years ago, but even then only on pain of being accused of utopianism, a charge leveled at Marx and Engels, for all their good sense and their reluctance to paint pictures of the future society. It was partly to avoid this that, in their early writings, they took it for granted that abolition of private ownership of the means of production would put an end to *all* alienation. But today we can start from our own reality and its developmental tendencies; we are not compelled to invent a socialist society: we are living in one.

Let us begin with the state.

It can hardly be denied that the state exists in a socialist society. Not only do we admit this, but in the ordinary run of things we pride ourselves on its power. But the state is an alienated force.

This is not only a matter of the armed forces and the threat of war, although such is the key issue of the world today, in which— despite all the differences that divide us from the capitalistic world —we all have a stake. It is obvious, surely, that a world in which man has reached the peak of his powers and attained mastery over nature, and is at the same time faced with a palpable threat of total destruction, unable to control the forces he has himself released, is an alienated world; not only is it independent of man, it actually menaces his very existence. In a world like this, man must feel threatened, even if he lives in a socialist society. It is not surprising that he responds to the uncanny world of Kafka's *Trial* or *Castle* even though we fortify him with the help of socialist realism. Nor is it strange that he is attracted to Marx's theory of alienation, even if we warn against the trap of existentialist pessimism into which he may stumble.

But in this respect, alienation is bound up with the existence of the capitalist world; the state as a system of coercion should disappear together with the disappearance of this world. The crux of the matter lies elsewhere.

As a system of coercion, the state is a force that is directed not only outwards but also inwards. Its capacity for alienation is well illustrated by the period of the so-called "cult of personality," indeed as it affected all the socialist countries. This was, after all, a story of appalling alienation as the forces created by man in the best faith and with the noblest of humane intentions tore themselves out of his hands, turned into a hostile power, and began to crush and annihilate their makers. This is a problem that still awaits sociological analysis; so far Marxists have gone beyond the surface.

Let us assume the best of the possible alternatives: that alienation will be abolished with the disappearance of a hostile external environment and the dying away of classes within society. But there still remains the alienation of the state, and moreover in a sphere apparently suspected by Marx or Engels. I have in mind the state as a machinery of administration, a system of managing things. According to the founders of Marxism, the state was to wither away as an apparatus of coercion but it would retain its function of administering things. Marx and Engels had no doubts on this point, although in their struggle against the anarchists they could not know the enormity of the functions and power of the apparatus that was to remain. The state is responsible for the planning of the whole of social life and its development, for the management of the entire nationalized economy, for the direction of science, culture and art, social welfare, health services, transport, and so forth. In its capacity of administrator, the state has become a gigantic machine, embracing, with the progress of technology, ever greater expanses of human life: at a rate that could not be foreseen a hundred years ago. Even in a near-perfect democracy, approaching that free and voluntary association of producers that was the ideal of the founders of Marxism, modern conditions would, for purely technical reasons require central management of the various spheres of social life. Consequently, the state would remain what it is: a Moloch that, owing to progressive specialization, is inevitably an organization of professional experts. Bureaucracy, despite all the democratic restraints that subordinate the state apparatus to social control, remains a necessity in modern conditions. The best that can be achieved is to have a competent and sensible bureaucracy; we should have no illusion that we can hope for anything more. As an administrative machinery, the state will not wither away; this is a dream, which neither Marx nor Engels in their maturity, and certainly not Lenin, ever cherished. The struggle against bureaucracy should therefore be conceived as a struggle against a bureaucracy that is bad, unreasonable, incompetent, top-heavy, etc., but not as one against the administrative machinery, against bureaucracy "in general." It is sometimes suggested that, since the present situation makes it impossible to fulfill Marx's postulate of the withering away of the state as an instrument of coercion under socialism, we should begin with what is practicable —the disappearance of the state as an administrative machine— but this whole approach rests, from the Marxist point of view, on a painful misconception.

This state of affairs, and it seems incontestable, entails a variety of far-reaching consequences as far as alienation in the socialist system is concerned.

In the first place, there remains—and apparently must remain— an extensive machinery of power, which, even if it does not fulfill the functions of an instrument of coercion, still stands over the individual. This must be so in a world of ever more universal relations, which, linked as they are with modern techniques of production and means of communication, are bound (quite apart from all other problems and difficulties) to upset that idea of self-governing "associations of free producers" that was born in the minds of the utopian socialists and was not without influence on the views of the young Marx. Given all the transformations of the modern world, all the radical reforms that help to democratize social life, that life must be centrally organized at a certain level and must be administered by a highly specialized machinery, compared with which the individual is a very atom. This need not be a bad thing, but in certain circumstances it may be so and all the more, since it is questionable whether *such* an apparatus of administration is radically different from a system of coercion. These are matters that certainly deserve attention.

But much more incisive in practice is the second kind of alienation of the state under socialism: its social effects.

According to Marxist theory, the communist society should be stateless and classless. Liquidation of social classes is by definition connected with the abolition of private ownership of the means of production, the class status being defined in terms of relationship to the ownership of these means. But such class division is not the only, or at any rate the only possible, division of society. Within the framework of a class society there are groups, for example occupational, social, and other groups that lead to a certain division of society along lines of prestige, position in social hierarchy and the like. Similar divisions cannot be ruled out in a society that has abolished private property and classes, on the contrary, previous experience indicates that their existence needs to be taken for granted.

Among the many possible divisions and their criteria (on the assumption, of course, that absolute equality is a fiction) a division based on the exercise of power—if only administrative power as described above—seems to be uppermost. It is surely obvious that if the vast and complicated state machinery of administration has to remain, there must also be a group or stratum of people to carry out these administrative functions. The larger this apparatus becomes as a result of technical necessities, the more numerous the stratum of administrators will be; and the more complicated and rigidly hierarchical the administrative machinery (also as a result of technical necessities), the greater the role this hierarchy will play in the structure of this stratum. Does this not create an additional danger of social alienation?

In Marxist quarters, the attitude to these problems tends to be defensive. They counter an anticommunist propaganda that leans heavily on talk of a "red bourgeoisie" or a "new class" and is designed to weaken communist attacks on the class structure of capitalist society. This theme can be found in Huxley and Orwell, in Burnham (with his "managers") and Djilas (with his "new class"), etc. But it is important that these defensive reactions should not obscure our view of the actual problems.

A social class, as has been said before, by definition cannot exist in a society that has abolished private ownership of the means of production. It is therefore easy to prove that what Burnham, Djilas, and others have to say about the class character of socialist society is sheer nonsense. But this is not, essentially, a matter of names or of sociological categories; the real issue lies in the sphere of alienation. And it certainly deserves reflection.

We are not prophets and we cannot foretell the final effect, in terms of social alienation, of the social distinctions of society based on position in the state machinery (and, let me repeat, that means that the apparatus *for managing things* cannot disappear and hence it can indirectly become an apparatus for *ruling people*). But we can and should see *the problem*.

This is all the more necessary since, at least in the period of transition, disparities in the field of social status and prestige are linked with a very down-to-earth factor: differences in financial and material situation. It would be difficult to make any hard and fast forecasts about how Marx's postulate of complete satisfaction of human needs under communism will be fulfilled in practice. We should bear in mind, however, that what is involved is not a *particular country* (and the problem *must not* be seen in these terms if we do not want to undermine the very foundations of communism) but the whole world, and that this world is still to an overwhelming degree a world of starving or merely vegetating people. Then it can only be said that, unless this postulate is simply a utopian throwback (a difficulty that could be circumvented by skillful interpretation of "needs" as "reasonable needs" with an additional explanation of what is meant by "reasonable" at a given time and in given circumstances), its full realization will have to be delayed for many, many years yet. In the meantime, however, it is necessary to live under normal conditions, that is, with a limited supply of goods that have to be distributed properly among the members of society. By what principle? Marxism has rightly never preached an abstract equalitarianism—neither the socialist "to each according to his work" nor the communist "to each according to his needs" are abstractly equalitarian: both of them accept differentiation. Clearly those who give more to society should receive more in return. But there can be further complications, not only because of a possible distortion of the meaning of "more," which (as we know from experience) is quite a real danger.

Today, with the experience of a much longer and more involved evolution than anything Marx could imagine, one should perceive these difficulties in a much sharper light. Among them are the dangers of alienation arising from the necessity of the survival of certain forms of statehood.

The second major aspect of alienation in socialist society is the alienation of labor.

To Marx this was an element of economic alienation, something wholly natural since his analysis concerned capitalist society. Together with private property, socialism abolishes alienation in the form in which it was known in capitalism. But this eradication is by no means complete: in a modified form all the elements of this alienation as specified by Marx remain, at least in socialism (in the sense of the first stage of communist society).

The product of human labor remains a commodity, and this means that the laws of the market continue to operate in some form. In the Marxian sense of the word, alienation has not disappeared, although its mode of operation has been changed by the abolition of private property. I have brought up this question since it might be claimed that in a developed communist society commodity production will disappear, although present experiences makes this contention seem debatable.

On the other hand, there is no doubt that what Marx described as the alienation of labor does, and will, persist.

As we have seen, the mature Marx did not cling to his dream of an "end of labor" and its supersession by "freely chosen activity." Given the development of industrial society, this would have been as chimerical as the vision of a "universal" man who knows everything, can do anything, and changes his occupation whenever he pleases. These ideas, I think, had better be written off as the naive whimsies of their young author. Even if the day should come when total automation and robots enable man to live in such a paradise, it is not for us to indulge in utopian prophecies which do not take us a single step further in the organization of our life today. All such suggestions were, of course, categorically rejected by Marx in his maturity.

In other words, even in socialism it is necessary to work; this according to Marx, is an unpleasant necessity. It could be said that he should not have included labor in the category of alienation. That he did was closely connected with his concepts of the "essence of man" and "species-being" and—following the advice of Marx himself—this interpretation of alienation can probably be safely shelved, together with these other youthful structures. Experience has shown that under the right conditions men can grow fond of their work; though it is still the "labor" of Marx's language, it is at the same time that "freely chosen activity" the absence of which makes men unhappy.

However, we are on more embarrassing ground with the question of the alienation of the labor process and that vast set of problems connected with the division of labor and specialization. Marx analyzed the crippled human nature of this alienation under capitalism. Unfortunately, the technical aspects of the problem cut across all systems—for example, work on an assembly line is inherently the same regardless of government; the only possible difference is in its conditions. To make matters worse, technical progress since Marx's day has only aggravated the situation. It is not my task, nor my intention, to go into the details of this specialized and involved problem. I wish only to call attention to the existence of this form of alienation under socialism, and to emphasize that the only way to overcome it is by reducing working time—that is, by a shorter work week and a shorter working day. Thus, unable to rid ourselves of this alienation (at least not until *human labor* is completely replaced by automation), we can only aim at alleviating and curtailing its rigors.

To document the workings of alienation in socialism, let me discuss one example taken at random: the institution of the family.

Marxism has exposed the social character of the family as alienation. In this field, too, a social product of man—institutionalized relations between people—has not only become autonomous, and begun to lead its own life, but has also subordinated man to itself. Marxism showed that the family changes its character in accordance with changing historical conditions—and so does the situation of women within the framework of the family and the prevalent morality. In the light of Marxist theory, it was easy to predict that the type of family that had come into being in a class society, and had adapted to its property relations, would be basically altered with the destruction of the foundations of the class system. Also what is true of modern industrial society in general, as a result of industrialization and urbanization the traditional socio-economic functions of the family (now being increasingly transferred to the factory, the school, and other social institutions), once the safeguard of its cohesion and durability, would be undermined. It could also be foreseen that the chance of conditions would bring a complete transformation of the profoundly human phenomenon, so critical to the individual's development and happiness, of love between men and women.

We can now observe for ourselves that these changes are in fact taking place. The position of women has shifted radically even in so normally conservative an area as moral judgments. Ideas of love are altering: the pattern of family relations is being remodeled, with respect both to their permanence and to those between wife and husband and between parents and children. Nevertheless, the traditional *form* of the family has not only survived, but also it defies any reasonable forecasts about its further development.

This is not the only instance of an alienated social institution that has been taken over lock, stock, and barrel by socialism from the capitalist system. Another example—which would have seemed absurd at one time—is the alienation of the nation and of those national feelings, which lead to nationalism and even racism. Naive speeches about the total eradication of such problems by the socialist revolution are hardly sensible when the facts obviously speak against them. Yet these are dangerous developments, not only because of their harmful effects on human personality and their glaring inconsistency with the image of man under socialism, but also because they obstruct in the most direct way the construction of a new society.

And so alienation can be found in socialist society, not only as a relic of the past, but also as something more durable and more organically linked with the new social conditions. At any rate, the problem is real, and demands thought and care.

It is quite clear that in social relationships between men the problem of the individual's development, and of the full evolution of his personality, is primarily dependent on the existence and nature of alienation. If man wants to communicate with others, he must constantly externalize his inner mental life, and objectify and reify his activities if he desires, as he must, to live in society.

Such objectification and reification may, under appropriate conditions, lead to alienation of human activity and of its products. Making man the slave of things subjects him to the blind necessities of a spontaneous elemental reality and alienates him by frustrating that fully conscious activity that, in nature, is characteristic only of the species *Homo sapiens.*

The estranged man, living and acting in a world of alienation, is curtailed in his development, and mutilated in his personality. The ideal type of man in the age of communism is one who has liberated himself from the rule of alienation; the total, universal man. This ideal may be unattainable, like the limit of a mathematical series, but even so one can and should try to reach it. The way, of course, is to resist the various kinds of alienation. But if this struggle is to be conscious, we must know the situation well, know where alienation lies, or may lie, and in what form, instead of closing our eyes to the realities and dogmatically asserting that the new system has put an end to alienation because it is by definition impossible in this new society.

If Marx had actually said this, it would have to be rejected as false. Fortunately, we need not go so far; he never made *any* such radical claim. It is true that in his early writings, particularly the *Manuscripts,* there is a substantial dose of utopian ideas on this subject [26]—all alienation is to disappear automatically with the abolition of private property. But these youthful errors are absent from his mature work. Not long after the *Manuscripts,* in *The German*

Ideology, Marx speaks of the *process* of eliminating alienation under communism, but not of its instant abolition:

"Communism is for us not a *state* of affairs which is to be established, an ideal to which *reality* will have to adjust itself. We call communism the *real* movement which abolishes the present state of things." [27]

Here we have the answer to our problem: alienation and its threat must be seen clearly and resisted consciously. That there is alienation under socialism is not a bad thing in itself; the trouble begins when no conscious efforts are made to combat it. Socialism is superior to capitalism, but not because it is free of all alienation, but because it provides better conditions for its consciously fighting it. All that is required is to turn these advantages to good account, and this means, among other things, not, as a matter of "principle," to wish away alienation when it actually exists, but to investigate and overcome the evil.

Chapter 3
The Individual and History

(The Problem of Freedom)

> *History* does *nothing;* "it possesses *no* colossal riches,"
> it "fights *no* battles." Rather it is *man,* actual and living
> man, who does all this, who possesses and fights; "his-
> tory" does not use man as a means for its purposes as
> though it were a person apart; it is *nothing* but the activ-
> ity of man pursuing his ends.[1]

The Marx who upholds the role of the individual in history, the Marx who treats "history" as a hypostasis, the Marx who identifies history with men's conscious activity: what a contrast with the stereotype of Marx writing only of classes and class struggle, objective laws of historical development, its economic determinants inclusive of human consciousness, and so on and so forth. Yet this is a perfectly genuine Marx, and, moreover, a point of view that was continually reiterated not only to the end of his work but also by Engels. The most important point, though, is that it is absolutely compatible with the doctrine of Marx, who—as Engels said at his graveside—"discovered the law of evolution in human history" and did for history what Darwin did for natural science. Nevertheless, it is a point of view that opens up new insights into Marx's thought and bids us consider it afresh.

There is a critical moment at which every theory of man, like every school of history, comes up against the central problem of "the individual and history"—which is simply another way of saying "the individual and society." Ordinary observation no less than scientific observation, reveals two sets of facts whose apparent contradiction demands reflection. On the one hand, we have human individuals acting in a conscious and purposeful manner and commanding, as we know from our own experience, a wide range of choices; on the other, there is historical development, which often runs counter to these endeavors and obviously conditions the choices made by men in their conscious actions. The individual and history; conscious activity and spontaneous development; freedom of choice and the factors determining this choice—these are only some aspects of the question, which must be an object of inquiry for any philosophical anthropology, any theory of history, any sociology that has not renounced theoretical ambitions and wishes to avoid the confusions of constructing a system that is internally incoherent and so destined for conflict.

This analysis can be carried out in one of two ways—taking either society or the individual as the frame of reference. In view of the requirements and the specific perspective of this book, I have chosen the latter course. Accordingly, the reader will not find in these pages the usual account (by now traditional in Marxist studies) of the role of the individual, particularly the "great individual," in history. It is omitted, not because it is unimportant, but because it is already familiar, and in this particular case, it is not the crucial factor. Let us, therefore, take this as given and concentrate on the problems from the perspective of the individual. We will thus obtain a kind of complement to our considerations of the Marxist concept of the individual, and above all, of his ontological status.

Is the human individual autonomous? This is the question with which any such analysis must begin. It will be as well to clear up exactly what the term means.

A discussion of autonomy, and independence, only makes sense if we identify the context; in other words, autonomy of what, and with respect to what? Independence in relation to whom or what? Thus, we usually have in mind such questions as: is the individual independent in the sense of being distinguishable from and independent of other individuals and their organized collectivities—society? Is he in his distinctiveness and independence an unrepeatable whole? Does he, as an unrepeatable whole, and in this sense as an individuality, constitute a specific microcosm?

In my formulation of this question, and its semantic interpretation, I have deliberately adopted the language and approach current in non-Marxist literature, particularly personalist and existentialist. This is not because I agree with these ways of presenting the problems, but because it is the only way of confronting their views on the issues. In any case, I believe that there can be no development of the contemporary Marxist theory of man without a comparative study of Marxist, personalist, and existentialist doctrines, from which basis their heuristic value can be shown. I would like to do this myself one day, and if I have not applied the comparative principle in this book, it is only because the absence of any serious studies of the Marxist treatment of this subject makes the task extremely difficult, if not impossible. This, however, does not mean that such assessment and confrontation should be avoided. Far from it.

Thus the question of the autonomy of the individual, as posed in theories of human nature, in philosophical anthropology, has more than one meaning; it involves a series of different though interrelated problems.

Is the individual a *distinct,* and in this sense an *independent,* whole relative to other individuals and society? If this question concerns the individual as a being distinguishable in the sense of constituting a psychophysical whole characteristic of the living reality of the species *Homo sapiens, nobody* will demur—either from the biological or the psychological side. After all, it is precisely *as wholes,* as specific *structures,* that these psychological entities are born, live, and die. They cannot be divided—in this respect what is the attribute of the whole is not the attribute of its parts; and they cannot be integrated into larger wholes, composed of individuals as organic parts. But this kind of "autonomous being" is proper to every living creature—with the exception of the lowest species—and to say that the individual being has *this* kind of distinctness is a truism. It is not this which is involved in the question of the autonomous existence of the human individual.

Is the human individual, as a whole entity distinct from nature and society, *independent* in his existence from other individuals and from society? The answer to this question is no longer unanimous, depending as it does on the assumptions adopted. It is here, indeed, that the various schools clearly part company.

Naturally, no one in his senses would now deny that man lives in society and that he is in various ways dependent upon others. But again this is not what those who hold the thesis of the individual's autonomous existence have in mind; the individual's dependence on society (and nature too), they say, is true of the animal side of human existence, and in this respect man does not differ from the animal. What is specifically human, they argue, concerns man as a person, and so as a spiritual being whose attribute is freedom of choice. When so conceived, personality is said to have been given to man from nature; it has nothing to do with society or other men and cannot be reduced to them. It is in this sense that the individual is said to be autonomous, that is, independent of nature and society, as a specific spiritual entity.

Such a concept of the autonomy of the individual can, as has been pointed out, only be accepted by those trends of thought that *by definition* link personality to this interpretation of the autonomy of individual existence. Be it noted, however, that such a definition of the *person* requires certain metaphysical assumptions: either the existence of the person as a spiritual being, which, created by God, participates in the divine being (Christian personalism); or the existence of the Ego as a spiritual monad, which, in view of the impenetrability of other monads of this type, is "doomed to solitariness" (Heidegger's *Geworfenheit*). In both instances, acceptance of such premises (which, in the case of existentialism, are camouflaged in esoteric language) necessarily depends on an act of *faith,* which, for all their other differences, is common to both religious anthropology and atheist existentialism. Now, not only is there no obligation to undertake such an act of faith (there are no rational arguments in its favor, nor have any even been suggested) but, indeed, it is downright impossible for anyone who is a rationalist (in the sense of being anti-irrationalist).

In fact, in the case of personalism, the advocate of the autonomy of the individual (in the above sense) conceals in this autonomy a notion that implies the exact opposite: for a person who only participates in God's essence and existence cannot be regarded as autonomous in the sense of his independence (the person is presumed to be independent of other men and society, but at the same time fully dependent on a supernatural being). Existentialist metaphysics is free of such contradictions, but even so it requires considerable courage to profess this new edition of monadology when confronted with the evidence of modern sociology and psychology. That this can be done is best attested by the existentialist philosophers, but their example is certainly no argument that it *must* be so as is borne out, in turn, by so many opponents and critics of existentialism.

Marxism utterly disagrees with such an interpretation of the "autonomy" of the individual. Its opposition comes from the basic tenets of its concept of the individual: as a specific part of living nature, the individual is a product of society, and in this sense a totality of social relations. Seen thus, far from being "autonomous" in relation to society, he is, on the contrary, its product, dependent on it. When a Marxist talks of autonomous anthropology, he means that the world as a product of social man's self-creation is independent of any superhuman factors; he is far from asserting the individual's autonomous existence in the personalist or existentialist sense. Such a claim must be opposed by a consistent autonomous anthropology of Marxism.

But when we are discussing the autonomous being of the individual, we cannot confine ourselves to consideration of his special position in nature and society (in the sense of his independence of society). For we are still left with another crucial question: the unrepeatability of individual existence. The point, as already mentioned, is not the unrepeatability and uniqueness of the individual as a physical structure, but more importantly the uniqueness of his psychological structure, which we call the personality of the individual, the sum total of his views, attitudes, and dispositions. For personalists or consistent existentialists, it is *only* this aspect of the individual's existence that matters; the Marxist—and here his position is by no means an isolated one in modern anthropology —will stress the organic unity of the physical and mental characteristics making up human personality. But, however different his approach, the Marxist will still *accept* the theory of the unrepeatability, and thus uniqueness, of the human individual. In doing so, he will also recognize that each individual, precisely because of his uniqueness, constitutes a certain *value,* particularly in the sphere of morals. As with the question of the exceptional place in nature, differences of ideological background do not prevent various schools from being unanimous about the individual's unrepeatability. If this means recognition of the autonomous being of the individual, then Marxism acknowledges such an autonomy.

This, however, has further implications for one possible version of the question about the individual's autonomy: is not the individual, as an unrepeatable entity, an unrepeatable psychophysical structure, a specific microcosm? And so does his death not represent the death, the end of a certain world?

This question has been raised by existentialism, and for obvious reasons. But it is also a fully legitimate question for Marxism; and, given a proper interpretation of the words "individual," "unrepeatable structure," and "microcosm," it must, to my mind, be answered in the affirmative. Yes, every individual is a specific microcosm and his death means the end of a certain world.

Acceptance of this statement must lead to further analysis on the borderline of politics and morals.

While rejecting the personalist and existentialist metaphysical conception of the individual autonomous being, Marxism recognizes that the human individual is physically distinct and psychophysically unrepeatable—and thus a specific microcosm. Accordingly it corroborates what is essential to the concept of the individual's autonomous existence, but repudiates all the mystical assumptions and their implications.

This point has to be made clear before embarking on further considerations of the relationship between the individual and history.

What is characteristic of Marxism is not that it develops an original theory of the autonomy of the human individual, but that it provides a consistent analysis of the objective laws of historical development that does not exclude, but indeed presupposes conscious and purposeful action by these autonomous individuals (autonomous in a specific sense of the word). This is the most profound meaning of the materialist approach to history and it is the bedrock on which the intellectual structure of Marx's "scientific socialism" is erected.

Men act consciously; their consciousness, however, is not a spiritual monad, which is independent of the objective world, but it is conditioned by this reality. That it is not consciousness which determines men's existence, but on the contrary their social existence that determines their consciousness was a discovery made by Marx as early as the works of his youth.[2] But at the same time he admitted that the individual is, in a certain sense, "bound" by society—both because, as an ensemble of social relations, he is its product, and because he is enmeshed, as an active element, in the objective laws of social development; these he helps to create, but at the same time he is subordinated to them.

This basic thesis of the materialist conception of history, which once was a great shock to the idealist concept of man and history (and still is to all varieties of personalistic mysticism), has now so permeated the modern science of society that it is no longer peculiar to Marxism. This is perhaps the highest tribute a scientific theory can receive.

This is not the place for a discussion of the objective laws of historical development, nor are these problems of interest to us here. It is enough to say that belief in such laws is *incompatible* with the idea of the individual's autonomy as conceived by personalism or existentialism. The alternatives are obvious: either we consistently extend the concept of the individual's autonomy and accept *voluntarism* in history, or to avoid this consequence, we adopt some kind of theory of objective laws, of historical development, and then we must discard any radical interpretation of the individual's autonomy. This is an uncomfortable alternative, since the luxury of believing the individual to be autonomous, in a certain sense, can only be achieved at a very high price—the loss of scientific prestige. What historian, sociologist, or economist would be prepared to accept the consequence of historical voluntarism? One can perhaps "philosophize" in this style, but it is no way of pursuing a science.

Rejection of *one* interpretation of the individual's autonomy does not mean, as we have already pointed out, disowning other, more moderate versions. On the contrary, it would be impossible to deny the autonomy of the individual, in a certain sense of the term, nor the connected problems of his relationship with history.

What is meant, when speaking of this autonomy, is primarily the individual's freedom to make choices of alternatives through which he makes history. But what kind of freedom can this be if we consider that the historical process is objective, that is, independent of human will and subordinating the individual to itself? Given such a concept, can the Marxist thesis that man is the creator of history be maintained? And is there any room for the freedom of choice without which not only does the theory of moral responsibility fall to the ground but even common sense is threatened with bankruptcy? Perhaps, after all, there is something to be said for those who, like Gabriel Marcel, in order to save the idea of man's freedom and his creative role in history, speak of "man *against* history." [3]

The problem of freedom may be discussed metaphysically, but it is also possible to treat it operationally.

In the first case, we ask "what is freedom?"—and wait for a definition. When the question is posed in this way the situation is hopeless. Adoption of one or another particular definition of freedom obviously depends on the whole system within which the definition has been formulated; and it follows from certain philosophical assumptions, requiring the acceptance of some and the rejection of others, to keep internal coherence. Any debate over the meaning of freedom, therefore, inevitably leads to a confrontation of philosophical systems and cannot be resolved without it. This means that at a certain point one can only state where and how opinions differ, and close the discussion, since it is irremediably deadlocked. As a result of this, the history of philosophy abounds with all sorts of statements about the "essence" of freedom, and it seems safe to say that here, too, there is nothing new under the sun. At any rate, the odds against originality are formidably long.

In our context, however, there seems to be no reason for despair. For when we speak of the relationship between the individual and history, and between the freedom of human actions and the objective laws of historical development, we are not primarily interested in an answer to the question "what is freedom?"; instead, we want to know something more practical: has man, when he acts, only one possibility of action to choose, or has he more? In this way we move from metaphysical to operational grounds—instead of asking "what is it?", we ask "how is it done?" It is here, in my judgment, that the key to the problem lies.

I do not challenge the need for inquiring into the nature of freedom. What I do deny is the claim that only these questions are necessary, and that they must first be answered before the problem of the freedom of human action can be discussed. What is more, I am convinced that the first type of investigation is not always helpful—unless its limits are clearly perceived—in the study of human actions.

If I were to say, with the personalists, that freedom is a characteristic feature of the person, I would only utter my voluntarist philosophical creed but I have really said nothing about the nature of concrete human actions. And if I say with Spinoza and the dialectical materialists—as I personally would certainly do—that freedom is a recognized necessity, I am only indicating the problem of the social conditioning of human actions, but despite appearances, I have said nothing about the possibility or impossibility of the individual being able to choose between a number of alternatives. For it is not true that man *always* complies with a known necessity, and it is even less true that he can act *only* if he recognizes necessity. On the other hand, it is a fact that, in his conscious actions, man always makes a choice that, although determined by a variety of factors, is normally the outcome of thought and consequently free—if only because it is not forcibly imposed, since he could have chosen otherwise.

Nor is the problem of human freedom, and seen from this angle the individual's relationship to history, a matter of abstract reflections on the essence of freedom; it is really a question of specifically considering the ways in which men concretely choose between various alternatives. This truth is appreciated not only by Marxists, but also by thinkers who are very remote from Marxism. Let me once more quote Gabriel Marcel, who makes the same point in other words:

> It appears that the question "what is a free man?" cannot be usefully investigated in the abstract, that is without reference to the relevant historical situations treated, at that, with a maximum of flexibility. For it is a characteristic of man that he finds himself in some situations—something that a certain kind of abstract humanism too easily forgets. Thus what matters is not what a free man is "in himself," as an essence—for this is perhaps quite immaterial—but how in the historical situation which always exists and which we must face *hic et nunc* this freedom can be conceived and documented.[4]

This is precisely the point: to understand how it is that man, socially conditioned and subordinated to objective historical processes—by now the voluntaristic concept of history may be quietly consigned to the stock of personalist fairy tales—can act in a conscious and planned way, and make the right choices from a variety of possibilities.

Seen thus, freedom is not absolute, but even so its range, although "bound" by the social determination of human personality, is still immense. And this is why we can regard man—a *product* of history—as the *maker* of history. At any rate, we can say that the more conscious his choice of actions directed towards a certain end, the freer he is—even if this choice is made in the belief that a certain development is inevitable for reasons beyond man's control, in other words when free choice means a deliberate subordination to necessity. For what matters is not that the choice made by man should be unconditioned, but that it should be made of his own free will and not the result of coercion by some external force. Man's freedom is not measured by the degree of his self-containment and detachment from social determinants (which in any case is a fiction) but by the extent to which he understands his purposes and the ways of achieving them through choice of the proper action. In this interpretation, freedom of the individual is the opposite of spontaneity in historical development, but not opposed to its objective character (in the sense of independence of the will of each individual). But here again we are clearly dealing with the concept of freedom as recognized necessity.

Let me return to the question of whether individual freedom can only be maintained if we adopt the notion of "man *against* history." Gabriel Marcel's dictum may be countered with another that is more realistic, and also activist: "man *makes* history."

These two solutions certainly express two different attitudes to the problem of "the individual and history." Behind the first is the *voluntarist notion* that recognition of the objectivity of historical processes does not so much limit as simply eliminate individual freedom, which is either absolute freedom or no freedom at all. On the other hand, the second motto is based on the view that freedom is to be found wherever the individual can, without being forced, choose between a number of courses of action, even though his choice is determined by some social or individual factors and can be explained in terms of them. From what has been said in the preceding pages, not only the philosophical nature of these alternatives, but also the reason for rejecting the first should be clear: the personalist concept of the individual's freedom is mere philosophical speculation without any real foundations.

But in accepting the Marxist solution do we not restrict the area of individual freedom so greatly that it is, in effect, lost? By no means, provided that we do not associate the problem of freedom with the personalist position.

When Marxism talks of the economic determinants of social development, it is not preaching some kind of economic fatalism but simply analyzing the controlling factors of development, which proceed from the mode of production and eventually affect the dispositions of men to accept certain views and attitudes. And that is all. What is said, therefore, is not that historical development must inevitably acquire this or that form, but only that it moves in this or that direction, assuming that very engagement of *men's conscious activity* which is part of the necessity of development. But this activity remains a matter of *choice* and for this very reason may not be forthcoming—if only because of the impediments or delays caused by the ideological superstructure. If Marxism did not recognize the importance of this factor, which can upset the probable course of events to the point of social disaster (and this is clearly stated by Marx in the *Communist Manifesto*), the call for ideological struggle would be meaningless.

According to Marxism, human activity is always socially determined but never a foregone conclusion. Thus, amid objective processes, there is still room for a choice of human activity—determined, it is true, but not compulsory, based on conscious deliberation and in this sense free. Hence man is not a blind tool of some force over and above him but the creator of history—not only because he creates by *acting,* but chiefly because he acts *consciously,* making a calculated choice between various possibilities. Proof of this lies in the fact that despite their social conditioning people do not act identically but differently—both because these determinants are diversified, if only by their class interests, and because individuals vary in their phylogenesis and ontogenesis alike.

Thus in the Marxist view, man is the maker of history not as a monad of utterly unconditioned free will, which belongs in the realm of philosophical phantasy, but as a *product* of history and so a real, socially conditioned psychophysical individual who makes certain *choices.* This may not seem much compared with the personalist utopia, but it actually goes much further, since what is involved is not an imaginary but a real freedom. From such a point of view, we do not need to resort to such desperate constructs as man versus history; it is enough to examine his actual situation as a maker of history. But this is a subtlety that can only be understood by comprehending the entire abyss between the philosophical positions of dialectical materialism and personalism.

Thus the problem of freedom presents itself to us not as a metaphysical conception, but in its real form as a choice of *alternative courses of action.* A point of special interest in this context, particularly from the point of view of morality, is the question of *choice in situations of conflict.*

Every conscious choice, and this is the essential meaning of individual freedom, is made within the framework of a certain system of values that establishes a scale of what is and is not worthy, good, noble, right, socially useful, etc. Such a system of values is formed socially and is instilled in the individual through various forms of social education. This is one of the ways in which the individual becomes socially conditioned. But within such a socially evolved and socially imparted system of values there is still considerable freedom of movement. This is so not only because the scale has many degrees and the individual chooses his station according to the balance of various factors, but also because in normal life different values tend to combine or even clash. Finally, as already pointed out, human personality is itself a value—and so an individualizing factor in every balance of values. When the question of individual freedom is seen in these terms, analysis of the conditions of its fulfilment is seen to be extremely complicated.

In such an investigation, two situations must be carefully distinguished. The first involves a choice between *different systems of values*. Typically this occurs when an individual has to decide in his social activity between a conservative or a revolutionary program, with all the consequences of either option. All individuals are socially conditioned, but their choices in this respect varies. In making it, they are realizing their freedom (even though the choice is to a certain extent determined, both socially and individually), but at the same time they are in a sense restricting it by committing themselves to a certain pattern of future choices. Here our analysis could be very involved indeed, since it would touch on both social and personal determinants. The position, however, is fairly simple: the selection of a given system of values clinches the direction of the subsequent choices through which the individual, if his attitude is consistent, fulfills his freedom.

The real complications begin with the second type of situation in which the individual, making a choice within a certain scheme of values, comes into conflict with this system, regardless of his option. This happens when a choice of any kind challenges some accepted value. Such dilemmas often occur in life and are the most frequent source of personal tragedies. Traditional moral thought, based as it was on the blissful conviction that every contingency in life could be made morally unequivocal, simply by drawing up a code of commands and prohibitions, completely overlooked the problem of conflict situations. The credit for bringing this issue into sharp focus belongs to existentialism, particularly its French version; it is characteristic that its exponents have failed to appreciate the importance of their discovery or of their contributions in this area.

It was, in fact, the significance of conflict situations that led the existentialists, in their analysis of the problem of individual freedom, to talk of the individual being "lonely," and "doomed to freedom," etc. These are questions that require serious study by the Marxist philosophy of man, if only because of the long years in which they were entirely neglected. At any rate they cannot be washed away with sneers about decadent philosophy or with platitudes about man not being lonely under socialism as he is under capitalism. Such smugness springs either from a failure to understand the problem or from a crude and one-sided interpretation of subtle expressions. In a certain sense of these phrases, man is as "lonely," "doomed to freedom," and "terrified" when making his choices under socialism as under capitalism. Bizarre and shocking though it may seem, this language conceals a real problem of human life that is *not peculiar to any political system;* it requires serious thought rather than disparaging clichés. These may be emotionally satisfying, but they do not advance analysis one bit, while those going through the agony of real dilemmas are looking not for clichés but for answers to the questions troubling them. No philosophy, on pain of courting defeat in the ideological struggle, can afford to ignore these issues, however novel they may be, or however much they go against the grain of its established tradition.

What is the essence of a conflict situation? Basically, it means that, having *freedom* of choice, a man *must* choose something, but cannot decide what. This is not only a matter of purely subjective factors: given a thorough knowledge of a system of values and the commands and prohibitions it involves, *every* choice inevitably entails the breaking of some rule and *every* attempt at doing good is inevitably coupled with doing evil. How shall one choose? Which good is better, which evil worse? There are no prescriptions. To work out an answer, a careful calculation must be made, taking into account the subjective factor, without which the sum is impossible. These are the situations when one says; "I'd do this or that if I were you, but you must decide for yourself." There is nothing more that can or should be said. In *such* predicaments, man is alone because he has to decide *by himself,* and because in most cases, like it or not, he is *obliged* to take some decision, he is *condemned to freedom.*

As far as this goes, the existentialists are right; their observations spring from the fact that man is an unrepeatable individuality and constitutes a specific microcosm. On the other hand, there is no justification for their subjectivist and voluntarist generalizations of this perception, from which it does not follow that man is a monad of consciousness or that the world is an arbitrary product of his will. Nor does it mean that man is alone and thrown back on his own resources in society or that he weaves his own rules of behavior out of himself, like a spider spins his web. But these fallacies do not confound the truth of the proposition about the nature of freedom in conflict situations. A theory of man that avows the objective character of the laws of history not only can but must recognize this postulate; if it does not, it cannot understand and account for an extensive and important sphere of human life—a deficiency that is an inexcusable error in any philosophy of man.

In the operational approach, the freedom of the individual is thus reduced to the possibility of choosing between various courses of action. Man is free in so far as he can proceed in one way or another, embark on or abandon a certain action. Deprive him of this *possibility* of making a choice and his freedom is taken away or curtailed.

This general statement is of particular importance in the field of creativity, which is simply inconceivable without freedom, that is without the possibility of unconstricted choice of action. This is undoubtedly the specific feature of this area of human activity.

Theoretically, this is a truism: no one in his senses would claim that science and art can thrive except in an atmosphere of free discussion and clash of opinions. But in practice, including that of socialist construction included, this becomes a major problem. For many reasons, above all because of its links with the political struggle within society, creativity has never and nowhere been completely free, wholly relieved of external pressures and resultant restrictions. A society building socialism is no exception in this respect. But the dictatorship of the proletariat is only a stage on the road to communist society, and under communism, the pressure of man's alienated products on his creative endeavors should dissolve along with the withering away of classes and the state. In view of this, it is essential to be perfectly clear in one's mind about the existing restraints on freedom of creativity, the nature of these restraints, and the necessity of hastening their disappearance as quickly as possible.

Here it might be useful to recall a familiar fact that is well worth repeating: Marx, who thoroughly understood the social and political implications of science and art, was passionately and radically opposed to any political interference with creativity and any restriction of the artist's freedom on political grounds. His criticism, it is true, was directed against the political interference of the bourgeoisie, but his remarks have a more general bearing. Thus, when reading his passionate tirades against censorship, it would be wrong and perverse to console ourselves that he was referring to the Prussian authorities with their clearly feudal complexion. Anyone who is familiar with Marxism knows that Marx retained his convictions on this point to the end of his life, that they are of a more general character; and indeed they are closely connected with his reply when asked by his daughters what was his most sacred principle: *de omnibus dubitandum est*. Without appreciating this dose of Cartesian scepticism that gives Marxism its flavor, I doubt whether anyone can really understand it.

Let us now listen to Marx on the search for truth and attempts at interference with inquiry:

> The pursuit of truth, not to be impeded by censorship, is qualified as being *serious* and *restrained*. Both modifications point to something outside the content of the pursuit rather than to the matter to be investigated. They distract from the pursuit of truth and bring into play an unknown third factor . . . Isn't it the first duty of the person in search of truth that he proceed to it directly, without glancing left or right? Don't I forget the substance if I must never forget to state it in a prescribed form? . . .
>
> You admire the charming variety, the inexhaustible wealth of nature. You do not demand that the rose smell like the violet. But the richest of all, the mind, is to exist only in *one* way? . . . *Grey on grey* is to be the only permissible color of freedom. Every dewdrop in the sun glitters in an infinite play of colors, but the light of the mind is to produce only one, only the *official* color! . . . The essence of mind is *always truth itself,* and what do you make its essence? [5]

Many years later, after Marx's death, the German social democratic leaders refused to approve a re-issue of Marx's criticism of Lassalle. This led to a quarrel with Engels, who was moved by this dispute to write a letter to Bebel on May 2, 1891.

> You, the party [he said], *need* a socialist science, and this cannot exist without freedom of movement. It is therefore necessary to put up with certain annoyances, and it is best to swallow them with a good grace and without petulance. Even a slight misunderstanding—let alone a dispute—between the German party and German socialist science would be an unparalleled misfortune and disgrace. It is obvious that the Executive, or you personally, have, and must have a considerable *moral* influence with "Neue Zeit" and all other publications. But this can

and should satisfy you. "Vorwärts" has always prided itself on its inviolable freedom of discussion, but it is hard to see why. You have no idea how strange this tendency to use coercion seems to someone living here, in a country where people are used to even the most senior party leaders being called to account by their own party. . . . And besides you must not forget that in a great party discipline cannot be as severe as in some small sect. . . .[6]

Thus, these views are not simply a matter of the young Marx and the pre-communist period in the work of the founders of Marxism. There is no consolation to be gained here; the matter is much more serious and involved.

Does this mean that Marxism postulates absolute freedom in the intellectual sphere? Are the restrictions in this field, which can be found in socialist society, merely a result of errors and distortions? Though both questions must be answered in the negative, this does not yet dispose of the underlying problem.

In the case of intellectual creativity, of science and art, there are two interacting sets of rules and requirements: those concerning the development of science and art per se, and those relating to their operation *in society*. There are interconnected but not identical, and it is this that gives rise to a variety of perturbations and complications.

It cannot be denied that the best atmosphere for the advance of science and art is created by free argument and unfettered discussion—simply because this is a field of creativity par excellence whose special feature is that no one has, or can have, advance knowledge of the results and that the truth can only be eliminated in a clash of opposed views continuously verified in the crucible of practice. This is the core of the dialectic and should above all be respected by Marxists.

If this is so, as it undoubtedly is, then *any* interference from the *outside* in the affairs of science and art in the sense of placing *restrictions* on freedom of expression, discussion, experimentation, etc., is *detrimental* to their development. The justification of such encroachments by the need to root out erroneous theories or reactionary doctrines does not bear criticism. Apart from certain extreme, and banal, cases, it assumes that there are people and institutions who have been granted—*ex officio* as it were—a knowledge denied everyone else; namely, what is truth. This is indeed a strange belief, since it seeks to replace the *quest* for truth, which can only be realized in the course of struggle, often by trial and error, by decrees. On what authority? A religious believer might be pardoned such a sentiment, but a Marxist—never. For Marxists, it must be an axiom that *scientific* work can only be reached through the *investigations* of *scientists,* and *artistic* truth through the *explorations* of *artists.* For their part, the seekers should adopt as their supreme principle the Cartesian scepticism recommended by Marx: *de omnibus dubitandum est. No* dogmas, *no* petrified opinions; everything must be reexamined when the facts seem to challenge the certainty of the doctrine.

The situation would be exceptionally clear and straightforward if science and art evolved in a vacuum. But, as everyone knows, this is not the case; they develop within society and consequently not only is their development affected by society, but, conversely, science and art also have an obvious influence on the development of society. And this is where complications and conflicts set in—for what is good and desirable from the point of view of one frame of reference is not always admissible from the standpoint of the other, and may even be decidedly harmful.

The best conditions for the development of science and art are created by full freedom of discussion, when *all* opinions can be heard, since even false or socially reactionary doctrines may contain a grain of truth or at least embody something specific that is a stimulus to further reflection, and so contributes to the final cultural product. From this point of view, it is worth risking contamination by misguided theories (whose noxious elements will, in any case, be eventually eliminated by the organism of science), for the beneficial influences that they may bring. Most important of all, by avoiding such bans, one forestalls the danger of censorship which might not stop at the limits of what is patently wrong and reactionary. Who for that matter can say anything about such a matter in advance, since it is preeminently one where the proof of the pudding is in the eating?

At this point, however, the politician enters with his veto. And right he is—for from the social point of view these problems are neither abstract nor neutral. A theory which is false or socially reactionary and which forms men's beliefs leaves its mark on the historical shape of society. This is something that no one responsible for its destinies can tolerate, whether he is defending traditional social relations against scientific theories and new revolutionary outlooks expressed with the help of art, or vice versa. In view of the social implications of science and art, practice of *absolute* freedom *cannot* be, but also *should not* be. Socially, its fulfillment would be harmful.

Thus there is an obvious clash between the purely cultural and the social aspect of scientific and artistic development. How should we behave in such a situation? Specifically, what should be the reaction of a Marxist politician?

He must above all remember that from the point of view of *cultural* progress any interference on his part in the freedom of scientific and artistic activity is always harmful, although it may be *socially warranted,* or even necessary. He must, therefore, be able to *justify* each and every act of trespass and not proceed in the blissful conviction that he is exercising a healthful influence on the development of science and art. For this is certainly not the case—and the least we should expect is observance of the minimal principle: *interfere no more than strictly necessary.* This may seem too modest a principle to the maximalists, but its acceptance by the politicians would mean a big step forward indeed!

The dictatorship of the proletariat placed restrictions on the freedom of science and art, since this was made necessary by the social struggle. There is no reason not to be frank about this; it is nothing to be ashamed of. As far as criticism from bourgeois quarters is concerned, it can be treated with contempt: to point to the mote in another's eye without considering the beam in one's own requires either a good deal of nerve or a truly Jesuitical hypocrisy. But let it go at that: tempting though it is to score against our critics, it is hardly worth the trouble in this place. For the main point is not that we are being read lectures from the other side of the fence, but that we are faced with an internal brake on our own development, something distressing enough as it is. We had to circumscribe creative freedom because a social struggle was being fought and we were too weak to give our antagonists free run of the field. The enemy meant not only those who came with guns, but also those who mobilized people's minds against us. Bourgeois economic, philosophical, and sociological theories were sometimes more potent than open political agitation. And what about plays, films, novels, even poetry? *À la guerre comme à la guerre.* Provided that such restrictions are not regarded as a virtue but as a necessity —a sad *but passing* necessity—the position is perfectly clear, and self-righteous liberals can only be advised to look closely at the history of their own political institutions. Will these restrictions be removed one day? Certainly, together with the progressing stabilization of our political system and the reduction of the practical influence of hostile ideologies.

In any case, what matters are not the restrictions themselves, but their overzealous application, their alienation. There are at least two possibilities here: the extension of constraints upon freedom to nonideological fields, and their transfer from hostile persuasions to Marxism too.

Why action is taken in the case of attempts to spread hostile economic sociological or other theories is evident: these theories are simply a part of ideology and as such shape the consciousness of the masses. They are connected with politics and political struggle. Now as regards the social sciences, and even philosophy, the politician has certain qualifications and in some cases (for instance, economics or sociology) the practitioner may have a clear advantage over the theorist. But what can the politician have to say in the field of, say, physics, chemistry, or biology? Naturally, nothing at all; his interference here is totally unfounded, even from the social point of view, and its effects are usually lamentable: restrictions on the freedom of research bring the development of science to a halt, and thus of practice is impeded, too, a consequence for which a high price must be paid.

It is also evident why action is taken in the field of art, when the theater, cinema, or literature are used as a medium of hostile political propaganda. But why encroach on such non-semantic arts as music, abstract painting, architecture, which purvey no messages and of which the politician *qua* politician knows nothing at all?

Finally, it is obvious why the Marxist politician interferes with and restricts the freedom of artists and intellectuals when they represent opposed ideologies and use the language of science and art to preach hostile political views.

But why should he interfere with and restrict the freedom of those artists and intellectuals who proceed from a Marxist position although he knows and even admits that without freedom of discussion Marxism can only stagnate? Why should he oppose the emergence of schools in Marxism, why should he act as if it were possible for all Marxists to have identical views, even though this is denied both by history and by the modern development of Marxism in various countries? Does he not know that there are national modes of thinking, which is tantamount to predicating different schools of thought based on national traditions and character?

These and similar questions can best be answered by social and individual psychology. But something can be added by sociology, which concerns itself with the alienation of power. Is it not true that interference in cultural matters (based as it was on the not groundless view that the creators of cultural values are not neutrals in the ideological struggle and are sometimes lacking in political intelligence and good sense to boot) began to show a tendency towards diffusion? Certainly, there have been many more factors: a wrong assessment of the relationship between culture and politics; the unwarranted use of methods of political struggle in the field of culture; an equally wrong extension of ideologically valid criteria to science and art in general, and so on. But the most important role has been played by a certain stereotyped model of political power and democracy, stemming from a distorted interpretation of the dictatorship of the proletariat—according to which the party *leadership* is identified with administrative management from above in matters for which this is not only harmful but politically unnecessary.

This is not the place for a detailed analysis of this fascinating and complex problem—I only wish to draw attention to it. It is the conclusion that is important: from the point of view of Marxism there are no grounds whatever for limiting the freedom of the creators of culture and art, with the exception of periods of transition when politics make it necessary to control those fields of creative activity that exert an influence on the political struggle itself. On the contrary, the communist ideal is a man who fully develops his personality, and so is free of all those restrictions of freedom that are imposed by alienation in a class society. If, under socialism, this freedom has been subjected to constraints, these should be eliminated as quickly as possible.

From this two practical conclusions follow.

The first, for those who exercise power in a socialist state, and deal with the politics of culture, is that freedom should never be restricted to a greater extent than is strictly necessary, and that leadership in matters of culture should never be confused with the right to a high-handed arbitration in intellectual and artistic controversies.

The second, for the artists and intellectuals, is that they should be aware of the bonds between culture and politics and approach problems of science and art with a sense of full responsibility for their political implications. At the same time they must hold to the conviction that in all controversies objective truth should be the supreme goal. This principle must be defended with a clear understanding that cultural and artistic creativity is a vocation involving moral responsibility for how honestly and uncompromisingly it is pursued.

Brecht's *Galileo* makes the point in his final, harrowing speech. I doubt whether it could be more beautifully put—or that anything need be added:

> Even a wool-merchant, apart from buying cheaply and
> selling dear, must also be concerned that trade in wool

can be carried on unhindered. In this respect the pursuit of science seems to me to require particular courage. It is concerned with knowledge, achieved through doubt. Making knowledge about everything available for everybody, science strives to make sceptics of them all. . . . I, as a scientist, had a unique opportunity. In my days astronomy reached the market-places. In these quite exceptional circumstances, the steadfastness of one man could have shaken the world. . . . I have betrayed my profession. A man who does what I have done cannot be tolerated in the ranks of science.[7]

What is more important, the individual or society?

Posed in these terms the problem defies reasonable discussion. How many times in the history of thought has an ill-framed question proved a major obstacle to enquiry. It is this kind of woolly-mindedness that nurtures phrases like "man against history."

But the fact remains that various theories dealing with man and society have concerned themselves with questions worded in this way, and of course, arrived at varying answers, some of which grant priority to the individual, others to society.

In *The Stormy Life of Lasik Roitschwantz*—a little known book by Ilya Ehrenburg that I consider his best—there is a passage about the relationship between the individual and history whose trenchancy is worth many philosophical treatises. Roitschwantz is on a train going to Tula and a fellow passenger tells him about a Doctor Rostovtsev from Byelgorod, who was taken by the Whites for a Cheka agent of the same name and executed. "The times are like that, aren't they," the man comments. "No reason to get upset; when you cut down a tree, chips are bound to fly." [8]

But this was too much for Roitschwantz. The floodgates of men's resentments against history burst open:

When hundred per cent history goes promenading the street, the only thing to do is to die at once, with eyes blazing with triumph. That's your Chinese twice two's four, clear to any man. But you and me are not history. We are only luckless fellow passengers in one of many splintery coaches, and without hesitation we at once can ask why the synonymous doctor had to pay for a great epoch. Perhaps that doctor even had his own dear little ones, perhaps he would simply have liked to live another twenty-five years. . . . You think that when a man is killed and a filing seal stamped on him, as if he were not a living corpse, but twice two of a remarkable future, blood ceases to be blood? [9]

The problem has been posed with the crispness of *Candide:* is it right to sacrifice the individual to the higher aims of history?

Roitschwantz's answer is no—and he gives it in a charming little story about the Zaddik of Berdichev, who almost convinces God that it is necessary to send a Messiah down to Earth to save humanity, but cuts short his pleading because a prolongation of his absence could have killed the wretched Hersch. He told God:

Perhaps I am being very foolish. I ought to finish proving to you that it is impossible to wait any longer. Then you would save the whole mass of humanity. But I cannot talk to you any longer just now; I have no time; if I stay here in Heaven a minute longer, old Hersch, who does all Berdichev's shameful washing, will be sure to die. And where is it written that I have the right to purchase the happiness of the whole of complex mankind with old Hersch's life? [10]

Here is a momentous question of philosophy and practice, which must have taxed all those who have ever been confronted with the difficult choice between the individual and the good of the community. The suggested answer may seem attractive in its evident humanism, but it is in fact profoundly anti-humanist.

Where is it written that one has the right to purchase the happiness of all mankind with the life of one Hersch? Nowhere. But who has claimed that one has the right to purchase the life and happiness of the individual with the life and happiness of millions of people? This, too, has never been written.

Take the general who, to save his army, must assign a battalion to the suicidal task of stopping the enemy's advance. Has he the right to act like this, to sacrifice the lives of a hundred men in order to save thousands—or millions—since one lost battle may cost incomparably more than the casualties actually suffered in it? No general will hesitate in such a situation, if he has no other way to save his army. And how should this be assessed from the moral point of view? Surely it is inhuman, deeply antihumanist, to sacrifice thousands of lives to save one individual. These casualties are not an abstraction; they are thousands of *human beings,* living, concrete human individuals.

But the dilemma is not confined to war; similar situations are frequent in normal life, particularly in politics, when a conflict arises between the interests of the individual and society, the masses of man. What can be said in this case of the morality of those who believe in the absolute priority of the individual and insist that this is humanism? The Zaddik of Berdichev argued well, but nevertheless badly.

But let us take the reverse case and have a closer look at those who think that the individual is a cipher compared with society. Are they right? Certainly not—and history has taught us many a painful lesson about the results of such views and ideas. Lazik Roitschwantz was undoubtedly right when asking ". . . when a man is killed and a filing seal stamped on him, as if he were not a living corpse, but twice two of a remarkable future, blood ceases to be blood?"

Blood does not cease to be blood, human misery remains misery, even if the blood is shed for the sake of a glorious future. One must never shrug off this suffering with indifference or with hollow phrases. The price of such callousness can be high, even degradation—a danger which should always be borne in mind.[11]

And so both alternatives are false. But in any case the choice itself makes no sense.

In a polemical article on the political emancipation of the Jews, Marx wrote:

> All emancipation is *restoration* of the human world and the relationships of *men themselves*. . . .
>
> Only when the actual, individual man has taken back into himself the abstract citizen and in his everyday life, his individual work, and his individual relationships has become a *species being,* only when he has recognized and organized his own powers as *social* powers so that social force is no longer separated from him as political power, only then is human emancipation complete.[11]

The question of "individual or society" can only arise when society and the individual have become alienated from each other, when the interests of the individual differ from those of society. In such a society, with its atomized interests, the dilemma appears "natural" and can indeed be made of a basic principle by those philosophies that approve of this state of society. But these are appearances, nothing but appearances. It is enough to transform social relations, to overcome the dramatic cleavage of the individual into *bourgeois* and *citoyen,* to bring about an identification of private with public interest—and the dilemma loses all meaning. Not, as some fear, because the individual will then cease to exist as an individual, as if he were constituted by the opposition between his own interest and that of society, that is, could only exist in accordance with the stereotype of bourgeois society. Rather because society will no longer be hostile to the individual.

This brings us back to the two rival mottos: "the individual against history" and "the individual as the creator of history." These reflect not only abstract theoretical stances but also, and perhaps primarily, attitudes to life. They generalize definite, mutually opposed visions of the relationship between the individual and society. Their choice is not only determined by one's attitude to the class system and its alienations, but also by the wider complex of one's concept of humanism. For this is the highest generalization of everything that is connected with man and society, and the choice of one of the many competing humanist conceptions is the culmination of all choices in the field of human affairs. This or that concept of humanism is thus both the result, and the basis, of human behavior and of reflection on human affairs. Herein lies the importance of the victory of a certain conception of humanism and the meaning of the struggle for this victory.

Chapter 4
Marxist Humanism

Ours could easily be called an age of clashing humanisms: not only are there many currents of thought that claim this name but they compete with one another or even fight each other. For we are living at a time when the growing importance of the problem of individual life often causes political struggle to take the form of mutual accusations of a lack of humanism, or even of anti-humanism. Such charges are not a proof that the accuser is himself a humanist, nor an insurance against countercharge. This popularity of humanism and the growing number of conflicting varieties show only one fact: man, whose very existence is now threatened as never before, wants at least the consolation of hearing about human happiness.

Nor is there a shortage of phrases concerning man and his happiness, particularly in propaganda. This is probably why these words have now lost so much of their meaning, and it is surely because of this that men sceptically test words with actions. The conflict of humanisms is primarily resolved in practice. But this does not mean that theory has been completely devaluated. For one thing, practice is seldom self-evident, nor does it provide direct solutions to our problems; and when we refer to the future we must resort to interpretation, and thereby to theory. Another reason is that, despite the growing incredulity of the public, ideologies still play a great role in shaping the minds and emotions of men—and every humanism is an ideology.

The ideological struggle has, therefore, been fought out with humanisms. Not surprisingly, all the sides are sharpening, or at least rattling, their weapons. The wonder is that Marxism held back for so long from this struggle, particularly since it is so well equipped for it.

What do we mean by humanism? Without an answer to this

question the dispute—none too precise as it is—-threatens to become completely confused.

The learned scholar could easily demonstrate that the word "humanism" has more than one meaning. This is certainly the case, and I do not intend to enter upon a semantic analysis of the word. Instead, I will try to distinguish its meaning more accurately as it is used in such phrases as "Marxist humanism," "Catholic humanism," etc.

Thus, by humanism we mean a system of reflections about man that regard him as the supreme good, and aim to guarantee in practice the best conditions for human happiness. Within this broad humanist framework, there is naturally room for various currents of thought, and, depending on their interpretation of the individual, society, and human happiness, and on their assessment of the effectiveness of the various paths to happiness, they may not only differ considerably but even be directly contradictory. Hence the controversy about which of the rival varieties of humanism is "true" or right. Naturally, this depends on what definitions are accepted, and these in turn depend upon an accepted philosophical system and its related system of values. It is, therefore, a debate that cannot be decided on its own merits, in isolation from a wider theoretical context and from practice. On the other hand, what can be done is to argue about effectivenes from the point of view of the ultimate goal, which is to create the best conditions for human happiness, and thus to win people's minds to a system of values related to one particular version of humanism.

Marxism is humanism, a *radical* humanism, which, through its theoretical consistency and its organic unity with practice and action, is greatly superior to all its rivals. Therein lies its attraction to all the oppressed who seek not only verbal consolation, but actual liberation from everything that bars the road to happiness.

"To be radical," Marx wrote, "is to grasp things by the root. But for man the root is man himself. . . . The criticism of religion ends with the doctrine that *man is the supreme being for man*. It ends therefore with the *categorical imperative to overthrow all those conditions* in which man is an abased, enslaved, abandoned, contemptible being. . . ." [1]

This is precisely—as we have repeatedly pointed out—the point of departure of Marxism: man as the supreme good, and the struggle for the changing of the social relations that debase him. This starting point, which bestows on the whole Marxist system of thought its special character, also gives it its humanism. Marxism is humanism—but, naturally, humanism of a specific kind. The most important thing is to pin down this difference which earmarks Marxist humanism and distinguishes it from the many other varieties of humanism.

Above all, then it is a *real* humanism, as Marx himself once described it, although it should more properly be called *materialist,* in contradistinction to the idealist, or even spiritualist, types. As it happens, Marx himself emphasized the contrast. *"Real humanism,"* he wrote, "has no more dangerous enemy in Germany than *spiritualism* or *speculative idealism* which replaces the *actual, individual man* with "self-consciousness" or "spirit.". . .[2]

Here clearly the character of humanism is associated with the conception of the human individual, which Marx takes as his point of departure: if the starting point is provided by the real, concrete individual (concrete from the point of view of his social ties as well) then this humanism is *real;* but when we start from the idealist speculation about "self-consciousness," "spirit," and the like, the humanism constructed on such foundations is *spiritualist*.

With which of them Marx sides is obvious—it is only real humanism that can be coherently related to his views about the world and society.

Closely connected with the reality of Marx's humanism is another of its most characteristic features: it is consistently *autonomous*.

This question has been discussed in detail in an earlier chapter, and need only be briefly recapitulated. Marxist humanism starts from the real individual and real society, and its doctrine is based on the assumption that man, in the course of *transforming* objective reality, *creates* his world and indirectly influences his own development. Hence this humanism is consistently *autonomous* in the sense of interpreting the human world as a result of the play of its own forces, without resorting to any ultra-humanism and thus heteronomous forces. This divorces Marxist humanism not only from all speculation of a religious nature, but also from objective idealism, which, for instance, takes a *heteronomous* view of the world of objective values. Man, real man, is not only the point of departure, but also the autonomous forger of his destiny, the maker of his world and of himself. Only such a humanism that denies interference in human affairs by forces *over* man can be described as consistent. This is the only possible humanism *sensu proprio*.

To this fundamental feature, this world view of Marxist humanism a further characteristic is wedded: it is a *militant* humanism.

Objections are often raised, particularly by Catholic philosophers, to the appropriation of the adjective "militant" for Marxist humanism alone. *Cannot,* for example, a humanism that is based on Catholic thought be described as militant? Certainly, and one could even quote examples. But what matters in this case is whether the attitude of a *militant* humanist is a logical consequence of his theoretical premises or is independent of them, an accidental appendage.

Viewed from this angle, a humanism based on real individuals and their social relations, and recognizing man as the supreme good, *must* challenge everything that debases man. The attitude of *militant* humanism is in this case resolutely logical: to abstain from the struggle would mean a lack of conviction, an inconsistency. On the other hand, if humanism proceeds from "spirit," "person," "self-consciousness," and the like, it *may* but *need not* oppose evil in *practical* life, since it is not practical life but philosophical speculation that is its province.

In this respect, Marxism is a full-blooded humanism and is deeply rooted in practice: it not only preaches certain principles but draws practical conclusions from them. This is precisely why Marx as a young man had already made *revolutionary struggle* a conclusion of his humanism.

> Just as philosophy finds its *material* weapons in the proletariat so the proletariat finds its intellectual weapons in philosophy. And once the lightning of thought has

penetrated deeply into this virgin soil of the people, the Germans will emancipate themselves and become *men* . . .

The emancipation of Germany is only possible in *practice* if one adopts the point of view of that theory according to which man is the highest being for man. . . . The *emancipation of Germany* will be an *emancipation of man*. Philosophy is the head of this emancipation, the proletariat is its heart. Philosophy can only be realized by the abolition of the proletariat, and the proletariat can only be abolished by the realization of philosophy.[3]

There is no doubt that the militant attitude of Marx's humanism was an integral part of his temperament. A man who answered his daughter's "questionnaire" about "happiness" by saying that happiness meant "struggle" and unhappiness "surrender" could hardly be satisfied with merely contemplating the causes of human suffering. But this aspect of Marx's humanism is also a logical consequence of his theoretical presuppositions.

In elaborating his view of the world, Marx dissociated himself no less firmly from a purely contemplative position than from idealism. This, in fact, is closely connected with what we have already pointed out in earlier chapters: *that the key to Marx's view of the world should be sought in his theory of man.* Marx begins with the living, real individual, not from contemplation but from action, from transformation of the world. Like Goethe's Faust he says that "in the beginning was the deed," and the "deed" to him is human practice. Consequently, the passive speculation of traditional philosophy, materialism included, was alien to him. He acknowledged the superiority of idealism in this respect: it developed the active side of philosophy although it did not, and could not, arrive at a theory of practice. This trend in Marx's thought culminated in his critique of Feuerbach's philosophy, and the famous eleventh "Thesis on Feuerbach" contains his credo: "The philosophers have only *interpreted* the world in various ways; the point however is to *change* it." With *such* an approach to philosophy, Marx could not, naturally, be satisfied with a humanist contemplation of human fate. A man who saw philosophy as the spiritual weapon of the proletariat and the proletariat as the material weapon of philosophy *must* choose a *militant* humanism.

It must not be thought, however, that this trait of Marx's humanism was arrived at by deduction from his general philosophical premises. The reverse was rather the case, although it seems likely that this is a classic example of mutual interaction.

As already pointed out, *militancy* is the logical outcome, primarily of the starting point of Marx's humanism, a consequence of the fact that this was a *real* humanism, which interpreted the human world as an *autonomous* world, created by social man and only by him.

If the world of man and man himself are products of *self-creation,* then man cannot and should not expect to be liberated from his sufferings by some superhuman force—good or evil—but must set about freeing himself. In other words, belief in self-creation means that one must also accept the idea of self-emancipation. And it is precisely the basic idea of the self-emancipation of the proletariat that must liberate the whole of mankind in order to liberate itself as a class, that is at the foundation of Marx's socialism; consequently, his humanism must accept the principle of struggle for its fulfillment and thus become a *militant* humanism.

It is only on the basis of self-emancipation and militant humanism that one can understand the Marxian theory of class struggle and of the historic mission of the proletariat in the formation of a classless society—so masterfully condensed in the *Communist Manifesto*. It is only through these ideas that we can grasp the dialectic of that which is class conditioned and that which transcends classes, the dialectic of general social interests, in Marxian socialism, as well as the dialectic of love and hatred that comes to be in the course of its realization.

Man is the point of departure of Marx's socialism; and man is also its point of arrival, its goal.

We know already that the man of whom Marx speaks is no abstraction—indeed, he criticized such an approach—but a concrete, real individual, involved in social relations and the resulting conflicts and struggles. Thus, in proceeding from real individuals,

Marx at the outset predicated his argument on actually existing social classes and social strata. In this way he made his discovery of the proletariat and its universal social function.

But Marx's point of arrival, the object of his endeavors, is man in general, the happiness of *every* human individual. This is where the profound meaning of the dialectic of his humanism lies: not in the purely sentimental theory "love thy neighbor" or with mumbo jumbo about "integral" humanism, it strives precisely toward the fulfillment of *integral* humanism, since it embraces the whole of mankind and is concerned with the full development of *every* personality. More than that: thanks to its realism and its guarantee of fulfillment through a struggle, *only* this humanism can *truly* be called *integral* by virtue of its aims—although it is resolutely opposed to the catchword of integral humanism in the sense of a repudiation of a genuine struggle for realization of humanist aims.

With this dialectic of struggle, the interaction between what is class-conditioned and what is all-human, is connected the dialectic of love and hate in the pursuit of universal human ideals.

Since socialism—in *every* form—takes man and a revolt against the dehumanization of life as its point of departure, it thus starts with *love of man* and a sense of distress at man's dehumanization, debasement, unhappiness. Socialism *is* in a sense *identical* with love of man, while a socialism that hated man would be a contradiction in terms. Yet Marxist socialism shuns all wishy-washy and abstract injunctions of the "love thy neighbor" brand; it is a doctrine of struggle and so enjoins hatred of the enemy in the *name* of love of neighbor. A contradiction? Only on the surface. In fact, this is a far more consistent, and so authentic, conviction than the lukewarm slogans of "integral" humanism, which, while sometimes subjectively honest, are in most cases hypocritical and mendacious.

Socialism is a doctrine of neighborly love both in its point of departure and in its goals. But since it approaches the problem of love not abstractly but in a concrete way—that is, on the hard ground of struggle for its related basis and goals—Marxist humanism must struggle against what contradicts this love, and so against all that makes man debased, oppressed, exploited—in a word, unhappy. But "struggle" is not simply a phrase, it means *action* to frustrate and render harmless all those who, in the name of their private interests, bar men's way to happiness—and so deny love of mankind. For in a class society, there have been and still are *enemies* of this love—whether their behavior is conscious or unconscious. Anyone who understands that also understands that the enemies of brotherly love—enemies of the cause of humanity— must be fought actively—and this is inseparably connected with feelings of hate. Love of man is far from excluding—in fact, presupposes—hatred of those who act objectively in the name of hatred (and how much more abominable if subjective awareness goes along with it). The Nazis are the classic example of such men. Despite appearances, anyone who in such a situation denies the necessity of struggle—and so of hatred of the enemy—acts not as a humanist but as a typical *antihumanist*. For by preaching a love of man that forbids harming another human being under any circumstances, one *does harm* to thousands and millions of innocent people who are victims of class, national, racial, or other kinds of oppression and violence. That *no* sensible person would behave like this in practice is a different matter; but the very profession of such principles—and they are often put forward in self-interest to bring intellectual chaos and confusion among one's enemies—is tantamount to asserting antihumanist ideas. On this point there should be theoretical clarity.

And so we have a love of neighbor, a love of man, which does not exclude hatred, since it does not exclude struggle, but on the contrary postulates it. But having adopted such a position *and following it through in practice,* we must exercise particular caution, which is also indispensable in the development of the relevant theory. In both cases, the *most important* thing is to remember that the crux is man, while hatred is always subordinated to another cause—*the love of man.* Unfortunately, in matters like this, it is always difficult to keep within the proper limits. This is one more reason to remember and recall—if only for didactic purposes—that what is really decisive is the problem of man. Here again, as on many other occasions, the idea has been strikingly and thoughtfully expressed by a poet; it was Bertolt Brecht who wrote these beautiful and profoundly humanistic lines:

Auch der Hass gegen die Niedrigkeit
verzerrt die Züge.
Auch der Zorn über das Unrecht
macht die Stimme heiser. Ach, wir, die wir den
Boden bereiten wollten für Freundlichkeit,
konnten selber nicht freundlich sein.
Ihr aber, wenn es soweit sein wird,
dass der Mensch dem Menschen ein Helfer ist,
gedenkt unser
mit Nachsicht.

A recent English translation for the above lines follows:

Even the hatred of squalor
Makes the brow grow stern.
Even anger against injustice
Makes the voice grow harsh. Alas, we
Who wished to lay the foundations of kindness
Could not ourselves be kind.
But you, when at last it comes to pass
That man can help his fellow man,
Do not judge us
Too harshly.[4]

Finally, there is one other characteristic that distinguishes Marxist humanism, particularly in our day: it is an *optimistic* humanism.

Reading the classic Marxist texts on man under communism, one sometimes gets the feeling that they are utopian. No doubt they do contain a residue of Utopia. But it may also be that, limited as we are by the narrow perspective of our own time, we lose sight of the more distant vistas adumbrated by the founders of the system. If it is advisable to beware of too bold flights of fantasy, it is equally necessary to avoid the mistake of keeping our feet too leadenly planted on the ground. In the light of the modern technical revolution, with automation of production and liberation of atomic energy, should we not take a different view of such goals as the elimination of the disparities between manual and mental labor, between work on the land and in the city, or the possibility of a practically limitless satisfaction of human needs—all of which only several decades ago belonged to the realm of fantasy?

Modern industrial technology certainly gives rise to a number of new problems, some of which were not foreseen. But if the right social context were created for it, technology also offers possibilities of solving ancient unsolved problems; if nothing else, it can bring a shorter working day.

It is interesting to see, particularly from the viewpoint of social psychology, how *the same* social phenomenon—industrialization and technical progress—can be interpreted in different ways according to the social perspective of the observer.

On the one hand, it forms the background of a philosophy of despair that treats society as a sum of isolated, atomized monads, moving meaninglessly on the stage of life in a setting of a depersonalized mass culture totally devoid of any human values. This is a grotesque exaggeration of certain features of the modern social and cultural situation in bourgeois society. That *only these* traits are perceived is undoubtedly due to a preoccupation with the perspective of a "dehumanized world"—to use a phrase of the young Marx. But this point of view makes for a pessimistic vision of the world. If existentialism is humanism—as Sartre with justice claims —it is the humanism of a dying world and therefore tragic and *pessimistic*.

But *the same* phenomenon can be seen in another light, as a harbinger of the new that the future will bring. This is the attitude of socialist humanism, whose perspective is determined by a completely new social situation, or at least by the prospects of such a situation. The technical revolution, which is disintegrating the old world, also holds out the possibility of creating a new world. For the first time in history there is a real chance of making mankind's most ancient dream—a happy life *for all men*—come true. Can this dream be *fully* realized? The future will show: personally, I am sceptical. But there is certainly the possibility of a *better, happier* life; this is already a great deal, and more can surely be expected. When things are viewed in this light—and this is feasible only from the appropriate social perspective—the vision of the further development of the individual and society at once changes.

This does not mean that the vision of Kafka's *Castle* or Sartre's *Nausea* must be replaced by a social-realist brand of optimism in which virtue always triumphs like the honest sheriff in American cowboy Westerns. Matters here are certainly—and fortunately—more complicated. But it is undoubtedly an *optimistic* humanism, not because it irrationally believes that man is good and that good must triumph (just as Sartre's existentialism holds, or held, the opposite belief), but because of its conviction that the world is a *product* of man and man himself is a product of *self-creation;* consequently, since his possibilities of transforming the world are practically boundless—as proved, among other things, before our eyes by the present technical revolution—man has in practice boundless possibilities of transforming himself.

Such optimism is not an act of faith but a *conviction* based on facts. Thus, it is not an axiom but a working hypothesis of high probability and tremendous practical importance from the point of view of mobilizing the social energies of man. Such a hypothesis is a component of ideology, but its heuristic value is no less great than many other propositions in the social sciences. And that is enough.

Every fully developed system of humanism contains its own theory of happiness. In a sense, each humanism is a theory of happiness, for any reflection on man and his affairs must culminate in a discussion of the conditions for a happy life. Marxist humanism is no exception. It also contains a theory of happiness, or at any rate *implies* one; to make it *explicit* is indispensable for a better understanding of the character of this Marxist humanism.

The problem of happiness can be approached from either of two directions: its positive side—which we call "happiness"—or its negative side—which we describe as "unhappiness." The difference between these approaches is crucial, particularly from a practical point of view, and cannot be reduced to the simple matter of inserting a "not" in certain affirmative propositions.

The first method is the traditional one, tested in various theories of happiness that have made their appearance during the history of human thought. But experience has shown that the positive approach does not—and cannot—yield any results, or only very modest ones. What a wealth of pronouncements we have had on this subject and how different, even contradictory, have been the attitudes behind them! No wonder: a condition that basically consists of subjective feelings, responses, and sensations can hardly be defined (apart from definitions that are so general as to be practically meaningless), and still less codified by means of norms and injunctions. I may go on for years telling somebody that he should be happy in a given situation, seeing his circumstances through *my* eyes, or thinking of one of the standard definitions of happiness— that of the Stoics, for example—and yet this will change nothing: the person in question will continue to be unhappy and may even commit suicide because in *his* mind the situation has become intolerable. It is in this discrepancy between *my* and *your* perception of a situation, one that cannot either be ignored or skirted, that the crux of the matter lies. For what is involved—and philosophers have often forgotten this—is not an abstraction, but living, real men who often enough differ from each other fundamentally as well as in details, men who constitute specific structures, specific microcosms. The problem of happiness may not be *fully* reducible to the subjective factor, but it is so closely, so organically linked with it that to take no account of this when trying to construct generally valid—and thus abstract—definitions is bound to be self-defeating. We all know, and need not be surprised, that what makes one person feel happy can make another unhappy, even within the same social framework, the same historical period, and the same system of social determinants. Some rejoice in exercising power, while it would make others suffer deeply; some delight in a permanent siesta, while others are driven to despair from lack of active work; one man will exult in promiscuous love affairs, another would regard it as intolerable drudgery. And so on, and so forth. It is also psychologically true, paradoxical as it may seem, that to feel contented some people must be unhappy, or at least have something to grumble about—and they go out of their way to find a cause for dissatisfaction. In a word, people are not alike and cannot find gratification in the same things. Since the feeling of happiness is always an individual sensation, which is organically bound to the psychophysical structure of the perceiving subject, any attempt to settle the problem in a "general" way, by means of sweeping definitions, or even worse, by laying down when and in what circumstances people *should* be happy is doomed to failure; and in the case of a state embarking on *practical* activity to this effect, it may bring real human misery.

A socialist society should pay particular attention to this problem—not only because the possibilities of centralized action are greater under socialism than in other systems of government, but also because the temptation of trying to decree the conditions for human happiness is a real danger.

It is not irrelevant to point out that it is precisely this formula that has provided the basis for various anticommunist utopias: a society that, to achieve a fusion of individual and public interests, strives to enforce a *generally binding* model of human happiness must inevitably end with a horrifying tyranny that stifles the individual with a totally dehumanized life. Let me illustrate this with the example of a little-known book, Zamiatin's *We,* probably the most original work of its kind. I have chosen this novel not because I approve its tenor, but because, like Orwell's *1984,* it takes to their logical extreme some of the tendencies in socialist ideology and certain developments in socialist countries, and thus helps us better to visualize the dangers.

The message of Zamiatin's book is as follows: when the idea of a complete fusion of individual and society is carried to its extreme (note that the Marxist postulate of a fusion between the *interests of the individual* and society has been twisted into a non-Marxist notion implying the *disappearance of individuality;* without this intellectual trick, the novel would not work), this must necessarily result in a denial of the right to individuality and individual happiness. By abolishing individual identity, the state imposes the same stereotype of happiness on everybody (in the book this is carried as far as the compulsory removal from the brains of all citizens of their "imagination center," which is responsible for their individualistic tendencies). Hell begins here. Do not deprive individuals of their individuality, is the author's single message; do not enforce your own ideas of happiness, for in doing this you can only dehumanize human existence, only make man unhappy.

Zamiatin is right, although it could easily be objected that he is fighting shadows since nobody ever sought to bring about the situation he describes, or that he has deliberately distorted the Marxist ideals by talking of a fusion between individual and society in terms of the liquidation of individuality. These criticisms are to the point, but even so a hard core remains in the book and deserves meditation.

Working with a specific literary convention, Zamiatin reduces certain observed tendencies to absurdity and shows what would happen if they were given full rein. Later, the same procedure was adopted by Orwell. It is true that this results in a grotesque or tragicomic distortion of things as they are. But the fact remains that this mirror reflects a certain reality which deserves closer inspection.

Although Zamiatin's anticommunist utopia is false, there are some kernels of truth in this falsehood and these should not be ignored. When definitions of happiness begin to be elaborated and a corresponding code of behavior is made binding on all men for their own good, of course;—what has not been done in history in the name of salvation and happiness!—then people are threatened under socialism too, with the danger of being "made happy" by decree, forcibly, according to the accepted model of happiness; and this may lead to massive general unhappiness. After all, a certain restriction of human freedom is then required—and every such constraint tends to reduce rather than increase the chances of happiness. Fortunately, experience has shown that such tendencies are typically a symptom of the childhood diseases of left-wing communism and usually fade away with the stabilization of life under the new system of government. Consequently, it is enough to conclude these remarks with just one warning: since *there is not*—and fortunately *cannot be*—a single type of happiness for everybody, any attempt to construct identical stereotypes should be avoided. Socialism does not oppose human individuality—on the contrary. Let us then give this individuality free play in the pursuit of happiness and let each person be happy in his own way—even if what he needs is a hobby, or if he insists on being slightly eccentric or different. That's his own business. Recognition of this freedom— which can do no harm to socialism—is one of the pre-conditions for genuine, authentic happiness of all men.

Thus, if the positive approach to the problem of human happiness does not yield any results—and even holds a danger of doing mischief—our interest should be all the greater in the opposite inquiry: what causes unhappiness, and what are the characteristics of this condition.

No generally binding definition of human happiness can be given, since, in view of its individual nature, such a definition is simply impossible. On the other hand, it is fairly easy to name the causes of general human unhappiness: hunger, death, disease, imprisonment, all kinds of exploitation and oppression, etc. People have changing needs and they cannot be codified positively from the point of view of general happiness. But they can be codified *negatively:* no normal man can be happy unless he can satisfy a minimum of his own and his family's needs, if he suffers hunger and cold, if he is sick, if he is threatened with death in war, when his country is enslaved, when he cannot enjoy his freedom in various ways, etc.

Here is a reasonable basis for action on behalf of human happiness—not in the sense of making man happy, but of *eliminating the causes of general unhappiness.*

The militant character of Marxist humanism is closely connected with this concept of happiness: it calls for an uncompromising struggle against the causes of human misery as a mass phenomenon —and thus against its *social* roots. This is a realistic objective, the aim being to create the *chances* of a happy life. Nothing more can be achieved by any social order, since no one can *guarantee* happiness. This after all is an individual matter. Even in ideal social and economic conditions people can individually be unhappy—no economic or social system can protect them against disease, the death of their near ones, unrequited love, personal failures, etc. Nor is this the point—it would be as impossible and unpracticable an objective as trying to make people happy by force, or to eradicate all sources of individual misery. But it is fully possible and practicable to root out the causes of widespread mass misery, whose sources lie not in the individual, but outside him, in social conditions and relations. Thus Marxist humanism does not promise any utopian paradise and does not claim to provide a key to individual happiness for everybody. It does not even guarantee that new barriers to human happiness will not emerge in the future; even this cannot be guaranteed, although it his highly probable that a rationally organized society will consciously combat such situations. But Marxist humanism calls for something else: *the liquidation of the existing social causes of human unhappiness.* This is a great deal— and it gives this humanism its appeal to all those who suffer under the prevailing social relations. It is this that determines its rebellious and militant character, as it strives to fulfill Marx's words cited above: "The criticism of religion ends with the doctrine that *man is the supreme being for man;* it ends therefore with the *categorical imperative* to overthrow *all* those conditions in which man is an abused, enslaved, abandoned contemptible being. . . ."

Chapter 5
Communism and the Individual

The starting point of Marxist socialism—the real man and the conditions for his happiness—determines its goal: a social order that assures the optimum provisions for the development of the human personality, and so for its happiness. Seen thus, the goal of social development, and of the proletarian revolution through which it is realized, shows the genuine meaning of communism as a movement and as a higher stage of the socialist system. Hence the shortest, and at the same time the most essential, definition of Marxian communism: communism = *humanism in practice.*

This was Marx's idea from his youth. He wrote in the *Manuscripts:*

> Atheism as the annulment of God is the emergence of theoretical humanism, and communism as the annulment of private property is the vindication of real human life as man's property. The latter is also the emergence of practical humanism, for atheism is humanism mediated to itself by the annulment of religion, while communism is humanism mediated to itself by the annulment of private property.[1]

And on another page:

> *Communism* is the *positive* abolition of *private property,* of *human self-alienation,* and thus the real *appropriation* of *human* nature through and for man. It is, therefore, the return of man himself as a *social,* i.e., really human, being, a complete and conscious return which assimilates all the wealth of previous development. Communism as a fully-developed naturalism is humanism and as a fully-developed humanism is naturalism. It is the *definitive* resolution of the antagonism between man and

nature, and between man and man. It is the true solution of the conflict between existence and essence, between objectification and self-affirmation, between freedom and necessity, between individual and species. It is the solution of the riddle of history and knows itself to be this solution.[2]

If communism as a social objective is conceived to be humanism in practice, then this goal is organically linked with the character of the revolution that furthers the goal—the social revolution. This, according to Marx, is essentially a protest against inhuman life, an act of human self-emancipation, consciously directed towards the realization of humanism.

> Social revolution involves the standpoint of the whole because it is a protest of man against dehumanized life, even if it occurs in only *one* factory district because it proceeds from the standpoint of the *single actual individual,* because it is the reaction of the individual against his isolation from that *community* which is the *true* community of man, i.e., from human existence.[3]

Hence communism is visualized by Marx primarily as a society in which man, liberated from alienation, is revealed as a complete, universal man, developing his personality to the fullest extent. For Marx this remained, from his youth to his full maturity after writing *Capital,* the principal goal, everything else serving as a means of achieving it.

Marx quickly realized that the word "human" and "inhuman" had a historical meaning. *The German Ideology* contains an important gloss to his thesis about the protest against "dehumanization" of life, which needs to be examined before we present a positive picture of Marxian communism.

For Stirner, Marx wrote, the process of human emancipation means that men have created a human ideal and liberated themselves to the extent that they have lived up to it. But, he retorts, actually men have liberated themselves not to the extent that they are bidden by the human ideal, but only so far as the existing forces of production made possible. And so far these forces have been so limited that the corresponding production has made development possible only when some people satisfy their needs at the expense of others.

> This explains, on the one hand, the abnormal "inhuman" means with which the oppressed class satisfies its needs, and, on the other hand, the narrow limits within which commercial intercourse, and with it the whole ruling class, develops; hence this restricted character of development consists not only in the exclusion of one class from development, but also in the narrow-mindedness of the excluding class; and the "inhuman" is to be found also within the ruling class, . . . The positive expression "human" corresponds to the definite conditions *predominant* at a certain stage of production, and the way of satisfying needs determined by them, just as the negative expression "inhuman" corresponds to the attempt, within the existing mode of production, to negate these predominant conditions and the way of satisfying needs prevailing under them, an attempt that this stage of production daily calls forth afresh.[4]

Thus, the "human" and "inhuman" are not absolute notions, but historically related to the given mode of production. But within this context they are also defined from the point of view of social protest against "inhuman" life and thereby of human endeavors to create an ideal of a "human" life.

Now, within this historical framework, a "human" life is only possible if all alienation is eliminated, especially economic. As far as Marx is concerned, this is the chief task of communism as a social system.

Stirner's contention that individuals have "proceeded from themselves" is not challenged in *The German Ideology*. Marx only denies that the individual is socially detached, since human needs force him to enter into various reciprocal relationships. Since we are not dealing with a pure "Ego," but with individuals at a definite level of needs, their behavior towards each other creates social relations as they are. In consequence, the development of each individual is socially determined.

From this angle, Marx observes the advancing reification of mutual human relations and the transformation of individual into objectified behaviors:

> In the present age the domination of material conditions over individuals, the suppression of individuality by chance, has assumed its sharpest and most universal form, thereby setting existing individuals a very definite task. It has set them the task of replacing the domination of circumstances and of chance over individuals by the domination of individuals over chance and circumstances . . . demanded liberation from one quite definite mode of development. This task, dictated as it is by present-day conditions, coincides with the task of the communist organization of society.[5]

The communist organization of society is, therefore, for Marx, identical with the need to develop a society in which people consciously control the conditions, not vice versa. This is only possible "within the communist society, the only society in which the original and free development of individuals is not an empty phrase. . . ."[6] This theme frequently recurs, also, in the work of the mature Marx: Communism as a social system is an organization of society in which alienation is abolished, and thereby a full unrestricted development of personality is made possible.

I will not discuss at this point the prospects of a complete elimination of alienation under communism; this has been considered in a previous chapter. Marx, at least for some time, believed that the liquidation of private property would bring about the disappearance of the various forms of alienation, including the division of labor (and labor itself would be replaced by free creativity). It must be admitted that in the light of the further development of technology and of the social division of labor, Marx's views on this subject sound clearly utopian, particularly when communism is presented as a society in which man can change his occupation as he pleases, where even activities based on special gifts, such as painting, are the domain of everyone.[7] But this is not the point; what matters is the fulfillment under communism of the ideal of a complete universal man. This postulate runs through the whole of Marx's works, from his youth to the end of his life: communism should ensure to all a full development of their personality.

In *The German Ideology* Marx wrote:

> The transformation, through the division of labour, of personal powers (relationships) into material powers, cannot be dispelled by dismissing the general idea of it from one's mind, but only be abolished by individuals again subjecting these material powers to themselves and abolishing the division of labour. This is not possible without the community. Only in community with others has each individual the means of cultivating his gifts in all directions; only in the community, therefore, is personal freedom possible.[8]

Barely two years later, Marx and Engels wrote in the *Communist Manifesto:*

> When, in the course of development, class distinctions have disappeared, and all production has been concentrated in the hands of a vast association of the whole nation, the public power will lose its political character. Political power, properly so called, is merely the organized power of one class for oppressing another. If the proletariat during its contest with the bourgeoisie is compelled, by the force of circumstances, to organize itself as a class; if, by means of a revolution, it makes itself the ruling class, and, as such, sweeps away by force the old conditions of production, then it will, along with these conditions, have swept away the conditions for the existence of class antagonisms and of classes generally, and will thereby have abolished its own supremacy as a class.
>
> In place of the old bourgeois society, with its classes and class antagonisms, we shall have an association, in which the free development of each is the condition for the free development of all.[9]

And many years later, in 1875, Marx reaffirmed these views in his *Critique of the Gotha Programme*—stressing the uniform nature of his conception of communism:

> In a higher phase of communist society, after the enslaving subordination of the individual to the division of labour, and therewith also the antithesis between mental and physical labour, has vanished; after labour has become not only a means of life but life's prime want; after the productive forces have also increased with the all-round development of the individual, and all the springs of co-operative wealth flow more abundantly—only then can the narrow horizon of bourgeois right [justice] be crossed in its entirety, and society inscribe on its banners: from each according to his ability, to each according to his needs.[10]

Engels was of the same mind as Marx, while stressing additional emphasis on certain ideas. In *The Principles of Communism,* which prepared the ground for *The Communist Manifesto,* he says:

> Production carried on in common by the whole of society, and the new development of manufacturing that follows, will require utterly new people and will create them. Joint production cannot be the work of people like those of today, each of whom is subjected to one branch of production, fettered to it and exploited by it, each of whom has developed only one of his abilities at the expense of all the others, has knowledge of only a single branch or merely the offshoots of a particular branch in the whole production. Even today industry has less and less need of such people. . . . A society organized on communist principles will give its members the possibility of all-round utilization of their fully developed abilities. . . .
>
> Hence the conclusion that the contrast between town and country will also vanish. The same people, not two distinct classes, will be engaged in work on the land and

in industry. This, for purely material reasons, constitutes a necessary condition for communist association.[11]

Many years later, when he undertook the task of a polemic with Dühring, Engels repeated these thoughts and stressed that through its abolition of alienation communism creates the conditions for true freedom for men. Liquidation of private property abolishes the domination of the product over the producer, and with it the anarchy of the market.

And at this point, in a certain sense, man finally cuts himself off from the animal world, leaves the conditions of animal existence behind him and enters conditions which are really human. The conditions of existence forming man's environment, which up to now have dominated man, at this point pass under the domination and control of man, who now for the first time becomes the real conscious master of nature, because and in so far as he has become master of his own social organization. The laws of his own social activity, which have hitherto confronted him as external, dominating laws of nature, will then be applied by man with complete understanding, and hence will be dominated by man. Men's own social organization, which has hitherto stood in opposition to them as if arbitrarily decreed by nature and history, will then become the voluntary act of men themselves. The objective, external forces which have hitherto dominated history, will then pass under the control of men themselves. It is only from this point that men, with full consciousness, will fashion their own history; it is only from this point that the social causes set in motion by men will have, predominantly and in constantly increasing measure, the effects willed by men. It is humanity's leap from the realm of necessity into the realm of freedom.

To carry through this world-emancipating act [Engels concludes], is the historical mission of the modern proletariat. And it is the task of scientific socialism, the theoretical expression of the proletarian movement, to establish the historical conditions . . . of this act.[12]

This is the vision of communism as a practical humanism faithfully reconstructed, where possible in their own word, from the writings of Marx and Engels.

At this point we might ask: what is the actual value of this vision of communism? what is its true meaning for those who, in the actual conditions of our time, are building socialism, in a different situation, and thus in a different way, than was envisaged by Marx and Engels?

There are two obvious approaches to the problem.

One of them—in my view unacceptable to a Marxist—consists in a literal and dogmatic embracing of this vision which inevitably entails acceptance by definition that communism is a system which has completely abolished alienation and hence that every society which claims to be communist *is* thereby *free* of alienation. This, of course, is the purest dogmatism, incompatible not only with empiricism, but quite simply with healthy common sense; unfortunately, some residues of this kind of thinking can still be found in Marxist propaganda, and even in what purports to be scientific literature. As propaganda, it cuts little ice; as science, it hardly bears examination.

In the second approach—and I feel the only legitimate one—the views of Marx and Engels on communism (both in their youth and their maturity) are registered as historical facts, and this is followed by analysis of the conditions to which Marx tied the realization of his vision, by assessment of the merits of his views within his particular frame of reference, and by empirical investigation of possible changes in these conditions and the practical consequences these bring for societies in our own times.

While Marxism itself leaves no doubts on this score, it seems only precautionary wisdom to point out that attempts to "defend" Marx's infallibility by a dogmatic interpretation of his writings are illusory and contrary to his own teaching. Marx was no prophet, but a scientist. His vision of the future—and as a communist he certainly had such a vision—was of a scientific character: it arose from description of facts, investigation of the laws of development, and evaluation of actual conditions. Such a vision can never claim to be final; it is a function of the current state of knowledge about reality, and it is bound to change accordingly. If Marx's views on communism contain, as they do, some residues of utopian socialism, they are there *despite* the endeavors of Marx himself, who made such a strong point of the contrast between the *scientific* nature of his socialism and that of the *utopians*. Psychologically, there seems to be a certain regularity in this process: even when he is uncompromisingly attacking established views a man usually remains under their sway.

Even a revolutionary fighting certain conditions and opinions, is in some respects their product and bears their stamp, particularly on his mentality. It is therefore advisable to appreciate the symbolic value of Jehovah's decision to bar the Promised Land to all those born in slavery—including the man who led them in their march to freedom.

In any case, Marx himself, as early as his youth, expressly disowned any such "defence." Throughout his life he was reluctant to make "prophecies" about the future society; he refused to answer questions about its structure (except in its most general outlines), assuming no doubt that the men of the future, with practical experience to go on, would be wiser than any "visionaries"; all the more as he had a fresh memory of the prophesying of the utopian socialists, who not only "knew" how best to organize people's life under communism but were prepared, like Fourier, to indulge in predictions about the anatomy of future men. This was probably why the young Marx wrote to Ruge:

> Even greater than the external obstacles seem to be the inner ones. Even though there is no doubt about the "whence," there does prevail all the more confusion about the "whither." It is not only the fact that a general anarchy has broken out among the reformers; each one will have to admit to himself that he has no exact idea of what is to happen. But that is exactly the advantage of the new direc-

tion, namely, that we do not anticipate the world dogmatically, but rather wish to find the new world through
criticism of the old. Until now the philosophers had the
solution to all the riddles in their desks, and the stupid
outside world simply had to open its mouth so that the
roasted pigeons of absolute science might fly into it. Philosophy has become secularized, and the most striking
proof for this is the fact that the philosophical consciousness itself is drawn into the torment of struggle, not only
outwardly but inwardly as well. Even though the construction of the future and its completion for all times is not our
task, what we have to accomplish at this time is all the
more clear: *relentless criticism of all existing conditions,*
relentless in the sense that the criticism is not afraid of its
findings and just as little afraid of the conflict with the
powers that be.[13]

In this explicit statement, we have Marx's own blessing to correct
his views on communism, or at any rate to take a critical view of
them if they run counter to his own principles.

To this general point must be added the specific condition upon
which Marx made his vision of communism and of man under
communism dependent: *a great development of the means of pro-*
duction as well as the victory of communism in the whole world:

This *"estrangement"* (to use a term which will be
comprehensible to the philosophers) can, of course, only
be abolished given two *practical* premises. For it to become an "intolerable" power, i.e., a power against which
men make a revolution, it must necessarily have rendered
the great mass of humanity "propertyless," and produced, at the same time, the contradiction of an existing
world of wealth and culture, both of which conditions
presuppose a great increase in productive power, a high
degree of development. And, on the other hand, this development of productive forces (which itself implies the
actual empirical existence of men in their *world-histori-*

cal, instead of local, being) is absolutely necessary as a practical premise because without it want is merely made general, and with destitution the struggle for necessities and all the old filthy business would necessarily be reproduced; . . . . Empirically, communism is only possible as the act of the dominant peoples "all at once" and simultaneously, which presupposes the universal development of productive forces and the world-intercourse bound up with communism.[14]

This idea of the material conditions for communism, without which "all the old filthy business would necessarily be reproduced" and "each extension of commercial intercourse would abolish [any merely] local communism," was never abandoned by Marx. It may be added that on this point he had the support of all Marxists, including Lenin. For, even when Lenin's analysis of imperialism led him to see that the chain of capitalism could be broken *in one country,* he did not by any means claim that this could be the only country building socialism, but merely the one from which the world revolution would *begin.* The thesis about the possibility of establishing communism in one country was advanced by Lenin only later, when the revolutionary tide in the world was ebbing while in the Soviet Union the revolution had already triumphed.

Marx did not foresee the situation in which socialism is actually being realized today. It would, of course, be foolish to resent history for having taken this rather than another course. But it is equally foolish to remain blind to the fact that this course has been *different* and has taken place in conditions other than those originally envisaged, and to cling to old formulas that were suited to other conditions.

Thus our task today is to analyze the changes that factually have occurred in the conditions for the realization of communism, and to draw the relevant conclusions about the ways of its accomplishment as a function of the changed conditions.

Viewing the problem from this angle, we can say that there has been a tendency to brush aside too lightly the question of modifying

Marx's postulate of the necessity for a simultaneous, worldwide victory of communism. This is not to question Lenin's analysis of imperialism, which created the possibility of breaking the chain of capitalism at its weakest link; its correctness has, after all, been confirmed by history. Our complaint concerns the evaluation of the effects of such a change on the vision of communism—above all the problem of man under communism. Marx's vision of him, as a universal man with a fully developed personality, was based on the material presuppositions both of a production level that would ensure the full satisfaction of human needs (Marx was a realist and saw that, failing this, "all the old filthy business would necessarily be reproduced") and of the emergence of a political situation that, with the victory of socialism all over the world, would provide conditions for the rapid withering away of the state, and therewith of a particularly grievous form of alienation. At the same time, however, *implicit* in the Marxist conception was the precondition that those who were called upon to build the new social order would have a high level of qualification and democratic preparation through a long tradition. However, if the problem is broached at all in analyses of the level of productive forces (and such treatments proceed too gingerly, usually with the spurious qualification that the problem belongs only to the past and plays no part today—which is obviously false given the fact that industrially underdeveloped nations like China are being drawn into the orbit of socialism), the analysis rarely mentions the problem of the state and entirely passes over the matter of the *human base* of communism. How false! Especially since communism is above all concerned with man. And man changes as a function of the whole ensemble of social relations, and this includes the cultural background and the traditional forms of social life. It is relatively easy to make up for a lag, a backlog, in the development of the means of production; the experience of the socialist countries, and in certain circumstances of the capitalist countries, too (Japan, for instance), proves that this can be done fairly quickly. But it is much more difficult to modify the human factor in the production process, as can be seen from the varying effectiveness of the same technology at different situations of culture and civilization. But the human factor shows the greatest degree of resistance when faced with a change in the interpersonal relations that make up the general pattern of culture. This is precisely what is involved in Marx's ideal of man under communism—a man who is free of any alienations and consequently universal and possessing a fully developed personality. From this point of view, all social conditions, including the material base of society, are only a means to an end, not ends in themselves.

All this constitutes an involved and many-sided problem, which in most cases is quietly—although quite wrongly—ignored: what is to be done with the Marxian ideal of man under communism? How, and to what extent, can it be realized under the existing conditions?

There is no doubt that the drama is taking place on a different stage, and with a different cast, than was ever imagined by Marx. No wonder, then, that the action has departed from Marx's script— and it is pointless to keep reciting his text as if nothing had changed. What matters is whether the substance of the play, whatever alterations there may be in its form or action, is or is not to remain *the same,* if not identical. To this question the only possible answer is *yes.*

The creation of a new communist man is a principle that cannot be abandoned without abandoning communism itself. Communism —at least as Marx saw it—is practical humanism. Marx's views can be modified in various ways and purged of certain "youthful errors" to be explained as hangovers from utopian socialism or as the results of the inexperience of a young man, but the principle itself must not be violated. Thus the call for a new image of man under communism remains intact; what can and should be adjusted is the approach to its fulfillment. For in this case there is no automatic influence of the economic base of society on consciousness —such a belief cannot be ascribed to Marx, young or mature, if his theory is seriously studied; nor are our hands in any way tied by some kind of "loyalty" to Marx's opinions on the subject—not only because such "loyalty" would be tantamount to a dogmatism, alien to Marx, but also in view of the changed conditions that entitle, and even obligate, us to think the problem through once more.

Is it possible to abolish all forms of alienation in a socialist society? What kind of action can and should be taken to achieve this end? These are the principal questions in the theory and practice of developing the new man of communism.

The experiences of the socialist revolution, now no longer limited to one country, have clearly demonstrated that it by no means does away with alienation; this survives in various forms even after the victory of the revolution. Of course, it could be objected that the end of alienation will come at the higher stage of socialism—communism—which no society has fully achieved as yet (and cannot before the victory of the revolution throughout the world, if only because the state continues to exist as a political institution, while communism is by definition a stateless social order), and that it is premature to offer any judgment about alienation under communism. The objection is a valid one, although it does not at all follow that it is wrong to study the developmental tendencies of socialist society in this respect; these tendencies are significant and can tell us much about the probable way these matters are likely to be settled in the future. But in any case this is a stricture against the unconcerned carelessness of those who blithely assert, without any grounds other than a dogmatic interpretation of Marx's texts, that alienation vanishes in socialist societies, because, by definition, it should vanish (and this is wrong even as a literal interpretation of Marx's words, since he referred to communism, not to its lower stage—socialism).

The course of socialist revolution has shown that the various forms of alienation do not automatically disappear with the abolition of the *institution* of private ownership of the means of production; even economic alienation is no exception. Nor, of course, does it automatically do away with the division of labor nor of course the labor process (on the contrary, by intensifying industrialization it extends and hardens this division); nor, and this complicates matters still further, does it automatically and completely remove the alienation of the product from its producer, nor the alienation of money and its social function, nor—which is particularly distressing—human relation to private property. This last relationship displays a particular capacity for survival, although the institution itself has been destroyed, like a limb that continues to hurt after amputation. The simile may be incomplete, but there is something in it that deserves attention: if the patient feels a "pain" in his leg, although it has been cut off, it is so because his nervous system still has certain centers that cause a feeling of pain, misplaced though it is. Is this not roughly the position with attitudes to private property that in a certain form has been "amputated," while changes in the circulation of the social product have not been sufficiently far-reaching to remove all reminiscences from people's minds?

In any case, it is clear that even economic alienation does not automatically vanish in socialist society—and the efforts made to stamp out misappropriations of social property show the extent to which this alienation is still a serious problem.

As for other forms of alienation, such as political or ideological, they have in the light of historical experience also turned out to be much more durable and more deeply rooted than was originally expected. From the point of view of the formation of the new man, the most distressing symptoms of these connected types of aliena-tion are nationalism and racism, which, as the very antithesis of internationalism, are particularly grievous, and at the same time, as the development of socialist society shows, an extremely refrac-tory obstacle in the path of fulfilling the ideal of communist man.

As already pointed out, it seems doubtful, given the present state and possibilities of the organization of social life, whether these other forms of alienation can disappear, even when communism has been fully realized. What matters most is the state as the ad-ministrative framework of social life and the impact of the contin-ued existence of its necessarily bureaucratic and hierarchical ma-chinery on people's minds.

There is another important factor: socialism is being built in a world in which capitalism continues to exist and to exert its influ-ence on the consciousness of men in the socialist world, with con-tacts between the two systems becoming ever more animated and diversified. This is another thing Marx did not foresee, and it is a factor that makes it even more complicated to overcome the various forms of alienation, since, as is generally admitted today, this co-existence is of long duration. Under present social and political conditions, the transformations in the capitalist world (in the case of the highly developed countries) will in all probability have an evolutionary character, and it can hardly be imagined that the relations between the two worlds, socialist and capitalist, will be based only on a one-way influence of the socialist world on the capitalist partner.

All these remarks merely review the problems and difficulties involved and are intended to illustrate the somewhat banal but, as far as its consequences are concerned, not unimportant proposition that things have changed from what Marx had in mind when he discussed the future of man under communism.

What then can sensibly be said about this future from the point of view of practice? This is what matters most today, when it is abundantly clear that the situation is different and much more involved than was envisaged by Marx, if at the same time we refuse to abandon Marx's ideal of man under communism—at least as a guiding light?

I think the answer to this question is provided by Marx himself in his conception of communism as a movement changing reality and not as a steady state of affairs; the relevant passage has been quoted on another page, but because of its importance for our argument we shall quote it again:

"Communism is for us not a *state of affairs* which is to be established," Marx wrote, "an *ideal* to which reality [will] have to adjust itself. We call communism the *real* movement which abolishes the present state of things." [15]

These words are in complete harmony with Marx's protest against the utopian visions of communist society, with which, as early as his letter to Ruge, he contrasted his own radical criticism of the existing world. To change this world, to fight the actual evil, and not to play the prophet about an unpredictable future—that was Marx's motto. This, it is true, seems to be belied by some of his pronouncements about communist man, but, as already admitted, he did not—and for practical purposes could not—wholly shake off the grip of the utopian ideas that he himself assailed. To avoid this pressure was all the more difficult because his vision of man under communism as an ideal model, as a mathematical limit to which man approximates in an unending process, is indispensable for a complete picture of communist society. Marx, after all, merely tells us what the communist man should be like, but not how this is to be achieved. Some of his pronouncements, it is true, give the impression of a rather cavalier approach to this last question, but in view of the situation of the movement in his day and his contemporary state of knowledge and experience, this is certainly excusable. This particular problem was not a practical issue in his day. Today the position is quite different: from the point of view of socialist construction it is one of the most important, and perhaps the most difficult, of the problems that confront us.

Under the circumstances, the only reasonable procedure is to return to Marx's idea that communism is not a ready-made, preconceived *state of affairs* that is to be established, but a *process* of struggle against everything that a definite system of values denounces. In terms of the theory of man under communism, this means that the crucial task today is to educate a new man—that is, to inculcate views and attitudes that criticize alienation in social life and approve those situations in which this alienation is overcome.

This may sound commonplace, but, depending on one's approach and interpretation, it can also be richly meaningful and pregnant.

That men need to be educated is, of course, something that not only Marxists have known for a long time. For them it is a truism, and I would say, a depreciated one. Is there a Marxist who has not said that the new man has still to be created and molded, that this is one of the chief tasks of socialist construction, that communism should be a society of people of a new type, and so on?

But it is one thing to recite familiar platitudes, eventually forgetting that one is merely mouthing clichés and becoming indifferent to the contradiction between word and action, between theory and practice; and another thing to perceive the specific meaning of these phrases and follow through with their *practical* conclusions. Then and only then can the general requirement, that the new communist man must begin to be educated now, in our still imperfect social relations and conditions—a principle that is tantamount to attacking those undesirable characteristics whose sources lie in the various forms of alienation—acquire new color and meaning. At any rate, it will certainly cease to be a commonplace.

Am I suggesting that in the practice of socialist construction so far the question of forming a new man has been overlooked? That no efforts of theory and practice have been made in this direction? That no transformations of a far-reaching nature have been accomplished? Such an assertion would be obviously false. What I do maintain, and this is the main point of my remarks at this stage, is that this matter has received not only insufficient, but also the wrong kind of attention; that the transformations of human consciousness and attitudes in socialist societies have basically been spontaneous processes springing out of the ensuing social changes, that premeditated action in this field has been inadequate and misconceived, especially when the traditional phraseology was belied by practice; and consequently that it is possible and necessary to proceed differently in this sphere, more specifically and so more effectively. Let me try to illustrate this point.

The watchwords of the French Revolution, "Liberty, Equality, Fraternity," expressed in the actual pattern of social relations the social goals of a bourgeois revolution. But its content goes much deeper, since at the climax of the revolutionary struggle the bourgeoisie took upon itself—and had to if it wanted to triumph—the role of champion of the interests of the people. It is only natural, therefore, that the answers to our problems are to be found within the framework of the ideals already embraced by the French Revolution with regard to man and his destiny in society. The specific substance of these aspirations may change, but their general form and character remain intact.

The most promising features of the ideal man of communist society are those that are the antithesis of the views and attitudes of people shaped by the conditions of a class society, with its divisions and its economic and social inequalities. "Equality" as a motto expresses a protest against economic and social alienation which deforms the mentality and checks the full development of the human personality, not only of those who are exploited and oppressed, but also of those who, exploiting and oppressing others, become the victims of these same restrictions and deformations, though in their case they operate differently. This problem is manifested in at least two forms, both of which have remained pressingly relevant to a society whose task is to develop a new type of man: as economic alienation and as social alienation.

The main concern in forming the man of the new society is to evolve as fulfilled and versatile a personality as possible, removing the domination of autonomous products over man, who had been reduced from their maker into their slave. This problem appears most graphically in the sphere of economic activity. Here the autonomization of man's product's (and of human relations), which become independent not only of their creator, but in their uncontrolled operation, grow into a hostile force opposed to him, is particularly striking and sinister and threatens to damage human personality. Among the many issues lurking behind the term "economic alienation" we can single out those such as the consequences of the division of labor or the nature of the labor process, which are connected with the long-term development of the forces and relations of production themselves, so that little can be achieved by persuasion, and those like attitudes to private property and money, which are directly linked with personal views and convictions. In this case, of course, the subjective factor is a function of a certain objective situation and is largely dependent on changes in it, but to some extent, at least, human attitudes are autonomous, and as a result the educational element assumes a special importance.

The object of education can be briefly summed up: the private interest of the individual should, in his mind and so in his behavior, be felt to overlap with the social interest. This does not by any means imply, as it is sometimes wrongly interpreted, a destruction of individual identity or interests (not even in the economic sphere), but only the development of a *social* attitude, one that is not characterized by a narrow egoism. This does not rule out the individuality of each man or the maintenance of his specific interests, but only a totally crass self-centered approach, which ultimately is also incompatible with the individual's best interests. This requirement is self-evident in pre-class societies and with certain modifications, in pre-capitalist societies as well. The elevation of economic egoism into a principle of life is a product of capitalist society with its atomization of the interests of commodity producers for whom market competition is the basic form of economic endeavor and for whom money, in consequence, is raised to the status of supreme value.

Thus what is sought in this sphere is relatively modest and simple, though crucial in its consequences: the eradication from the minds of men of the effects of the market economy in a class society, and in particular of the results of capitalist market economy. In other words, the point is that they should act in the conviction that their best interests always require that they respect the interests of others, and so of society, and that the mentality so formed should frame a code of conduct reflecting standards of "decency" in the common meaning of this word. This is a formidable task, given the thinking now widespread; for the object is to make men regard not only such things as stealing as dishonest and indecent, but also any kind of selfish behavior which, by the standards of capitalist society, is perfectly compatible with honesty and respectability.

But this, of course, is the maximum ideal and obviously connected with long-term and deep-reaching processes of economic and social change. The attitude and mentality of egoism, typical of the commodity producer, is certainly not congenital, but the result of certain production relations. It grows up with them and dies with them. But this process of withering-away is not automatic, if only because these are phenomena from the field of consciousness; at any rate, its tempo is not socially unimportant.

Apart from these momentous, not to say epoch-making and revolutionary changes, there are, however, smaller matters which are present in everyday life and so more amenable to educational influences: the spreading of the standards of honesty accepted in every society. For instance, it is not asking very much that people should not steal. But as long as the elementary honesty is flouted—

and the cases of pilfering of public property in socialist societies cogently demonstrate that this is not infrequent—learned dissertations on the subject of the abolition of alienation and the merging of private and social interest will make sceptical reading.

Has a change of system contributed anything new in the area of these manifold questions? Undoubtedly yes. The effects of the revolution are in this respect enormous, and it would be wrong to lose sight of these changes simply because dishonesty has not vanished, because we are still plagued with thefts and embezzlement of public property, because private interest is still not identified with the social interest.

Take, for instance, the question of attitudes to money. One of the characteristic changes in the mentality of people living in socialist societies, a change moreover that comes rapidly, is the disappearance of that idolatrous worship of money as a means of hoarding value, which is so striking in capitalist countries, where it ruins not only the characters, but even the lives of people as they are dragged into the treadmill of acquisition. The change is very simply explained: hoarding is pointless. Property cannot be sold, insurance is not worthwhile, work will be found anyway, so why bother? This change is caused not by virtue but by circumstances, but surely such a change is better since it is likely to be more lasting. As far as its influences on human character are concerned, the effects can neither be calculated nor foreseen.

Now this kind of change that influences the general pattern of human personality is, so to say, automatically achieved by socialist revolution, and not only confined to the sphere of attitudes to private property. Another example is the fact that wealth ceases to play a role in assessing a man or to be a measure of his place in the social hierarchy. Obviously, money is not despised: hermits are not a mass occurrence in socialist society, but it is not money that decides social status. This is a situation diametrically opposite to that in America and undoubtedly more favorable to the proper development of human personality than is the situation there.

The general conclusion is that the abolition of private ownership of the means of production eradicates social privileges based on property, thereby changing public attitudes toward money as a symbol of social status. This in itself is a breakthrough and certain symptoms clearly become visible from the start, while others, though latent, also take hold of social life.

There is an interesting problem embodied in the following pragmatic question: what should be done to speed up this process of changing attitudes to private property and to accelerate the reorganization, from the point of view of socialism, of the relationship between private and social interest in human conduct?

It is obvious that such transformations, like all transformations of consciousness, are not accomplished rapidly and are a function of the actual changes in social life. It is these that I would now like to discuss.

The developments that should primarily be mentioned here are such matters as a weakening of acquisitive urges, since these are seen to be pointless, a reduction of the number of petty thefts of social property following a rise in the general living standards of the population, a hardening of popular criticisms of encroachments on the public good as socialist production relations become firmly established, and so on.

All these are changes that require time and persuasion, above all by means of *practical example* in keeping with the principle *verba volant, facta trahunt.*

There is a certain area of life that, remote as it may seem from these matters, exerts a considerable influence on their evolution and as a result its role, usually overlooked, should be clearly understood. I am thinking of the factors that shape the internal structure of society, namely the character and aspirations of its elite which contribute to the emergence of a certain hierarchy of social values and of a personal model which is reflected in the general run of the community. This is a very important agent of real changes in the life of society whose connection with the relationship between private and social interest is crucial though not always clear.

The educational problem facing us can be reduced to the need to overcome egoism in members of society, an egoism that, as we have said, is a product of capitalist society. This egoism, whose symptom is the desire to get rich at any cost, becomes the decisive element in the personality model of the stereotyped man of a specific society. Its characteristic feature is a determination to "get ahead," to dominate others, superiority being based primarily on wealth. The personality model of the communist man possesses traits that are the very reverse of this, chief among them in this context being a moderate equalitarianism. At any rate, ascendancy over others by reason of wealth plays no role, and there is no corresponding attitude. Of course, we are talking here of an ideal to be pursued, fully realizing that what is involved is an attitude that is exceedingly persistent, once it has appeared.

The matter might be put thus: the object of education is to disseminate through practical example and ideal persuasion an attitude of judicious equalitarianism that precludes the pursuit of wealth and the enlargement of individual property for the purposes of social elevation. It is not a matter of turning people into ascetics; on the contrary, communism seeks to help everyone to enjoy life fully in all its forms. Nor is it a question of making some kind of absolute equalitarianism, which is not only contrary to healthy common sense, if we consider the differences between people and their needs, but alien to Marxism as well. Thus communism preserves individual property and retains the differences among men in this respect too. It fights only to prevent the differences from affecting a person's social situation, and consequently endeavors to bring about a change in attitudes and personality patterns.

It must clearly be seen that the fulfillment of this goal is impeded not only by the pressure of attitudes bequeathed by tradition or seeping in from countries with a system based on private property, but also by all those things within the life of socialist societies that encourage and revive anti-equalitarian tendencies, and whose consequences through stratification, cause excessive differentiation in material situations and create an economically privileged elite. This arouses unhealthy appetites and urges in the community that find an outlet—since they cannot otherwise be satisfied—in an intensified courting of money as a means of living up to the style set by the powerful "big shots." *Exempla trahunt*— especially as the gap between the living circumstances of the various groups is considerable and the minimum standard still low.

In the development of socialist societies, there must inevitably be a long transition period during which, for various reasons clearly marked differences will persist in personal situations: not only material affluence, but also the disparities between town and country, or between manual and white-collar occupations, position in the administrative apparatus, etc. If for no other reason, there emerge in socialist societies, as the traditional classes tend to disappear, new social divisions and an intricate stratification. In this field, classic Marxist theory offers little guidance.

1. For obvious practical reasons it was concerned with analysis of the great classes that play a salient role in the anatomy of capitalist society and in its dynamics.
2. This theory was an account of the situation existing in capitalist society and could not, in a presocialist phase, foresee the future complexities of stratification in socialist society.

In the present stage of development, when the construction of socialism is not only a fact but firmly advancing, Marxist theory is confronted with the necessity of expanding its field of interest and developing its conceptual apparatus. This is obstructed by a traditionalism that tries to shrug off the gaps and deficiencies in Marxist theory in this sphere as proof that the problems do not exist, or are trivial, and by a psychological reluctance to drag up facts that are considered embarrassing and so better left unspoken—as if reticence could cancel out things that objectively exist or our silence could oblige the other side to be equally tactful. This method can produce only one result: only our opponents are heard, and all the louder.

These phenomena have encouraged anticommunist literature to such imaginery visions as "a new class," a "red bourgeoisie," and so on. Theoretically speaking, this is ridiculous: the elite emergent in socialist societies is, by definition, not a class, while the term "bourgeoisie" in this context can only be treated as a cheap gimmick. But this should not quiet us: it is easier to nail the deceptions of the enemy than to dispose of the problem itself. The point is that in socialist societies social groups do arise that enjoy a privileged social position. This is wholly natural and socially justified, and there is no reason to hush up the fact shamefacedly. But natural and even inevitable though it may be at a certain stage, it bristles with dangers, and for this reason at least should be carefully examined and pondered. The risk is that if certain limits of privilege are exceeded and the results of this are not countered, there inevitably will be undesirable consequences from the point of view of socialism, particularly in the sphere of education.

Here we come back to our key problem: the formation of a new type of man, of different spirit than the bourgeois "citizen," with his economic avarice and egoism, requires a change of model, a change in the stereotype of man. This is not only a matter of speech-making; it cannot be settled with a number of popular lectures on the nature of socialist man. In a certain situation, where there is a discrepancy between words and deeds, such homilies do more harm than good. For practice is all-important here. In the complicated system of social influence, not inconsiderable place is occupied by personal example, particularly on the part of those who are in the public eye, since in one way or another they are its leaders, they exercise authority. There is an ancient truth embodied in the popular saying that the worst service is rendered by those who preach water and drink wine.

Thus, it is important that the way of life of the elites, which arise unresisted in socialist society, are a factor molding the new man. This subject is by no means new, though indeed a delicate one. Fortunately, I can call on Marx himself, whose views on this matter were fully endorsed by Lenin. My object, however, is not unqualified acceptance of his recommendations. In his enthusiasm over the experiences of the Paris Commune, he was probably no less utopian than generous when he counselled that those who exercise power in a socialist society should earn no more than a skilled worker, be subject to frequent and unconditional rotation and so forth. But basically this notion is undoubtedly on the right lines and points to the crux of what is at issue; from the point of view of social education and the general formation of a new model of man, this is a problem of enormous moment.

Does this mean a call for absolute equalitarianism? Not at all. This would be at odds with common sense, quite apart from the fact that Marxism has never embraced anything so simple. The attack launched against latter-day "levellers" was also justified in its time, and rooted in Marxian theory, being a response to primitive and harmful equalitarian demagogy. But it should also be perceived that these reasonable objections were blatantly abused in the Stalinist period. These are questions that should be taken up in the searching sociological analysis we are still awaiting of the so-called "cult of personality," which had its roots in social phenomena and not in the personal character of an "individual." Suffice it to say that many of the undesirable elements in the educative model of socialist man can be traced to the Stalinist period and its distortions. Without a penetrating inquiry into its social roots and causes, it is impossible to understand these phenomena and so effectively to counter and overcome them.

The raising of men of the age of socialism requires not only eradication of the flaws inherent in the capitalist pattern, but also the implanting of attitudes that should distinguish the new model. Among the qualities that still need to be brought to a new and superior form, the most important are social commitment and public-spiritedness, characteristics that should be inseparable from libertarian principles. Contrary to the usual view, it is not only a matter of providing the members of society with a maximum of democracy and freedom, but also of teaching them to use this democracy and freedom. At the same time, there is an interdependence between democracy and the libertarian principle: it is not only libertarian attitudes that depend on the degree of the democratization of social life, but also, conversely, the degree of democracy achieved by a society is contingent on the vigor and profundity of the libertarian attitudes of its members.

The founders of Marxism had no doubts of this: although communism means "a leap into the realm of freedom," people still have to learn to exercise this freedom. The conditions of class society and its prevailing human relations are no good ground for the development of libertarian attitudes. This does not, of course, mean that they are altogether impossible in a class society; on the contrary, we know from experience that in this kind of society splendid exponents of this attitude can be found. But they are rare exceptions, in the category of rebels. What is needed is the creation of an average man in this mold. How else are we to pursue the goal of a man with a fully developed personality, what Marx called a universal man? Lenin's contention that in a communist society each housewife should be capable of managing public affairs is an expression of this ideal.

No communist has ever denied the justice of this requirement. For that matter, who would dare? Lenin's remark has been repeated so often that it is in danger of becoming a platitude that is approvingly quoted, but without any awareness that approval entails certain consequences, and indeed very important ones. For what is involved is a matter that is of truly first importance as far as the tasks and prospects of forming a new model of man under communism are concerned.

Does this mean that Lenin's admirable sentiment has remained a hollow phrase, a piece of wishful thinking? Far from it. The development of socialism in the Soviet Union and in the other socialist countries has brought with it enormous, truly revolutionary changes precisely in this sphere, the social commitment of the masses of people and their social activism, their powerful drive towards freedom. The socialist revolution, regardless of whether it is accomplished by force or by peaceful means, is synonymous with a tremendous intensification of the social activism of the masses that carries over into the post-revolutionary phase, as the other side of the economic and social changes, the incalculable cultural revolution, etc. What is happening in the socialist countries as far as this is concerned is perhaps the most encouraging development of all, one that reaches most deeply into men's souls, and constitutes a real guarantee of the fulfillment of Marx's call for a metamorphosis of man under communism. The judgments and forecasts of western "Marxologists" and "specialists" on the socialist countries who, with a quite remarkable one-sided purblindness, fail to perceive any of this, fastening only on what is wrong, backward, and apparently anti-libertarian, testify only to the great weakness of Western Marxology. They fall into that most grievous, but also most frequent, error of ideologues: they are concerned not with discovering the objective truth, but with telling their sponsors what they want to hear. It is irrelevant or at any rate only of interest to their biographers whether these "experts" deliberately distort the truth or simply succumb—which is a frequent and psychologically understandable lapse—to the myopia of the ideology they espouse. Suffice it to say that this kind of "Marxology" may produce venomous propaganda, but as a weapon in a serious, long-term struggle it is ineffective and even self-defeating. By providing a false picture, it misleads, and precisely those people who need to know the true state of affairs if they are to hold up their side of the argument. This remark, for that matter, is applicable not only to bourgeois ideologues.

As far as this is concerned, therefore, we can laugh at the bourgeois "Marxologists." Contrary to their pious hopes, man under socialism is being made over rapidly and radically, developing an articulate public spirited and a many-sided commitment in social matters, both as a result both of the spontaneous transformations in human consciousness that follow changes in the base of society and of ideological persuasion and educational endeavors.

But just because socialism can point to successes and achievements in this sphere, it would be a silly mistake to beat the triumphal drum so loudly as to drown out all dissonant sounds. After all, disconcerting notes are making themselves heard in no faint fashion, disturbing the general harmony. Let us not behave, therefore, like the very bourgeois ideologues we criticized à rebours. If we want to achieve progress, we must remove the evil that stands in the way. If we want to reverse a negative state of things, we must above all understand it in precise detail, give an account of it, discover its causes, and so on. The ostrich policy is no help, but only an impediment to a conscious educational effort.

The development of libertarian attitudes, expressed in the social commitment and activism of the members of our existing socialist societies, does not by any means follow a straight path: along with a tremendous upward swing, there have also been negative turns which limit progress. Apart from the commonplace observation that such processes, by virtue of their complexity, are never simple or straightforward, the phenomenon in which we are specifically interested has at least two main causes: one lies in the specific nature of the human base of the societies that actually are building socialism, the other in the nature of the errors committed during the period of the "cult of personality."

The first of these matters has already been noted. From the point of view of socialist construction, it is significant that the countries concerned are not equipped with a tradition of bourgeois democracy and all its attendant institutions. This is of importance primarily as regards the development of human attitudes. For all their class limitations, the libertarianism connected with bourgeois democracy, the centuries old traditions of social commitment consequent upon bourgeois parliamentarianism, and the struggles associated with it (for the victory and expansion of its institutions and for their proper functioning), have profoundly affected the outlook of the members of these bourgeois democratic societies, inculcating certain attitudes and habits that eventually became part of social psychology and creating traits that have sunk deep roots. This point is all the more important in that it concerns the *whole* society, that is not only the "man in the street," but also the various elites. Public sentiments about what is or is not socially admissible or respectable, by which after all these powerful people are also swayed, operate more powerfully, because of the manifest and independent rights of members of society, than the best legal codes do if they are not a reflection of attitudes, habits, and feelings deeply rooted in people's way of thinking. This kind of entrenched tradition and outlook, founded on ancient social practice, comes out not only in trifles like disciplined behavior in bus queues, or in more serious matters like observance of food-rationing regulations in times of shortages and voluntary rejection of the black market as a dishonorable practice, but also in matters of the highest social importance involving the rights of the citizen. Let me repeat: this social schooling, for all its class-determined limitations, is a potent teacher, especially if it is of long standing. It is not irrelevant that the members of the current socialist societies have not graduated from such a school, and that the socialist revolution must, on the way so to speak, execute the business of the bourgeois-democratic revolution. This is not a comfortable situation in any sphere, but particularly not in this one, if only because of the significance and influence of the time factor, that is, the period needed to loosen the mental grip of certain conditions. After all, countries like Russia or Poland, though they have a stirring record of revolutionary upsurges against tyranny and oppression, unfortunately lack protracted experience of the functioning of parliamentary democratic institutions, however attenuated by a class character. On the contrary, the history of countries like Poland and to some extent of the others building socialism has elevated the insubordination and nonconformism, bred by a justified revolt against ruling conditions and oppressor states, into a national virtue cutting across all social classes. This is manifested not only in nonconformist rebelliousness, but also in a more deepseated and pernicious disrespect of the principles of social discipline, since these rules were imposed by enemies. The socialist revolution has, therefore, to carry out, *en passant,* no easy task, one that reaches deep to the heart of social psychology.

The second impediment is connected with the errors committed during the Stalinist period. Leaving aside the features of a clearly pathological character, we can reduce this problem to the doctrine of the sharpening class struggle under socialism and to the idea that the class enemy must be stamped out by terror. Of course, in such circumstance, the formation of libertarian attitudes and habits of democracy is, at the very least, checked.

The task facing a socialist society here is to develop a human personality preparing for the communist man, and instilled with a profound love of freedom in all its forms, a love which, backed up by personal courage and a sense of social responsibility for one's actions, guarantees a genuine commitment of the individual in social matters. But verbal agreement on the ideals of the distant future is not enough; what is needed is energetic educative action right now, if this ideal is not to become a hollow slogan, or at any rate if its fulfillment is not to be seriously retarded. But to be able to pursue effective and proper action in this direction, it is not enough to possess a repertoire of edifying principles and recommendations (for example, the raising of civic consciousness through a general improvement in the standards of education and culture, promoting Marxist knowledge about society and its laws of development, recruitment of the citizen to active participation in social life through work in social organizations, development of political and social life by a devolution of certain kinds of power, above all in the administrative field, to autonomous civic organizations, etc.), which are all justified in abstract but have one basic flaw: they give no specific answer to current questions and gloss over the difficulties and conflicts that stand in the way of their fulfillment.

Let me say a little more about one such conflict, in my view the chief one.

It is obvious and self-evident that if one wants to stimulate in a positive way not only an abstract love of freedom but also a concrete capacity for transforming this love into action; in other words, if one wants to foster the quality of courage in working for the common good, to promote commitment in social matters, it is essential to create the right conditions. Now the fact of the matter is that socialist societies cannot always afford this. This is something that needs to be openly admitted, and the resulting situation should be carefully analyzed, since the obstacles are of an objective character, not only derived from certain mistakes of a subjective nature.

If one of the tasks of a socialist society is inculcation of certain desirable attitudes and characteristics of personality, a no less important task is the consolidation of its political existence and its further development. In the current circumstances, this imposes certain necessities that do not always favor the development of the specific features of the new man. As I have already said, the fact that socialism has not triumphed all over the world at once, let alone in the countries that are militarily and economically decisive, entails far-reaching consequences that have not been discussed with sufficient objectivity or clarity. The prime result is that the period which Marx called the transition stage, the dictatorship of the proletariat, which was to be a relatively brief post-revolutionary phase, has not only been considerably prolonged, but it also has changed its character. Just so the nature of the class struggle inevitably had to change in the conditions of capitalist encirclement, which was distinctly more powerful economically and militarily than the first and at that time the only socialist state. Subsequently, the situation swung in favor of socialism: there are more socialist countries than before and they are incomparably stronger than they were. But the problem of external and internal struggle still remains, as do various difficulties of development. In these circumstances, can the socialist countries permit themselves as broad a development of democracy as they would like? Can they solve the problem of the personal liberties of the citizen as they would like? No, they cannot.

From this point of view, it is not important whether the freedom touted on the other side of the barricade is complete and genuine. Pointing out its limitations and deceptions does not change the situation on our side. For that matter, arguments *ad hominem* have never cut much ice in such debates. What is important, however, is that the shortcomings on our side do not spring from bad faith but from the objective necessities of a specific historical situation. Even if socialist democracy is already in many respects superior to the bourgeois democracies, no reasonable man would claim that it has achieved the zenith of its development, or that it has set aside all restrictions on freedom. Granted that bourgeois democracy is only formal, this is no reason for pleasure over the fact that some of these "formal" liberties are, for one reason or another, constrained in our part of the world. This is not a virtue but a necessity imposed by the struggle. For this very reason it is nothing to be ashamed of, but yet it should be frankly admitted, though not with pride (as sometimes happens in an excess of enthusiasm). At any rate, these are matters that require serious thought in order to find a way out.

For there is a way out of this kind of conflict: it lies through the deliberate, if gradual, lifting of unnecessary restrictions. If the obstacles to the formation of the new man include limitations of democracy and personal liberties, and if these are not merely the result of mistaken policies or deficient judgments, but of political necessities stemming from the configuration of forces, then the only solution to the ensuing conflict between the various tendencies in socialist society is a slow but sustained and judicious eradication of those that do not belong to its essence but only to a specific transitory pattern of conditions.

This general conclusion ceases to be a platitude if it is translated into concrete terms, and if the principle itself is not only socially propagated but also accepted. But in that once it involves certain guides to practice that policy makers at various levels should be prepared to follow even though as a result they undoubtedly will meet difficulties and inconveniences in the exercise of their duties, formidable enough as they are already. It is precisely here that there is a call for ideological enlightenment to bring home the gravity of the problem, since it is hardly likely that anyone will make things more difficult for himself of his own accord unless he is deeply convinced of the importance of what he is doing.

Here the general object of public education should be the utmost increase in independence of thought and behavior through active involvement of people in public affairs. In terms of daily practice, this is precisely what is meant by the cultivation of libertarian attitudes.

Where does this put the politician or anyone in charge of a sector of public life? In these matters, a conflict situation normally arises when the need for efficient execution of some particular task are weighed against the requirements of an educative influence on human attitudes. It is obvious that the most effective, if not always the most proper, way of carrying out an assignment lies in having one person in charge and treating it as an army exercise. The source of command is concentrated in a single place and action consists in the unquestioning execution of orders. If the risk of error is greater, so is the degree of efficiency. It is enough to believe in the infallibility of the judgment of those who give the orders for the system to be acknowledged as ideal from the praxological point of view. It is no accident that the thinking of the Stalinist period along these lines was usually clothed in such military language as "front," "combat tasks," etc. Add to this how convenient it is for those who are responsible for the leadership: orders replace protracted persuasion and discussions, when time is pressing. Execution of an assignment, for which men in the field are answerable to their superiors is assured wherever objections and disagreements might put it in jeopardy. It is uncomfortable to engage in arguments, and to give those of a different opinion an equal say, if you do not feel sufficiently secure and so are frightened of such a clash of views. Not surprisingly, in the hurly-burly of battle, political leaders are apt to rely on commands and administrative directives instead of leadership, and this inclination grows in direct proportion to their political and ideological weakness.

It would be banal to demonstrate that this mode of management is, in social terms, only apparently effective and convenient. It is not only that the risk of error is greater: but the sort of execution that consists in blind discipline, and so inhibits the initiative of those who carry it out, is, at the very least, imperfect. Politics and daily life are not identical with front-line operations—this is an unfortunate analogy if interpreted literally—and in any case, modern military doctrine long ago rejected the nineteenth-century model of the soldier as obsolete. Suffice it to say that the citizen of the socialist society cannot be regarded simply as a soldier in combat, and that other attitudes than unquestioning discipline and blind obedience need to be inculcated if we are seriously concerned with the emergence of a new type of man characteristic of the new communist society. On the contrary, seeing the shortcomings and flaws in the type of man formed by a class society, we should do everything to cultivate a new human personality that would be distinguished equally by commitment to social concerns and responsibility for them as by independence of mind and intelligent disobedience if this is required by the social good; and this includes the courage of expressing views even if they are not popular, especially with superiors. For without the latter, the call for commitment and responsibility for social matters will remain empty words.

What administrator likes critics and opponents? One can scarcely expect people to become masochists. Nor is this the point. It is not a matter of loving critics and opponents—this would require giving up one's own mind and deny the individuality of the manager—but simply of admitting the uncomfortable truth that we are not infallible, and that other people are not obliged to carry out our orders unquestioningly even though we may occupy the highest position in the social hierarchy. In other words, it is essential to accept not only that other people have a right to think for themselves but even a social duty to do so, and that they are entitled and obliged to give practical expression to this. From the point of view of democracy, and not necessarily in the socialist countries alone, this is a very small step, but it is also a momentous one, particularly in the conditions of societies that have no long-standing training in the functioning of bourgeois democracy institutions.

Specific advice on this matter is hard to give—indeed impossible if we remember the complexity of the situations that arise in life. The main point is to accept as normal a certain procedure for dealing with social contingencies, and as a result a certain method of behavior in others as well as ourselves. None of this might even be worth mentioning if the Stalinist period had not weighed so heavily on the style of life, thought, and conduct of all socialist societies, even those that in one way or another defied Stalin. A certain approach to the dictatorship of the proletariat—particularly in its practical action rather than in ideological declarations—is difficult to overcome, especially if it finds an ally in the resistance raised—psychologically at least—by consideration of the convenience of those who are responsible for the administration of various sectors of the socialist societies and—as has been frequently repeated—of the lack of a tradition of functioning democratic institutions.

Is the goal then a practicable one? By all means yes, since this is required by life, by the practice of the development of socialism, which sooner or later will force its passage, sweeping aside resistance and prejudice. But it is necessary to hasten this process and to ensure that it runs along sensible and well-reasoned lines. As far as this is concerned, much, though not everything, can be done by theoretical reflection that affects the formation of the prevailing ideology. And it is for this very reason that such enquiry should be courageous and radical in exposing errors and shortcomings, and also, as far as possible, in attempting to sketch a positive program.

The Communist Manifesto ends with a call that has become the general battle cry of the socialist revolution: "Workers of the world, unite!"

The meaning given to this watchword by Marx and Engels, however, only becomes fully clear in the light of another thesis of the *Manifesto,* namely that the proletariat has no fatherland. This may be variously interpreted, and it has provoked bitter controversies about the relationship between internationalism and patriotism, disputes which are far from spent and which naturally assume a different tenor depending on the period in which they are waged. But it is beyond dispute that *internationalism* is an inseparable part of the attitude of communists and that both the founders of Marxism and all their disciples and followers regarded it as one of the characteristic features of the personality of the communist man. It is also unchallenged that *internationalist attitudes* should be fostered consciously, that they do not arise spontaneously, least of all in periods laden with nationalist moods, but can only be formed in a struggle against nationalism and racism of all varieties and shades. Here, then, we have yet another salient educative task as far as shaping the personality of the members of socialist society is concerned, particularly in the specific conditions of the post-Hitler era, of a world torn by nationalist contradictions from which the socialist countries have not escaped either; the task is clear: *cultivation and nurturing of sentiments and attitudes of proletarian internationalism in a sharp struggle against all manifestations of nationalism and racism.*

The national question has taken a different turn than once was imagined by the leaders of the workers' movement. For example, if Rosa Luxemburg obviously underestimated the importance of the national question, even though she was undoubtedly one of the greatest Marxist theorists in history, this was so not only because her grasp of this issue did not go deep enough, but primarily because like all Marxists of her time, Lenin not excluded, she was sure that the socialist revolution would spread rapidly, if not at once, throughout the whole world and that in such a socialist world the national question, like frontier problems, would cease to be of any major significance. Looking at the world today, however, we need not shake our heads sorrowfully at this idea, since it contemplated wholly different conditions for the development of socialism, namely those envisaged by Marx; and nothing can be said about how the national question would actually have fared in such a context. Suffice it to say that our world is different and that for this reason the national question plays an enormous role quite unpredicted by the founders of Marxism. Had anyone in those days suggested that tensions of a nationalist or even racist character might appear in a socialist community—and not only in its initial phase—he would certainly have been dismissed as either ignorant or mad. Life, however, has shown that this is possible, once again demonstrating that reality is richer than any theory.

Is this only a matter of survivals of the past that still prey on people's minds? Undoubtedly, these are phenomena with roots deep in the history of class society: it produced the problem and its economic and social sources, and it nourished the corresponding attitudes and sentiments. But to reduce the whole matter only to survival and relics is so simplified as to explain nothing.

To explain the problem of nationalism in socialist societies we must go back to those factors that keep alive the relics of the past and offer a *new* stimulus to the feelings and attitudes that go with them.

These factors should be sought first of all in the division of the world in conditions where the socialist nations still lag behind the economically most advanced capitalist countries and, unfortunately, still have a long way to go before they catch up. This is the basic factor, since it upsets Marx's conception of the simultaneous triumph of socialism all over the world. That triumph would have assured a proper international division of labor and resources and would have eliminated the political battle between systems that inevitably seize upon nationalism as one of their chief weapons.

A second factor is the disparities among the development levels of the socialist countries themselves. This makes for different economic targets and tasks, since in a politically divided world there is a lack of those possibilities of a rapid clearing of economic arrears envisaged by Marx. It must be remembered that in the socialist as well as the capitalist world there are countries which are economically well-developed and others that are underdeveloped, that the gap between the development of the Soviet Union and the Democratic Republic of Vietnam, for instance, is in practice no smaller that that between the United States and South Vietnam. As a result, if the Soviet Union puts forward the task of overtaking the United States in the economic sphere, a goal due to the needs not only of the internal development of the U.S.S.R., but also of the progress and success of the communist movement in the West, such an objective is rejected by, for instance, China.

Third, we should add the fact that the countries now building socialism have traditionally been an arena of national struggles and communal strife. These antagonisms were a commodity which did not need to be manufactured in these countries; the only question is the extent to which the new conditions permit the persistence of old prejudices, attitudes, and conflicts.

Once again, it must be emphasized that the socialist authority has achieved a great deal in this matter, and in a very short time at that. Let us not forget that there still are survivors of the generation which lived under the conditions of that prison of the nations, Tsarist Russia. People who were brought up in the white heat of blazing national hatreds cannot be turned into angels of internationalism at a touch of the magic wand of communism. To think otherwise is cheap and foolish utopianism. It is true that the origin of these prejudices can be historically explained, but this does not in the least change the actual situation from which socialist construction began in these countries. Our enemies—and it says little for their intelligence—may be unable or unwilling to see the changes that have come about in this sphere, to perceive that these countries are radically different today from what they were at the beginning of the road.

There is one other category of blindness, about which I want to comment in this context: it is that of the disillusioned follower.

I have already written elsewhere about the difficulties of "socialism in daily life," but I must at least touch on this subject once more. We know that Marx's perspective for the revolution was too short: in 1848, he considered that the world was on the eve of a situation that has still to dawn a century later. We might generalize that although patience should be one of the qualities of the revolutionary, most revolutionaries tend to be impatient. This is psychologically natural, and in any case it is a matter of temperament. But the results of this may be extremely harmful, especially when theory gives way to practice, to the realization of ideals.

What Marxist is unaware that changes in consciousness, as a function of changes in social being, come about more slowly than economic transformations? What Marxist, in consequence, is unaware that the accomplishment of a socialist revolution in the sphere of dominant institutions does not automatically and immediately transform the whole of social life; that in many fields, despite the revolution, old habits linger on as if nothing had happened, and do not disappear nearly as quickly as he would like? *In theory,* therefore, every Marxist is prepared to understand that even after the revolution, the "old filthy business," as Marx called it, will stick to the new life and that any hopes of a sudden change are illusory. But *in practice* few people are capable of maintaining a stoic calm if their nostrils are assailed by the stench of the "old filthy business," if they come across dishonesty, stealing, hatred, nationalism, racism, etc. After the revolution this is more distressing than before: then it accorded with the stereotype, a part of the landscape, but here and now, it is out of place. It hurts that much more if individuals are involved who, at least nominally, are close to us ideologically. Men with alien ideologies—perhaps an enemy who is a nationalist and a racist—this one can cope with. But one of us? If we take this trouble to think about it, we will realize that an expanding mass movement cannot avoid social ailments, if these are widespread every society reaches whatever level of political and social integrity it can afford. But even so it is a bitter pill. This perhaps explains why veteran and seasoned revolutionaries, whom the prisons and tortures of the enemy had not been able to crush, broke like matchsticks when in the "past period" they had to face the misdeeds of people from their own ranks.

This psychology of disillusionment at having put so many glorious dreams into the revolutionary struggle and then seeing the revolution take place without bringing paradise operates in various fields and does considerable harm. I do not know whether analysis of this phenomenon can do much good: after all, this is an area in which irrationalism reigns supreme, since the people who commit this specific error of reasoning usually know how they *ought* to think currently about this. But perhaps it is worth trying, particularly where nationalist emotions are concerned, since this is where the phenomenon in question is probably most acute.

If it is wrong to react too impatiently, since reason tells us to allow for the time factor and for the gradualism of change, it is no less serious a mistake to allow such considerations to inhibit us from reacting at all. What is discreditable cannot be wished away, however successful we may, or may not be at accounting for its origin. A communist is always duty bound to oppose occurrences of this kind, to try to overcome them by education, even though he is perfectly aware that they are not accidental, but—quite the contrary—have deepseated social and historical roots. If we can see at one extreme the error of an exaggerated reaction ending in despondency and resignation, there is, at the other, the equally grievous though diametrically opposite error of ceasing to be outraged by wrongs because they are historically "documented," or refusing to fight them since they are—in a certain sense—in the regular order of things by virtue of their social conditioning. The mistake lies in overlooking the fact that changes in human consciousness are not wholly spontaneous; on the contrary, the *speed* of these changes is not irrelevant, and that every blot on the personality of a man casts a shadow over its whole. An unambiguous posture in this matter should be an integral part of the struggle for the education of the new man of the communist era.

Here we are brought back to our basic problem and for this reason the question needs to be formalized as concretely as possible.

The ideal of communist man is bound up with the concept that man is the supreme good for man. For it is only in such circumstances that the ideas of liberty, equality, social justice, and above all *brotherhood,* can become meaningful and luminous. Internationalism, too, in the Marxist system, is not simply a counsel of battle dictated by the need to unite the forces of one class against another on a supranational scale, but it is also a principle of equality that makes the notion of brotherhood realistic. As a result, if a communist is, by definition, a champion of equality and fraternity, of the ideal that man is the *supreme* good for man, he cannot indifferently make a little mistake and regard Negroes, Jews, Armenians, Greeks, or any other people, depending on the geography of racism, as nonhumans or at any rate as second-rate members of the human race. He is simply a racist and not a communist. Hence, the conclusion that if such attitudes and views are to be found among the members of socialist societies, and even among persons who call themselves communists, it is the duty of these societies to take vigorous action against such sentiments. Otherwise a mistake is being made that impedes the progress of socialism and even contains the danger of a permanent warp in its line of development. As we have said, the fact that a society is developing that is in a sense collectivist, and which has abolished the institution of private property, does not yet mean that a situation measuring up to the Marxian ideal of communist society will be automatically and unfailingly achieved.

In the European socialist countries, particular importance attaches to the battle against anti-Semitism and the necessary educational action within society this involves. Why exactly anti-Semitism of all the brands of national and race hatred that exist? Because it is historically rooted, and because it always involves ultrareactionary political consequences that have been further aggravated by Hitler's Nazism and its aftermath. There have never been any doubts in the revolutionary workers movement about the social implications of anti-Semitism, the working class movement has always fought it fiercely and uncompromisingly. The pattern of this struggle was set by Lenin, who immediately after the revolution proclaimed the struggle against anti-Semitism as one of the chief tasks, writing a number of articles and recording several speeches on this subject that were circulated widely. (It is notable that this fine example of proletarian party spirit has officially passed out of meaning, and its tradition not revived.)

The education of the new man cannot be treated in abstract terms. It must be concretely related to the actual shortcomings and problems of the societies building socialism. Hence, in cultivating internationalist attitudes, we cannot let it go with professions of solidarity with Negroes, since as long as the Negro problem does not exist in our part of the world, this will remain an abstraction. What needs to be done is to inculcate a spirit of brotherhood and identification with those peoples who live and work in our own midst, to concentrate on our own gravest of racist dangers, and to struggle against anti-Semitism.

To do this, we must start by calling a spade a spade and facing up to the truth. We have too many achievements that are legitimate sources of pride to equivocate on this point: plain speaking about these matters, if it is accompanied by resolute action, can only raise our moral stock and authority, even with our enemies. Given our countries and their history, it is straining credulity to imagine that anti-Semitism disappeared overnight: it is not discreditable that it exists; what is discreditable is that it is not being combatted. This makes it all the more misguided to resort to the humbug of pretending, by invoking general principles, that the phenomenon does not exist since it is, by definition, impossible under socialism. The fallacy here is that this by no means follows logically from the definition of socialism (communism is another matter), and anyway there is no hiding the fact that the disease occurs, since it sometimes assumes all too widely visible forms. Thus, this kind of denial neither does us credit nor increases trust in us, and moreover, it certainly weakens our struggle for a just cause.

How should we fight this phenomenon and what educational action should we adopt? It is not my purpose in these pages to provide a handbook of rules on how to proceed on each question involved in the shaping of the new man of communism. This would, in any case, be pointless and wrong. It is not possible to foresee all contingencies, nor is it a question of matters that are unknown to the workers movement. We have only to recall the already quoted example of Lenin's action after the October Revolution to be reminded of that. But one thing can be said for certain: this struggle is incumbent on socialist society, and above all on Marxist parties, in direct proportion to the degree of the danger of nationalism. For without developing an internationalist posture in socialist man, in other words without overcoming the influences of nationalism and racism on his mind and behavior, no one can build communism in the Marxist sense of the term. Since the guiding force in the development of socialist societies are their Marxist-Leninist parties, it is primarily on them—both with regard to the ideological purity of their own ranks and the outlook of society as a whole—that the political and moral responsibility rests for the realization of this urgent task.

The overcoming of all forms of alienation in communism may be expressed positively as the need to assure the all-round development of the human personality. The new man of communism was, in Marx's view, to be a universal, all-round, complete man. Each of these adjectives is the antithesis of the attributes of the man crippled by alienation, who has been robbed of a part of his personality, a part of his humanity, with his products turned into independent forces, reducing him to the status of a thing.

We know what Marx had in mind. We know also that this goal can only be achieved by changing man himself as well as transforming the base of society; he has to be educated according to a new model. But is this feasible? Are there not objective and insuperable obstacles standing in the way?

We have already touched on this problem when analyzing Marx's concept of alienation. Here let us return to this question in terms of the education of the new man.

Much is being said, echoing Marx, but also on the basis of actual observations, in modern anthropological and sociological literature about the increasing depersonalization of man in industrial society. This is a consequence not only of the reification and alienation typical of capitalist human relations, but also with more profound developments that have nothing to do with particular systems and spring from qualitative changes in the base of modern society.

Certain trends in contemporary literature (symbolized by Kafka and the response to him, in socialist societies no less then elsewhere), and in philosophy (here epitomized by Sartre) are cogent testimony to modern man's sense of isolation. Let me emphasize that I am not concerned with Kafka's style as a writer or Sartre's as a philosopher. These can be regarded as isolated idiosyncrasies that ultimately may be evidence of the decadence of certain social groups or even a symptom of individual disorders. What interests me is the influence of this kind of writing or philosophizing. If it appeals to the broad reading public, if it wins over readers in the socialist countries (the point is not that people do not read these works when they are banned, but that, if published, they are read not only on a mass scale but also—which is at least distressing from the ideological point of view—somewhat uncritically), this is a sign not of their decadence but that they contain certain ideas that touch a sensitive chord and that are not forthcoming from other sources and in better books. Prominent among these ideas is the sense of isolation of modern man, with all the implications and complications this involves.

For the Marxist the source of this phenomenon is more easily understood than it is for the representative of other philosophies, if only because he has a better understanding of how social consciousness is conditioned by changes in the base of society and because he is prepared to apply the necessary methodological principles in his analyses of cultural matters. And so, it is all the more embarrassing to find some people of Marxist allegiance trying to play down this problem with empty cries about decadence and the even more vapid cliché that a sense of isolation is natural in capitalist society but impossible under socialism. By definition perhaps.

Sociologically, it is understandable that progressive industrialization creates a number of by-products in the field of human relations. There is an increasing depersonalization of the relationship between the working man and the product of his labor as well as the very process of labor, for the process is increasingly specialized, divided and mechanized (as Hannah Arendt formulates this in her book *The Human Condition,* in industrial society *homo faber* is more and more giving way to *animal laborans*). Various kinds of social microstructures are being broken, and with them there comes a tearing or straining of such personal ties as neighborhood or family bonds in the broad sense of these words and these ties are replaced by new forms of urban or industrial association (political parties, trade unions, sports clubs, etc.). This leads to a growing atomization of personal life, even though the individual is more closely linked than before with society in the broad sense. There are profound transformations in family life, as mutual attitudes between working couples, children and parents, etc., change. Add to this the collapse of inherited systems of values, which once gave the individual a sense of stability with regard to his place in society, the rapid transformations withing a given community that challenge and sometimes even disrupt its structure, the tensions and insecurity in the international situation, which, given the present development of the destructive power of the weapons of war, confronts people all over the world with the danger of annihilation, and the feelings and attitudes of anxiety and isolation become not only understandable, but even explicable as the influence of objective factors. Of course, the social system exerts a potent influence in this field, too, —capitalism intensifying the atomization of society and the reactions that go with it, socialism mitigating this phenomenon. But it is neither the case that it disappears altogether in socialism since the factors behind it are connected with industrial society in general and are, therefore, to some extent at least, suprapolitical, nor is it said, by definition, that these phenomena must invariably take a more gentle course in socialism. If the processes of rapid industrialization take place in a socialist society with a predominantly agrarian structure and so create, as a result of the migrations of rural population to industrial centers, additional difficulties by breaking up the existing microstructure, the direct consequences of this on the consciousness of people may be more acute than in the stabilized and tradition-hedged capitalist society. As an example, we might take England and its entrenched intellectual resistance to existentialism, which is undoubtedly connected with deeper social causes.

Regardless of the details of this question, one thing is certain: industrialization and urbanization bring an atomization of society in their wake in the sense of an isolation of the personal and private lives of its members. This leads to a particularly painful form of alienation—the impoverishment of human personality. The more a society is atomized in terms of individual life and the more man is isolated, the greater the extent to which his life is alienated and depersonalized, since society, its relations, and institutions, are all the more opposed to him as an objectified and alien force. The more the surrounding world, including the relationships traditionally associated with the private sphere (like neighborly, family, or work ties), begins to be, or seems to be, external and alien to the individual, the more a man is alienated and as a result isolated. Here is a great problem for socialist society, which is after all supremely well equipped for the struggle against alienation and the depersonalization it involves.

But might all this be simply an intellectual fancy that is totally irrelevant to the proletarian backbone of society and utterly unintelligible to the working class? I have phrased the question in these terms, since they reflect an attitude that can be found in certain quarters with a traditional distrust of the intelligentsia (though they forget that, from the class and ideological point of view, most of it, the absolute majority, have long since become one of their own). Such a standpoint is evidence of a poor understanding of social phenomena. It is true that conscious introspection on these matters is to be found primarily among the intelligentsia, but the fact that other people do not *explicitly* formulate such problems does not mean that they do not feel these dilemmas; only that they are not clearly aware or articulate about them. The "existentialist" attitude to life is embraced not only by those who philosophize about the isolation of the individual, but also by those who display their "muddled states" in drunkenness, brutal sexuality, hooliganism, etc. This is a symptom of the same attitudes expressed in practice, not only in theory. Personally, I prefer the latter, since it brings less direct social damage.

This is, undoubtedly, a real and extensive problem that goes far beyond a narrow social group. It is a difficult one because it is also connected with the depersonalizing influence of the modern technology used in industrialization processes. These are irreversible and cannot be avoided in social progress. How then are their effects on human personality to be avoided? I doubt whether anyone today can answer this question, but it is one that has to be asked if we are to be clearly aware of the situation and able to devise some correct remedial measures.

Another problem of this type is the question of mass culture. Here we are interested in only an aspect of this problem, connected with the development of human personality. The term "mass culture" may mean *"culture spread among the masses."* Both as a postulate connected with the development and democratization of society (culture not only for the elite, but for the whole of society, since every one of its members has the right to a full development of his personality) and as a statement of the progress already achieved (it was clearly forecast by Marx in *Capital,* taking into account the need to raise the intellectual standards of the working class together with the advance of production technology and the attendant requirements for "know-how"), this definition arouses no objections. But it is obvious that "mass culture" has another meaning, equally widespread and rooted in practice, that provokes controversy and discussion: here it means simply "culture *for the masses*" in contradistinction to the culture of the elite, which is more esoteric, since it is more difficult and abstruse.

There can be no doubt that the differences in the educational standards of society bring cultural disparities among its particular classes and strata. The historical genesis and traditional structure of modern societies still prevents all cultural goods—especially those whose assimilation requires special preparation and knowledge—from becoming generally accessible. There is only one conclusion to be drawn from this, particularly from the point of view of the educative tasks of socialist society: everything must be done to fill this gap in the education of the masses as quickly as possible and raise them to a higher level, that is, make them into a cultural elite. This principle involves specific conclusions not only in the field of general education, whose standards are steadily rising and should, under communism, approach the level of Plato's Utopia, but also in the field of improving artistic culture, the tastes and esthetic preferences of the people, etc.

But this requirement, the only one that is right for socialism, is clearly opposed to the notion (and reality) of "mass culture" as a *special culture for the masses,* that is, a culture managed in such a way as to be accessible to, and accepted by, them. Since just such a "mass culture" is developing for various reasons, it aggravates in a certain specific way the phenomenon of alienation, frustrating the aim of an all-round development of human personality.

Let me here draw attention to two causes of the intensification of this phenomenon in modern societies, selected from among many others.

One is called "the commercialization of culture." Behind this term lurks an obvious desire to make the production of cultural goods—books, music, plays, films, radio, television, etc.—a paying proposition. This approach is disastrous in its social effects: pandering as it does to philistine tastes, instead of *teaching*, and raising standards, it lowers them. The result is a deluge of cheap thrillers, comics, western and "sexbomb" films and so on. This is not surprising in capitalism, indeed, within its framework these tendencies cannot be effectively combated. On the other hand, it is certainly astounding to see them appearing in socialist societies, where they go against the very nature of the social system. One of the saddest consequences of the ideological confusion in Poland in the period following the events of October, 1956, was that this sickness struck root in this country, too, and has not been fully eliminated to this day. Here it might be worth repeating a few truisms, for in certain situations even truisms have some value. The "profitability" of culture should be gauged by its effects on human consciousness, not by its financial returns. Spending on culture should be as high as a society can afford in a given economic situation; and it should be regarded as a kind of investment in the spiritual life of society, not as a profit-making venture. Culture is not a drain on money, but an investment that will one day bear fruit in a wholly different realm, not to be assessed in terms of money. Not to grasp this is simply to misunderstand the role of culture in social life and the workings of its mechanism. And the practical conclusions drawn from this misconception—the claim that culture should pay—are not only mistaken but even harmful to the educational endeavors of socialism.

The second cause is known as "intelligible culture for the masses." This requires more careful analysis, since it is specifically connected with socialism, and much more complex in character.

As in many other questions of the strategy and tactics of social development, policy in cultural matters must steer a course between two extremes: one of them is *avant-gardism*, which, presenting esoteric experiments to an unprepared and uncomprehending public, can only discourage it; the other is catering for the established tastes of the masses, resulting in a surrender to petty-bourgeois,

Philistine tastes—since, considering the structure of modern societies (including socialist societies where the majority of the working class come from a rural peasant background), these are still predominant. Consequently, what is necessary in this field is a sustained effort to educate the masses and to raise their cultural standards.

In this light the phrase "culture for the masses" has at least two meanings.

In one of them, it is a warning against stunning the "mass consumer" with a cultural production that he is not ready to assimilate and which—too bizarre to be intelligible to him—he must repudiate. In such a case, any educational activity is bound to prove abortive. And it is in this moderate sense that the frequently heard demand for a literature, art, or music accessible to the masses (that is, a culture for which they are prepared by sustained education) is undoubtedly right. On the other hand, it would be quite wrong—indeed nonsensical—to regale a peasant audience with a concert of so-called concrete music or a play by Beckett or Ionesco.

In its other sense, "culture for the masses" means that production of cultural goods should conform with the type and standards appreciated and readily accepted by the masses. Unfortunately, this second sense, although it is clearly tantamount to a lowering of cultural standards, can be seen creeping into various statements on cultural policy. It is not only dodecaphonic music, but also immortal works of genius, such as Beethoven's *Ninth Symphony* or Bach's *St. Matthew Passion* that are beyond the masses. So perhaps both of them should be scrapped? And should they be replaced with what is accepted by everybody—light music, jazz, pop songs—as the only musical fare, chosen by music ignorance? Shall we do the same with literary masterpieces (after all, the masses, unless properly prepared, will be puzzled not only by Joyce or Kafka, but also by Goethe's *Faust*), or painting (what about El Greco, the impressionists, let alone the more far-out trends), etc.?

These are, of course, purely rhetorical questions—I only wish to prove how false this doctrine is. Without the right to innovation—which as a rule goes over the heads of most of its contemporaries, and not only the masses—and without the right to swim against the prevailing current, culture would be doomed to stagnation, and thus to destruction. Without experiments, intelligible only to the cultural elite in the best sense of the word "elite," there would be no cultural progress or development. Thus, the fact that the masses do not like or understand certain elements of the culture of their time does not necessarily mean that these elements are wrong; it usually means that their eyes or ears—in other words, their tastes— have not been properly formed and trained. The conclusion is obvious: instead of bringing artists down to the level of the public, it is necessary to raise the masses to the level of leading representatives of culture. Consequently, one's own ignorance or poor taste must not be made a yardstick of beauty and progress. On the contrary, the lessons taught by the history of art—and culture in general— should be learned and humility exercised in relations with the experts, particularly the innovators, who are paving the way to new currents—strange as they may seem to us, since we are used to something else, but gradually becoming a commonplace for our children. Nobody can force us to like things that go against our tastes—but common sense should warn us against making our own taste an absolute measure and show us the need for moderation and modesty in these matters.

What practical conclusions can be drawn in this context for the educational action undertaken to assure the fullest possible development of personality? It is a normal law of social development that there are discrepancies between a society's established pattern of cultural standards and what may be the nucleus of a future culture; since it cannot be overthrown by any social system, it is necessary to counteract human conservatism with its tendency to perpetuate certain models and stereotypes. This can only be done by the right kind of education in which new models and their intellectual values are made accessible to the widest circles of the public. Here what matters most is that the choice (after all, it concerns society as a whole and results in the acceptance of certain ideas as a lasting treasured part of social culture and the rejection of others as "ideological shavings") should be made with a full awareness of all the issues involved. But to achieve this end, society and its administrative bodies must not play the role of censors who claim to know what no one can know about the value and future prospects of given trends and ideas, and who prevent them from reaching the public as allegedly worthless or even harmful. On the contrary, the administrative organs of society should act as information channels and as teachers, bringing all that is novel to the consumer of cultural goods and supplying him with a maximum amount of objective information about the history and kinship of the new ideas. In the final analysis, it is society that is the supreme —and only—arbiter in these matters, the only one capable of pronouncing final verdicts.

It is only along this road that we can comply with the socialist ideal of education and of an all-round development of human personality. It is only in this way that we can counteract the alienation of a given sphere of human life (in this case artistic tastes and opinions) and, by attacking conservatism, encourage the development of human personality towards that goal of unattainable perfection.

The last problem to be mentioned in this context is similarly related to the sphere of consciousness. I have in mind the process of scientific development, inevitably leading to narrow specialization and so to an ever greater disintegration of knowledge, while the goal of a full human personality predicates exactly the opposite evolution—towards a universal, integrated knowledge, utopian as this may sound today. Here is another of the many problems facing the communist man—even though, given the objective character of the processes involved, it transcends any particular system.

The ideal image of the wise men of ancient times—the philosopher, "a true friend of knowledge" or of the Renaissance thinker, with his universality and his all-embracing knowledge of reality, has long been out of date. Today, as Bertrand Russell has wittily observed, we tend to know more and more about less and less until the day when where we know everything about nothing. This is not because people are less intelligent today, or because of the class nature of society. It is an objective process: the bounds of our knowledge are spreading and can no longer be encompassed by any single mind.

In a period of a crashing flood of specialized literature, which no one, even in his limited field, can fully master, at a time when human knowledge is not only growing rapidly, but is undergoing a continuous revolution, the growing specialization of scientists, steadily narrowing down the field of their pursuits and isolating them from even closely related areas of interest, is an objective process, equally valid under capitalism and under socialism.

On the one hand, the process is not only necessary but even progressive, since it promotes human knowledge about the world and men's ability to control and transform this world for their own interest; and on the other hand, it is also undesirable and reactionary, since, as it disintegrates human knowledge and breaks up our picture of the world into ever more loosely (if at all) connected fragments, it tends to check the advance of knowledge and thus to reduce man's ability to understand the world, to master and transform it. Particularly distressing in this respect is the deepening abyss between knowledge of nature and knowledge of man. And so, we have a process that, as often happens, is characterized by opposed tendencies but that also—and this is much rarer—directly affects the formation of human personality.

Integration of science is one of the outstanding topics of intellectual life today: the most enlightened minds, capable of seeing beyond the purely technical aspects of their work, are dismayed by the growing process of disintegration. Unfortunately, little of practical value has so far been said on the subject. And, I fear, little more can be said unless we forget about the present conditions and, turning to the future, leave some freedom for a little fantasy. The history of science has taught us that predictions of future developments have more than once proved an important factor in the development of science.

It cannot be claimed that no efforts are being made to promote integration: for a start there is a great deal of discussion, and there are even attempts to get experts on related matters to "reach an understanding" and work out a common conceptual apparatus. These endeavors are, as a rule, abortive, and backfire by leaving— as far as I am concerned at least—a depressing impression, since they only prove how little specialists in related disciplines (and sometimes even in the same one) have to tell each other and how feebly they can communicate. (I personally have often seen this among philosophers, sociologists, or linguists.)

What can be done?

As I see it, the future society will have two choices.

One of them is connected with the need and possibility of a change in the educational system. This system is incredibly conservative—and whatever reforms have been introduced by socialism are insignificant compared with capitalist countries.

What matters above all is general education. It is only through a radical change in its very foundations that we can overcome the stalemate produced by the specialized dismemberment of our knowledge of the world and come closer to the ideal of an integrated science and a universal man. This is certainly true—but both the length and scope of general schooling militate against this objective.

Instruction today takes as much time and has the same program as at the outset of the nineteenth century. Yet human knowledge has so greatly increased, both in amount and quality, that we are actually living in an altogether different world. This fact is not reflected either in the length or in the curricula of education—not even as compared with Greek antiquity, which knew perfectly well that education in the arts (including the culture of speech still completely ignored in our schools) is one of the essential factors in the formation of the complete man as summed up in the phrase *kalos kai agathos*. Surprisingly, this can be only remedied by reverting to an ancient utopia—which now, at last, can be made real. According to Plato, those destined to manage public affairs—and thus a whole social stratum—were to study various arts and sciences until they were forty and only then, rich in knowledge and matured with experience of life, were they to be allowed to engage in the practice of government. But how insignificant the corpus of knowledge was in Plato's days compared with what we have to learn today, particularly if we are bent on educating a universal man.

Consequently, a considerably longer course of study is essential to provide a solid general grounding as a basis for specialization—which will then proceed smoothly and will not cripple human personality by turning man into a narrowly specialized "scientific craftsman," often embarrassingly ignorant of everything outside his own field. This naturally entails a thorough reform of curricula, which will have to be carefully integrated at all levels and supplemented with those branches of learning that do not form a part of the student's later specialized research—and this would be a radical departure from the principle now prevailing in both our secondary and our higher education. It is a problem in itself to understand man's contact with life and practice; this is particularly important at a time when students are much more adult, if other maladies are to be avoided. All these are open questions, barely touched on outside the realm of utopia; to answer them we must above all realize that these are *real* questions and *feasible* tasks. And we must know how long the necessary reforms will take and whether society will have sufficient time to execute them.

Is it practicable to extend the period of instruction? I am convinced that it is not only possible but necessary, since one day society will be faced with the problem of free time. This is directly connected with automation: as a result of the revolutionary changes in science, we are on the threshold of a new industrial revolution. Everybody knows this, but not everybody has sufficient imagination to visualize, even in the vaguest outlines, the effects of this revolution. Its most important feature will be automation—and this will not only fulfill the once utopian dream of the disappearance of differences between intellectual and manual work or between work in the town and on the land; it will also liberate man from Jehovah's curse: in the sweat of thy brow shalt thou toil. This is less remote than it seems—and, compared to the rest of the world, we are obviously trailing in our analysis of what can happen. For it must be remembered that such socially adverse effects of automation as large-scale unemployment will be experienced not only by the capitalist countries, but also by those societies that, although they have abolished the private ownership of the means of production and do not fear unemployment, will have to face mankind's mighty new problem—the problem of leisure. For the return to the Garden of Eden is neither simple nor easy. Work is not only a curse: it is also a source of satisfaction and there is no way of knowing whether man will be happy when rid of it. Neither can it be guaranteed that —without previous training—he will make the right use of his leisure. This seems to be the problem of Swedish youth, for instance, not infrequently driven to the verge of pathology by their easy, prosperous life; it only proves that in unfavorable social conditions, well-being can turn sour. Another important factor is that when not accompanied by proper measures to occupy people in their spare time, any rapid reduction of working time is bound to result in a growth of crime and not only in capitalist countries. Briefly, to solve the problem of leisure it is absolutely essential to frame special programs of interesting and socially useful occupations to keep people busy in their spare time. What can be more welcome in this situation than a comprehensive program of practical general education designed to achieve an all-round development of human personality?

All this can be done; what is more, it is socially indispensable that it should be done—not only because of the manpower surpluses that will be caused by automation, but also because of the need to form a human personality according to communist ideals. As far as the preliminary thinking and preparations are concerned, the task is indeed urgent. Granted, this is not a matter of the next few years—we have other, more immediate worries and sceptics may well smile when listening to these discussions. But these are foolish sceptics, very foolish indeed—for failure to visualize and understand the future developments, to have a realistic vision of the future, is only evidence of narrow-mindedness, not of wisdom or realism. It is not just a question of a single generation; the year 2000—a model of which is already being projected by thoughtful men all over the world—will not only mark the end of our millennium: it will also be the beginning of a new era. We are on the threshold of the greatest revolution in human history and we must not let it take us by surprise. As has been said, a prosperity for which society has not been prepared can be a source of difficulties and disorders, even of unhappiness. In this respect, socialist society has the extraordinary chance of staking out the path for the whole human race.

In any case, this new perspective radiates a gleam of hope in the seemingly hopeless dilemma—which is also a great threat to human personality—of the incompatibility between the general progress of human knowledge and its dismemberment and disintegration, threatening to cripple the human personality.

There is another factor that—at least as far as the vision of the future is concerned—may be of assistance. I am thinking of "electronic brains"—or machines with a "memory."

The great problem facing civilization today—and beginning to affect human personality and the possibilities of its development—is the tremendous amount of information necessary for the steadily increasing volume of our knowledge of the world: this is already more than the human brain can assimilate. One solution is to entrust this mass of information to the "memory" of the automatic machines to be placed at the disposal of every individual while reserving for the human brain the indispensable modicum of general knowledge and the function of its intellectual "processing." This is at present a very vague program indeed—what is more, there is little chance as yet of making it more precise. What do we mean by saying that machines will store information in their "memory" and man will only retain some general knowledge? It is arguable whether—and if so to what extent—this is in fact possible, even on the assumption that "general" information will be appropriately programmed as a certain synthesis of the knowledge acquired by people in an uninterrupted course of study with the detailed data collected by the machines. But it is incontestable that this is an extremely valuable aid in the amassing of knowledge and that the further development of these machines may open up new—as yet unpredictable—possibilities. In any case, this is one more indication that the difficult question of the full development of human personality can find a new and interesting solution in the future. The problem is worth thinking over—if only to prevent its slipping out of our concern.

Problems of the individual—and so also problems of the individual in the communist society—culminate in the question about the meaning of life. The human individual "exists" as long as he lives—and so all that concerns him falls within the great cycle of events with birth and death as beginning and end. Questions about life and its sense, although in most cases posed in vague and ambiguous terms, are from many points of view among the most important in philosophical reflection about man. But what do those who ask such questions actually have in mind?

When we ponder the meaning of life, we are above all concerned with the *value of life*—we want to know whether life is worth living.

A very old question indeed—whether it is asked in deadly earnest with the intention of drawing practical conclusions should the answer happen to be negative or simply for the relief that a bit of grumbling can give. Thus we read in the Bible "Vanity of vanities, all is vanity." The Stoics, on the other hand, maintained that instead of consoling men because of the inevitability of death, they should be persuaded of the reasons for living.

However that may be, the chief stimulus to meditation on the sense of life is the imminence of death, our own or more frequently the actual loss of someone we love. Despite their indubitable fear of death, men regard their own only as a possibility while that of a near one is felt in all its horror. In fact, it is only this experience that brings home to them the reality of their own death. If this were not so, if people were constantly aware of the implacable approach of death, they would certainly go mad. To lead a normal life, they must be conscious of the flow of time—that life blood in their veins —only on some special occasions. In Rilke's *The Notebooks of Malte-Laurids,* Brigge Nicholas Kusmitch found he could live no longer when he became aware of the passing of time and its value.

But the question *whether life is worth living* is not only prompted by death, which, by its very inevitability, challenges all human efforts and endeavors—particularly when these are viewed in the light of individual life as a frame of reference for all evaluation. It is also brought on by physical or mental suffering, which, particularly when undeserved, makes us ask: Why suffer? Is it worthwhile?

We may now have a better insight into this version of the question about the sense of life that makes us wonder whether life is worth living—but we still do not know how to answer it. How shall we justify our answer so that it can convince others?

We are, of course, interested in the affirmative answer, founded on the belief that although death is inevitable, and although there is no escape from suffering—particularly that caused by the death of those we love—life is worth living and in this sense life has a meaning. But why? If we are to carry conviction, and if our attitude is not to remain merely an expression of our purely personal and quite unsubstantiated sentiments, we must also answer this question.

This makes it perfectly clear how slippery is the ground on which we are treading and how much our thinking differs, not only from the exact or empirical sciences, but also from epistemological or ontological enquiries based on the special sciences. In the deductive disciplines we can speak of certainty, in empirical ones of probability, which may have various degres of justification but always depends upon facts. This is also true, although to a different extent and in another form, of scientific philosophy science. But the position is different in the question that concerns us here: for the object is not to ascertain the truth or falsity of certain assertions, but to appraise and evaluate. And, in this field it is disputable whether description can legitimately be followed by evaluation, since it is doubtful whether a true description automatically authorizes the passing of a judgment. It is not my intention to discuss the theoretical problems of axiology; I want only to emphasize how *varied* these questions are and how many additional difficulties they produce.

A logical positivist might object that my statements and judgments cannot unequivocally be reduced to verifiable facts and that I am in danger of lapsing into subjectivism. As far as this goes he would certainly be right. But he would *not* be right to argue that this is, therefore, a pseudo-problem that may not even be considered. If he did, he would be assuming something that requires proof—he would be by definition postulating a criterion of meaningfulness and science, which prejudges the matter at its start.

In actual fact, a philosopher dealing, for example, with the problem of attitudes to life, adopts a different procedure from someone concerned with the method of natural science. He *must* do so, since this is implied in the problem that interests him. But this does not mean that his mode of procedure is illegitimate or unscientific. He, too, generalizes the facts of experience and bases his findings on the results of such special sciences as sociology and psychology. But his procedure is different, since, as we have pointed out, he does not simply describe but evaluates. And evaluating means that he must choose a frame of reference, a scale of values. Naturally, the choice is not arbitrary but socially determined. But social determination does not exhaust the matter. There are also other factors, including psychological and physiological factors, involving what is clearly an individual element. The situation repeats itself whenever choice is implied—including the choice of a general outlook on the world. But this involves not only the intellectual, but also the emotional—and thus the stage is set for subjectivism. It appears in different forms and to a greater extent than in considering the method of natural science.

This is precisely why the very process of generalization also assumes a different form: the distance between the empirical ascertained facts and their philosophical generalization becomes greater —and so does the possibility of different interpretation and outlook. In this field, the philosopher's method is more that of the ancient sage, meditating on human life, than that of the experimental scientist, simply because the latter's mode of procedure is of little use in this case. We have here an altogether different sphere of analysis, and at least at the present level of our knowledge (although it is doubtful whether the progress of science will ever change anything in this respect), it does not lend itself to investigation by methods of the exact or natural sciences.

A very unpleasant situation, to be sure, and personally, I would be much happier if we could say something more secure and decisive about these questions. Unfortunately, we cannot. On the other hand, distressing as it may be, this situation neither removes the problem nor reduces its importance. Anyone who is peeved by the imprecise and uncertain character of the question, and in the interests of "science" refuses to contemplate it, will be defeated by the antagonist who is prepared to come to grips with these problems—even though he may often present it, indeed mystify it, with a totally untrue light. In any case, there is no blanket recipe to provide a scientific approach to different problems of investigation. One principle, however, should be observed: they must be treated in as scientific a spirit as the framework of the actual achievements of a given discipline allows. This is precisely why a philosopher working on the problem of the sense of life should not go beyond suggesting a choice of certain solutions. He should realize that this subject does not admit of a clearcut and authoritative decision. If this is not scientific philosophy, yet it does not mean—as it seems to the logical positivists—that it is unscientific. Such oppositions of "scientific" and "unscientific" is simply meaningless, here, since this is a type of philosophizing that does not lend itself to such classification. Logically, it would be equally fatuous to ask whether love is a quadratic, and from a negative answer infer that it is not a quadratic. We have said that in his reflection on such questions as the sense of life the philosopher resembles the ancient sage. But the sage and the scholar are two different things. Scholarly learning and wisdom often go hand in hand, but they are not the same. The scholar is someone who has mastered knowledge of a section of reality; the sage is a man who is intelligent and experienced; particularly with regard to the problems of relations with other people. It is not hard to see—and in any case practice points in this direction—that erudition in some specialized field is not identical with wisdom, either in the sense of general intelligence or of experience of life and the ability to get along with others. On the contrary, it is quite possible to be a wise man—a sage—without possessing any specialized knowledge.

In the field that interests us here, a philosopher behaves more like a sage than a scientific scholar: his work is appraised in such terms as "wise–unwise," "useful–useless," and not "scientific–unscientific." There is nothing disparaging in this—it is simply a different field of enquiry. In some situations, it is the wise and experienced person who can be of most help to his fellow-men. A philosopher, therefore, should be not only a man of learning, but also a man of wisdom. In this case, the element of scientific learning is not totally unimportant. Knowledge, a special kind of knowledge, is *helpful* in pondering life and human relations. Solution of such problems as "the meaning of life" depends on many factors, but primarily on one's general view of the world. Here there is an obvious connection with opinions that can be classified as "scientific" or "unscientific." But it must be stressed once again that the description "scientific opinion" or "unscientific opinion" cannot be directly applied either to the affirmative view that life has a meaning and is worth living or to its denial.

But let us revert to our main problem: how can we answer the question about the meaning of life (as interpreted above), and how can we justify this answer?

This is, of course, crucially dependent on the philosophical context of our reply. We have just pointed out that among the many factors on which a view of this problem depends, the most important is the general view of the world.

To a believer, the matter is simple: life is always meaningful (that is, it is under all conditions worth living), because even suffering, pain, and death are part of the design of a higher being who will compensate for these ills after death or who has imposed them as a punishment for misdeeds in this life. It must be admitted that in many cases, including this one, it is convenient to be a believer: even the most difficult problems become very simple. But the price is high—a sacrifice of the scientific attitude, and this is why it is more and more difficult to afford the "comfort" and convenience of this simple solution.

But in nonreligious terms—regardless of the philosophical point of view—it is impossible to answer the question about the sense of life in a general, and generally binding, way. Deciding, in a given case, whether life is worth living depends on an assessment of the conditions and prospects of that life—and this, obviously is up to the individual whose life is at stake. This evaluation must involve all the individually experienced elements that can be summed up and evaluated only by the person concerned. His fellow-men can only help him in drawing up the balance of positive and negative by reminding him of all that is good in life, which, under the impact of some exceptional strain, can easily be forgotten: that man has only one life, that time softens all suffering, that man has obligations towards his family and society, etc. But that is all; we can do no more. For unless we are ready to accept absolute moral injunctions, which are ultimately religious (whether or not we believe in supernatural beings), we cannot prejudge the individual's answer; we cannot make his choice *for* him—nobody can do it except himself. All we can do is tell him: if I were you, this would be my choice. That's all.

But those who ask about the meaning of life are also concerned with its *purpose:* they want to know why we live. This is closely connected with the first question—is life worth living?—but, nevertheless, not quite the same. It is surely, in practice, a more important and more interesting version of the question about the sense of life.

It is asked by everybody anxious to know *how* he should live. Our behavior—particularly in difficult conflict-laden situations—depends on what we consider to be our goal in life, on our hierarchy of values—of the ends that can be secured by our action or lack of it. Naturally, this is primarily true of those who consciously reflect on these things. But in those cases, too, where as a result of education in the broadest sense men are spontaneously swayed by personal models, the problems of the 'meaning of life,' and the influence of one or another answer given to it, make themselves felt, if only indirectly. For these answers are found not only in treatises and learned discourse, but also in the conduct of the hero who sacrifices his life for some ideal; of the traitor who goes over to the enemy for money; of the fighter for truth who ignores his private interests for its sake; or the opportunist who forgets his own convictions to curry favor, and so on.

Thus, if someone asks us about the sense of life so that he may find the purpose to which all his actions and choices should be subordinated, as to a supreme principle; in other words, when he wants to know how he should live, he is simply seeking *our* views on the subject and the reasons for it. This is different from the case when we are asked to make a decision for someone else—in a matter that is solely withing his discretion. In this case, I not only can answer the question which, after all, concerns my own attitude but

I also can and should defend—propagate as it were—all the valid points in its favor.

Once more a distinction should be drawn between the religious and the secular approaches—these are not only different, but they belong to diametrically opposed patterns of thought.

From the standpoint of faith, the question is again a simple and "convenient" one: man does not have to think, since he is bound by heteronomous rules, stemming from outside him, from God, to which he owes obedience. These norms prescribe the purpose of a decent life—and thus instruct man in the meaning of life in the present context. And that is all. There is no problem whatsoever— all that is needed is better understanding of the divine laws made known to us by Revelation. It might, of course, be argued that these norms are of human origin: it is not God who creates man, but men who create gods in their likeness. But no such arguments will convince a man whose mind is shut to rational propositions, or who stubbornly resists them for emotional reasons. To anyone who believes in Revelation the falsity of such arguments is a foregone conclusion. Even so there is only one way to deal with these atti-tudes: to draw continual attention to the contradictions between the religious and scientific standpoints, and to stress the necessity of choosing between them. This, I feel, is the only effective method of combating religious prejudice. And those who tenaciously insist on the religious solution can only be told that it is unacceptable to the scientifically minded and is beyond intellectual consideration.

What of non-religious attempts to fathom the sense of life? Here it must be pointed out that in view of the age-old preoccupation of philosophers with these problems, exhaustive classifications of all the possible approaches have long been made—and, apart from new names, it is hardly possible to think of some new solution. One might easily say with Solomon that there is nothing new under the sun.

Yet this would be a wrong conclusion, for if we go beyond ab-stract description and probe the social context in which our ends are pursued, the situation changes radically. If, therefore, as a Marxist, I recognize socialist humanism as my supreme principle of action, arising from the goals I have in view, then I shall see that my attitude fits into the pigeon-hole classification of "social eudae-monism" (in a specific sense of this term). But at the same time I can perceive the characteristics that distinguish my position from the others in this rubric. I shall also see that my sentiments on this matter are related to my general view of the world—to Marxism, in the broadest sense of the word.

I have already stressed the close connection between the answers given to questions about the sense of life and the world-views en-tertained by their authors. The relation is not simple and direct cause and effect; for example, a materialist does not necessarily choose altruism and the idealist egoism, or vice versa. Either of these attitudes may be embraced by the materialist or the idealist, the believer in a static theory of the world or a dynamic, etc.—as could be illustrated by hundreds of examples from the long history of the problem. These, incidentally, would be merely general, ab-stract descriptions of some ideal attitudes, which, in particular cases, can be variously interpreted. After all, pure altruism is, in real life, as much a fiction as pure egoism.

Social eudaemonism is the view that the supreme goal of life is the greatest happiness of the broadest masses of people as the only way to happiness (the identification of this view with a form of utilitarianism is, I think, both mistaken and historically un-founded). It can be professed by supporters of various ontological and epistemological doctrines. But socialist humanism cannot be avowed by a non-Marxist. For what matters in this case—(although this view, too, might be classified under the heading of "social eudaemonism" in a certain sense of the phrase—the phrase is so vague, after all, that it can be interpreted in a number of different ways)—is not a general formulation, to which adherents of various theories can subscribe, but a well-defined concept, so closely con-nected with other parts of a systematic outlook that it cannot be espoused without espousing the whole system.

The principles of socialist humanism and its practical guidance stem from definite theoretical attitudes. What matters is, first, a specific conception of the human individual as a social product as "an ensemble of social relations," which helps to clarify the prob-lem of human attitudes and their formation. Second, a specific approach to the relationship between the individual and society, based on the conception of social development represented by historical materialism. And third, with historical materialism, the contention that ideals can only be realized in the appropriate social conditions, otherwise they degenerate into utopianism.

As a result, instead of vague theorizing or wishful thinking we have a body of scientifically well-founded views—from which practical conclusions can be drawn as guides to action.

A supporter of socialist humanism believes that personal happiness can only be attained through social happiness—since it is only an expansion of the sphere of human personality and the possibility of satisfying the manifold aspirations of man in society that create a lasting basis for the fulfillment of one's own longings. But he is not satisfied with misty appeals for good will or brotherly love—although these are his most cherished ideals, the violation of which is the main cause of suffering. A believer in socialist humanism realizes that his goal can only be achieved by struggle and that the cause he is serving is socially determined, and requires specific changes in social conditions. In antagonistic societies, he is thus struck above all by the connection between the fulfillment of his objectives and the change in property relations together with the class system called forth by them. In the name of humanity and brotherly love, he proclaims the class struggle, and paradoxical as this may seem, it is his love of man that makes him avow hatred of those who oppress man.

A supporter of socialist humanism knows that man is a product of social conditions, but he also knows that these conditions are the work of man.

He is a dialectician—and this is precisely why he can fight, while professing peace.

His socialist ideal is most closely linked to his concept of humanism—hence his "socialist humanism." Socialism as an ideal is the logical expression of this humanism—but it is also the material fulfillment of humanist ideals. In the name of these ideals, the adherent of socialist humanism is prepared to make the greatest sacrifices—and so he can himself call for sacrifice and demand it from others. He believes in love of neighbor, but despises all those who pay lip service to this noble idea but betray it in their deeds. For socialist humanism is not merely an obligation to believe in certain ideals; it also means the waging of a struggle to make these ideals become reality. Perhaps its most important aspect is persuading other people that socialist humanism is right, transforming their outlook.

Is this social eudaemonism? In a sense, yes. But there is little meaning in this designation as such. What matters is a coherent system of opinions, which, in this particular form, is only possible when grounded on Marxism; it is its consequence, and in turn, its foundation. Thus, it is of deepest significance to the solution of the essential problem of the sense of life whether one is a Marxist or not. For only a Marxist can become a spokesman for the highest form of humanism: *socialist* humanism.

Conclusion

Mankind is now at a revolutionary crossroads. It sounds like pathos; it is just the banal truth.

Human knowledge, particularly technology, has reached a point where it can be both enormously beneficial and enormously destructive. Discovery of the uses of nuclear power has opened up practically inexhaustible sources of energy; these have ushered in the age of the conquest of space, and transforming man from a master of the earth into the potential master of the universe. Electronics has made the dream of full automation of production into a reality, and this means that many may one day be wholly free of manual labor. "Electronic brains," though still in their infancy, have so greatly intensified the functions of the human memory and other intellectual functions that dreams of an omniscient being seem near realization. At the same time, man has come close to the source of the mystery of life as he gradually unlocks more and more of Nature's secrets. When he finally learns how to produce synthetically animated matter; when he learns how to regenerate living tissues and prolong human life (and he is not far from this either); and when he can use biochemistry to influence the sex as well as other somatic and psychic traits of the human embryo (and human knowledge is making huge strides towards this objective as well) —then mankind, which has so long been climbing up the steps to the throne of the biblical Jehovah, will reach for His Scepter.

Never before has man's power been so greatly enhanced by his knowledge; and no preceding age—not even the days when Prometheus offered men the gift of the fire he had stolen from the gods —has been so rich in revolutionary change, in visions of a possible future when human experience will be equal to that of the mythical gods.

A century ago, the vision of communism must have seemed a utopia. Today there seems nothing utopian in the demands for a distribution of wealth according to needs; for freedom from physical labor, and thus the abolition of differences between manual and intellectual occupations, with all the social consequences; or the disappearance of differences between agricultural and industrial labor, with similar but even more important, consequences. All this, theoretically at least, is realistic, for the ways and means to achieve these objectives are already visible—and they steadily grow more abundant. To Marx's vision of progress we can now add many more elements, particularly in the field of health and eugenics, of which he himself could not even have dreamed and which he would have certainly—and rightly—dismissed as sheer fantasy, like Fourier's men with eyes on their tails.

For the first time in human history a brave new world, a genuine one, not the ghostly fantasy of Aldous Huxley, seems within reach. It is a world of men capable of satisfying all their material requirements, of physically and intellectually perfect man, suited to Plato's *Kalogatic,* close to the Marxian ideal of an all-round, universal human personality. For the first time in the history of man, this is all potentially here. The ideas of Marx's humanism and his vision of communist society are today firmly rooted in real possibilities. But everybody, even the most hardened dogmatist, is perfectly aware that the possibility is not yet reality. This gives rise to at least two issues:

Are these possibilities *bound* to become realities—and if not, what are the basic conditions of their fulfillment?

Will their transformation into realities *automatically* solve the problem of human happiness—in other words will it provide sufficient conditions for such happiness ?

To the first question Marxism long ago gave answer that has lost nothing of its freshness and splendor: the possibilities now looming will not become a reality by fate—it will depend on social conditions—and these in turn on human *struggle* and *action,* taken into account as an element of social forces and their laws of development.

In *The Communist Manifesto,* where he outlined his theory of transition from one socio-economic system to another, Marx was not naively optimistic about the *inevitability* of the victory of progress as a result of changes in the mode of production. The case of the Roman Empire showed that the struggle may end in disaster, not in progress. This is a general thesis; it follows that if a new socio-economic formation is to triumph, the conditions for its victory must be *fought* for by the whole of society; social development is not an automatic, spontaneous outcome of changes in the economic base—an extremely vital role is played by the human element, by *human activity*. In his own age, Marx could not foresee the destructive possibilities of the era of atomic energy—all the more so since he did not anticipate socialism's victory in only part of the world, the consequent political division of the world, and the extension of the class struggle to the sphere of armed conflict between states. But today we can see, with much more clarity, the horror of his purely theoretical dilemma of progress or disaster. What he conceived as a possible destruction of certain countries and systems is now assuming the ominous dimensions of global extermination—not only of mankind, but of all life on this earth.

That the brilliant possibilities of human development opened up by man's genius may also be the source of the destruction of mankind is already a commonplace to which people are slowly becoming accustomed, if not reconciled. And a sense of the alienation of these powerful forces—which man has created to serve him and which are now not only independent of their maker, but are in fact his enemies—has given rise to a widespread and far-reaching feeling of frustration. Directly or indirectly that frustration affects the life of modern society.

The Marxist answers to these problems have been proved during many years of practice: the only solution is a relentless striving for the conditions of progress. Since the only real danger is war—and the extermination of mankind as its result—the Marxist formula is pressed today as the "struggle for peace." Whoever understands Marxism will understand that in the present situation this is neither an opportunist nor a tactical catchphrase.

The battle for peace can take a variety of forms, from building up the power of the socialist states so as to deter the militarists on the other side of the barricade to an ideological struggle for the minds and hearts of the peoples of the world. In a situation where only genuine madmen can desire another world war, since even a criminal would balk at an act that would result in his own extinction, the ideological struggle acquires the decisive importance of which the young Marx once wrote. And it is this struggle that gives added weight to Marxist humanism and the Marxist philosophy of man.

In the struggle for defense of peace and social progress, there is no more powerful and effective weapon than humanism and the philosophy of man—if only because they are concerned with those matters on which all people feel insecure and with those questions to which all men seek answers. Here Marxism, at least potentially, is particularly well equipped: it possesses a realistic theory that has been proved historically to be closely linked with practice—and this appeals to the common sense of those who are particularly afflicted by the prevailing conditions. Another reason why Marxism should attach special importance to humanism and the philosophy of man is that its deficiencies in these matters—which, as explained in our introductory remarks, spring from historical factors—are today being seized on by its ideological opponents; and these attacks are particularly dangerous, since they tend to undermine its authority. In the Marxist camp, this can be ignored only by those who do not understand the essential meaning of Marxism or by those conservatives and dogmatists who, ignorant of the central creative character of Marxist ideas, wrongly believe that, since a certain interpretation and a certain language were accepted in the past, they must have been right and are the only authorized version today. The fate of such opinions is sealed—and if they are ever mentioned in the future it will merely be to recall that even revolutionary movements are not free of intellectual conservatism and traditionalism.

While relatively simple answers can be given to the first question, matters seem to be much more involved when we turn to the second.

Are the present possibilities of human development—on the assumption, of course, that they become a reality—a guarantee of human happiness in the new world?

The question is difficult because of the many meanings it contains; within the framework of Marxist theory there is an additional embarrassment: unlike the first question, it has never been regarded as a real problem for the simple reason that a positive answer was considered self-evident.

In trying to discover whether the present revolutionary changes in the conditions of human life will make men happy, we are actually asking one of the two questions: can man in the new conditions be happier than before? or will they eradicate all causes of unhappiness so that man will achieve the ideal of complete happiness?

In the light of what has been said about human happiness, the answer to the latter question can only be, No. Absolute peace prevails only in the graveyard. As long as he is alive, man's peace may always be troubled and—no matter how rich and powerful he is—he can have many reasons for being unhappy. Marxists are not charlatans, and they do not delude people with a utopian vision of absolute happiness—which in any case would be so boring as to be psychologically tantamount to frustration and unhappiness. What Marxists do promise is only the gradual elimination (not the abolition at one stroke) of the causes of general misfortune—that is, they are committed to creating the *possibilities* for a happy life for every man. They do not promise anything more—but what they do promise is a great deal.

The matter is much more involved when the question about future society is posed in more modest terms—when we want to know whether the new conditions will make men happier than before.

When interpreted in a certain way, the answer must be positive. Obviously, with the elimination of the causes of mass unhappiness, even of the normal adversities of life, men will certainly be happier than those who had to suffer because of these misfortunes. A well fed man is happier than a hungry man and one who can satisfy all his material needs is happier than when he is poor and needy. Similarly, knowledge is better than ignorance. The theory that the poor and ignorant are happier than the rich and educated was invented by the privileged to soothe their conscience. But there is a bit of truth even in these silly fables: wealth, power, knowledge, and so on, certainly cannot guarantee happiness—a cliché, perhaps, but with a profound meaning. It is worth remembering today, when, on the threshold of a new era of unprecedented wealth and human power, we wonder whether men will be happy in the future.

That this is not a matter of automatic necessity has already been made clear. But the problem cannot—and should not—be restricted to negation.

As long as men are men—even if each of them has his own aircraft, has nothing else to occupy him but the development of his personality, and spends his vacations on the Milky Way—they will face conflicts in their lives and will have reasons for personal unhappiness. And as long as various social alienations persist—and these can only be abolished by abolishing society and men themselves—there will exist the social sources and causes of these conflicts. Elimination of the social sources of unhappiness that existed in the past does not at all mean that there might not be new causes of an even greater unhappiness in the future society. It is, therefore, impossible to guarantee that the new conditions, although in a certain respect (from the point of view of the possibilities of a happy life) much better than the old ones, will not be worse in other respects. This is all the more impossible, since even today we are witnessing some adverse and unexpected effects of industrialization, mass culture, etc.

There is one thing that can and should be done in this field: observe the facts and, with due attention to the problem of human happiness, we must analyze these facts and consciously counteract those of the adverse effects which can be foreseen or, even worse, may already be detected. In this field, as in many others related to the individual and society, there is no absolute guarantee of success—we can only *fight* for a proper line of development.

This entails particularly responsible tasks for socialist society—and for Marxism as a balanced theory of its development. The tasks are even more difficult, since Marxism is a science that does not claim to have prophetic gifts; and so it has no ready-made recipes or formulas in this respect. What is worse, Marxism is full of gaps—historically justified, it is true, but nevertheless very distressing.

Pride of place here is due to a broadly conceived theory of the individual, his life, his relations with society, and his happiness. Such a philosophy of man—conceived as a scientific generalization of research in the various branches of science and not as pure speculation—means that Marxism must encourage enquiry in the fields of psychology (including the problem of the subconscious, problems which cannot be disposed of by condemning Freud's theories, although it is by no means true that Freudianism should be accepted as the only true theory of the subconscious), sociology in its various forms, social pedagogics and the other sciences of man. The general tendency should be toward an integration of all these disciplines.

Marxism has not—and, as has been pointed out, cannot have —finished answers to these questions. But thanks to its method, it has a better chance than other theories to arrive at the right answers. This is a great deal—but it must be borne in mind that this is only a possibility, a chance, which will depend on whether and how research is conducted. For only he who seeks shall find.

As far as the Marxist philosophy of man is concerned, two conclusions can be drawn from these remarks.

One is addressed to those who are still unwilling to admit that this is a legitimate field of research within Marxism. But its legitimacy is confirmed not only by historical considerations—the genesis of Marxist theory—but also by the sharp and immediate necessity to guide the social development of socialism on behalf of man and for the sake of man. In other words, it is necessitated by Marxist humanism.

The other conclusion is addressed to those who, although claiming solidarity with socialism, felt at one time, or perhaps still feel, that the problems of the individual can only be discussed outside Marxism—or even by *rejecting* Marxism. However, the opposite is true: it is *only on the basis of Marxism* that the philosophy of man can be cultivated in a consistent and effective way—in compliance with common sense and in close touch with practice. Marxism's deficiencies in this field only show that Marxists have for many years—and for diverse reasons—paid no attention to these questions; but they are no proof that they cannot, or will not, tackle them. As a psychological reaction to the narrow, dogmatic

Marxism of the Stalinist era, a belief has developed in some intellectual circles—it is an international phenomenon—that progress in the socialist movement can only be achieved by going beyond Marxism—not by promoting its development, but by denying its basic principles, rejecting it. But the truth is that genuine progress, true innovation in the socialist movement, can only be achieved within the framework of Marxist thought. Anyone who fails to grasp this truth is not only heading for intellectual disaster of his own; he is also harming a cause to which he is subjectively committed.

Endnotes

INTRODUCTION

1. M. Rubel, *Karl Marx, Essai de biographie intellectuelle*, Paris, 1957, Librairie Marcel Rivière, p. 14.
2. E. Thier, *Das Menschenbild des jungen Marx*, Göttingen, 1957, Vandenhoeck und Ruprecht, p. 3.
3. R. Tucker, *Philosophy and Myth in Karl Marx*, Cambridge, England, 1961, Cambridge University Press, p. 12.
4. J. Hyppolite, *Études sur Marx et Hegel*, Paris, 1955, Librairie Marcel Rivière, pp. 60–61. [Now available (1969) in English translation as *Studies on Marx and Hegel*, New York: Basic Books—Ed.]
5. *Cf.* S. Kierkegaard, *Tagebücher*, ed. Th. Haecker, I, p. 326 (after H. J. Schoeps, *Was ist der Mensch?*, Göttingen, 1960. Musterschmidt Verlag, p. 20).
6. A. de Tocqueville, *Oeuvres complètes*, V, Paris, 1866, pp. 461–462.
7. R. Garaudy, *Perspectives de l'homme*, Paris, 1959, Presses Universitaires de France, p. 8.
8. M. Buber, *Le problème de l'homme*, Paris, 1962, Aubier, p. 19.
9. *Ibid.*, p. 60.
10. *Ibid.*, p. 61.
11. M. Heidegger, *Kant und das Problem der Metaphysik*, Bonn, 1929, Velag für Cohen, p. 200.
12. M. Buber, *op. cit.*, p. 19.
13. *Der Kampf*, Vienna, 1932, pp. 224–229, 267–277.
14. *Ibid.*, p. 224.
15. *Ibid.*, p. 276 [my italics—A.S.].
16. S. Landshut, J. P. Mayer, "Einleitung der Herausgeber," in *Karl Marx: Der historische Materialismus, Die Frürschriften*, Leipzig, 1932, A. Kroner, Erster Band, pp. XII–XIII.
17. E. Thier, *op. cit.*
18. *Ibid.*, p. 3.
19. L. N. Pazhitnov, *U istokov revolyutsionnogo perevorota*, Moskva, 1960, Sotsekgiz.
20. *Ibid.*, p. 11.
21. In the course of writing this book, I had the opportunity to read a more recent Soviet work on the subject: V. Keshelava, *Mir o dvukh Marksakh*, Moskva, 1963, Politizdat. While rightly repudiating the "two Marx's" doctrine, the author repeats Pozhitnov's error: he thinks it necessary to disown the role of Marx's philosophical anthropology in the whole of his system, because the claims made for it have been used as a weapon by his opponents. Despite all the appearances of "ideological of-

fensive," this is a typically *defensive* approach: battle is accepted on the ground chosen by the enemy and "victory" consists in leaving him the battlefield—just to create an impression that there is nothing to fight for.

22. I have in mind the discussion following my article "Le vrai visage du jeune Marx," *Recherches internationales à la lumière du marxisme,* 1960, no. 19, in which I insisted that the views of the young Marx can be correctly appraised only in the light of his doctrine; it is only here that the effects of some early views and ideas are revealed. In this context I referred to a methodological assumption of Marx about man's anatomy being the key to the anatomy of the ape. My views were criticized by several French Marxists, notably by Louis Althusser ("Sur le jeune Marx," *La Pensée,* 1961, no. 96), who accused me of teleologism. All this seems the result of a serious misunderstanding, not only of my views but also *on Marx and Hegel,* New York: Basic Books—Ed.]

23. Bogdan Suchodolski, *Narodzing nowożytnej filozofii czlowieka,* Warsaw, 1963, PWN, p. 22.

24. J. Hyppolite, *op. cit.,* p. 110.

25. D. Bell, "The Debates on Alienation," in L. Labedz, Ed., *Revisionism,* London, 1962, George Allen and Unwin, pp. 200–201.

26. E. Metzke, "Mensch und Geschichte im ursprünglichen Ansatz des Marx' schen Denkens," *Marxismusstudien,* Zweite Folge, Tübingen, 1957, J. C. B. Mehr (Paul Siebeck) p. 4.

27. K. Axelos, *Marx penseur de la technique,* Paris, 1961, Les Editions de Minuit, p. 49 [my italics—A.S.].

28. Some of the ideas underlying the following remarks on sociology are the outcome of my conversations with Professor Erich Fromm in his house at Cuernavaca, Mexico, in September, 1963. While I am now unable to say which of them stem from him and which are my own responsibility or the result of an exchange of opinions, I must emphasize that the basic outlines of the conception are undoubtedly his contribution. This I gratefully acknowledge; during my several days' stay with him I learned a great deal, including matters which concern the understanding of Marxism.

CHAPTER 1

1. K. Marx, "Critical Remarks on the Article of 'A Prussian,'" *Marx-Engels Historisch-Kritische Gesamtausgabe* [abbreviated as MEGA—A.S.], Berlin, 1932, Marx-Engels-Verlag, I/3, p. 22.
2. Reprinted by permission of International Publishers Co., Inc. Copyright © 1939. K. Marx, *The German Ideology,* Parts I and III, edited by R. Pascal, pp. 14–15 [MEGA I/5, pp. 15–16].
3. *Ibid.,* reprinted by permission, pp. 6–7 [MEGA I/5, p. 10].
4. *Ibid.,* reprinted by permission, p. 76 [MEGA I/5, p. 69].
5. K. Marx, *Selected Writings in Sociology and Social Philosophy,* edited by T. B. Bottomore and M. Rubel, Penguin Books, 1963, p. 33 [abbreviated as Bottomore and Rubel], or in *A Contribution to the Critique of Political Economy, Introduction* (posthumous appendix), translated by N. I. Stone, Chicago, 1904, Kerr, p. 265.
6. Swieżewski, *Rozum i tajamnica,* Cracow, 1960, "Znak," pp. 224–225.
7. These problems are not my invention; I came across them in discussions during my seminars on philosophical anthropology in Warsaw University. They are, therefore, likely to linger on elsewhere as well.
8. K. Marx, *Economic and Philosophical Manuscripts,* translated by T. B. Bottomore, in Erich Fromm, *Marx's Concept of Man,* New York, 1961, Frederick Ungar Publishing Co., pp. 181–182 [MEGA I/3, pp. 160–161]. *Ed. note:* See also the translation by M. Milligan, *The Economic and Philosophic Manuscripts of 1844,* edited by D. J. Struik, New York, 1964, International Publishers.
9. MEGA I/1/1, Frankfurt a.M., 1927, pp. 426–427. *Ed. note:* See the translation of the *Introduction* to Marx, *Contribution to the Critique of Hegel's Philosophy of Law* in L. D. Easton and K. H. Guddat, *Writings of the Young Marx on Philosophy and Society,* New York, 1967, Doubleday, pp. 249–264.
10. *Ibid.,* pp. 446–447.
11. R. Pascal edition, *op. cit.,* quoted by permission, pp. 37–38 [MEGA I/5, p. 34]. *Ed. note:* See also the complete translation, edited by S. Ryazanskaya, Moscow, 1964, Progress Publishers, pp. 58–59.
12. Reprinted by permission of International Publishers Co., Inc. Copyright © 1964. K. Marx, *Economic and Philosophical Manuscripts of 1844* translated by M. Milligan and edited by D. J. Struik, p. 130 [MEGA I/3, p. 17].
13. K. Marx, *A Contribution to the Critique of Political Economy,* translated by N. I. Stone, Chicago, 1904, Kerr, pp. 267–268.

14. K. Marx, *Selected Works,* London, 1948, Lawrence and Wishart, vol. 1, pp. 472–473 [MEGA I/5, p. 535]. *Ed. note:* See the different translations in Easton and Guddat edition, *op. cit.,* p. 402.

15. MEGA I/3, pp. 227–232. *Ed. note:* See *The Holy Family,* translated by R. Dixon, Moscow, 1956, Foreign Language Publishing House; London, 1957, Lawrence and Wishart; New York, 1956, International Publishers Co., Inc.

16. "If from real apples, pears, strawberries, and almonds I form the general idea 'Fruit,' if I go further and imagine that my abstract idea 'Fruit,' derived from real fruit, is an entity existing outside me, is indeed the true essence of the pear, the apple, etc.—then in the language of speculative philosophy I am declaring that 'Fruit' is the substance of the pear, the apple, the almond, etc. I am saying, therefore, that to be a pear is not essential to the pear, that to be an apple is not essential to the apple; that what is essential to these things is not their real being, perceptible to the senses, but the essence that I have extracted from them and then foisted on them, the essence of my idea—'Fruit.' I therefore declare apples, pears, almonds, etc. to be mere forms of existence, modi, of 'Fruit.' My finite understanding supported by my senses does, of course, distinguish an apple from a pear and a pear from an almond; but my speculative reason declares these sensuous differences unessential, indifferent. It sees in the apple the same as in the pear, and in the pear the same as in the almond, namely 'Fruit.' Particular real fruits are no more than semblances whose true essence is 'the Substance'—'Fruit'." K. Marx, F. Engels, *The Holy Family,* in *Reader in Marxist Philosophy,* selected and edited by Howard Selsam and Harry Martel, pp. 318–319. Reprinted by permission of International Publishers Co., Inc. Copyright © 1963. *Ed. note:* See the Dixon translation, *op. cit.,* pp. 78–79.

17. K. Marx, *A Contribution to the Critique of Political Economy, op. cit.,* pp. 293–294.

18. Bottomore and Rubel, p. 41 [MEGA I/1/1, p. 607].

19. On this point, too, *The German Ideology* is an elaboration of the *Theses:*

"It shows that history does not end by being resolved into 'self-consciousness' as 'spirit of the spirit,' but that in it at each stage there is found a material result: a sum of productive forces, a historically created relation of individuals to nature and to one another, which is handed down to each generation from its predecessor; a mass of productive forces, different forms of capital, and conditions, which, indeed, is modified by the new generation on the one hand, but also on the other prescribes for it its conditions of life and gives it a definite development, a special character. It shows that circumstances make men just as much as men make circumstances.

"This sum of productive forces, forms of capital and social forms of intercourse, which every individual and generation finds in existence as something given, is the real basis of what the philosophers have conceived as 'substance' and 'essence of man,' and what they had deified and attacked: a real basis which is not in the least disturbed, in its effect and influence on the development of men. . . ." Pascal edition, *op. cit.*, reprinted by permission, p. 29 [MEGA I/5, pp. 27–28].

20. The problem is discussed in detail by Auguste Cornu, in the third volume of his *Karl Marx et Friedrich Engels,* Paris, 1961, Presses Universitaires de France, pp. 142–166, and in particular, on pp. 159–160.

21. Struik edition, *op. cit.,* reprinted by permission, p. 177 [MEGA I/3, pp. 156–157].

22. Goethe's *Faust,* translated by Louis MacNeice, 1954. Reprinted by permission of Oxford University Press and Faber and Faber, Ltd.

23. Selsam and Martel edition, *op. cit.,* reprinted by permission, pp. 316–317 [MEGA I/5, p. 534]. *Ed. note:* See the different translation in Easton and Guddat, p. 401.

24. Selsam and Martel edition, *op. cit.,* reprinted by permission, pp. 283–284.

25. A. Gramsci, *Wstęp do studiów nad filozofią, Pisma wybrane,* Warszawa, 1961, KiW, vol. 1, pp. 38–39. *Ed. note:* The original context is to be found in Antonio Gramsci, *Il Materialismo Storico e la Filosofia di Benedetto Croce,* in *Opere,* Rome, 1953, Einaudi. An extensive English selection is in Gramsci, *The Modern Prince,* translated by L. Marks, London and New York, 1957, Lawrence and Wishart, and International Publishers Co., Inc., especially pp. 58–75.

26. M. Fritzhand, *Człowiek-humanizm-moralność,* Warszawa, 1961, KiW, pp. 75–112.

27. Pascal edition, *op. cit.,* reprinted by permission, p. 7 [MEGA I/5, p. 10].

28. Struik edition, *op. cit.,* reprinted by permission, p. 113.

29. "The use and fabrication of instruments of labour, although existing in the germ among certain species of animals, is specifically characteristic of the human labour-process, and Franklin therefore defines man as a tool-making animal." Dona Torr, ed., K. Marx, *Capital,* London, 1938, George Allen and Unwin, and New York, 1939, International Publishers Co., Inc., p. 159.

30. MEGA I/5, pp. 215–216. *Ed. Note:* See the slightly different translation in Ryazanskaya edition, pp. 254–255.

31. MEGA, Moskau-Leningrad, 1933, Verlagsgenossenschaft Ausländischer Arbeiter in der USSR, I/6, p. 14.

32. *Ibid.,* I/6, p. 18.

33. Reprinted by permission of International Publishers Co., Inc. Copyright © 1964. K. Marx, *The Poverty of Philosophy,* edited by C. P. Dutt and V. Chattopadhyaya [MEGA I/6, p. 166.] *Ed. note:* See the different translation in Bottomore and Rubel, p. 109.

34. L. Feuerbach, *Grundsätze der Philosophie der Zukunft, 59,* in *Kleine philosophische Schriften,* Leipzig, 1950, Meiner Verlag, p. 168.

35. L. Feuerbach, 'Über das Wesen des Christentung in Beziehung auf den "Einzigen und sein Eigentum," ' *Kleine philosophische Schriften* (1842–1845), pp. 187–188, Leipzig, 1950, Verlag Felix Meiner.

36. *Ibid.,* p. 190.

37. *Mark Engels Werke,* Dietz Verlag, Berlin, vol. 27, p. 425.

38. "None of the supposed rights of man, therefore, go beyond the egoistic man, man as he is, as a member of civil society; that is, an individual separated from the community, withdrawn into himself, wholly preoccupied with his private interest and acting in accordance with his private caprice. Man is far from being considered, *in the rights of man, as a species-being; on the contrary, species-life itself—society—appears as a system which* is external to the individual and as a limitation of his original independence. The only bond between men is natural necessity, need and private interest, the preservation of their property and their egoistic persons." K. Marx, *Zur Judenfrage* [MEGA I/1/1, p. 595 (my italics—A.S.)] *Ed. note:* translation by T. B. Bottomore, *Karl Marx: Early Writings,* reprinted by permission of C. A. Watts & Co., Ltd., London, 1963, p. 26 and McGraw-Hill, Inc., New York, 1965; see the different translation in Easton and Guddat, pp. 236–237.

The question of "species being" is similarly answered by Marx in the conclusion of the same work:

"As soon as society succeeds in abolishing the *empirical* essence of Judaism—bargaining and its conditions—the Jew becomes *impossible,* because his consciousness no longer has an object. The subjective basis of Judaism—practical need—assumes a human form, and the conflict between the individual, sensuous existence of man and his species-existence is abolished." [*Ibid.,* I/1/1, p. 606 (my italics—A.S.)] Bottomore, *op. cit.,* reprinted by permission, p. 40; see also Easton and Guddat, p. 248.

39. K. Marx, *Grundrisse der Kritik der politischen Ökonomie,* Berlin, 1953, Dietz Verlag, p. 395. *Ed. note:* Karl Marx, *Pre-Capitalist Economic Formations,* translated by Jack Cohen and edited by Eric Hobsbawm, London, 1964, Lawrence and Wishart, p. 96; New York, 1965, International Publishers Co., Inc.

40. K. Marx, *Economic and Philosophical Manuscripts,* Bottomore translation as in Fromm edition, *op. cit.,* p. 101. See also *Karl Marx: Early Writings,* p. 127.

41. *Ibid.,* Fromm edition, p. 102; see also Bottomore, p. 128.

42. *Capital, op. cit.,* (Dona Torr edition) p. 622, note 2.

43. It is first posed in *The Sane Society,* then discussed in *Marx's Concept of Man* and *Beyond the Chains of Illusion*—an interesting sequence showing Fromm's gradual transition from Freudianism to Marxism in his discussion of the problems of human nature.

44. E. Fromm, *Beyond the Chains of Illusion: My Encounter with Freud and Marx,* New York, 1962, Trident Press—Simon and Schuster Book, p. 27.

45. *Ibid.,* p. 31.
46. MEGA I/1/1, p. 499.
47. MEGA I/1/1, p. 584. *Ed. note:* From Bottomore, *Karl Marx: Early Writings, op. cit.,* reprinted by permission, p. 13; see also Easton and Guddat edition, p. 225.
48. MEGA I/1/3, p. 131. Struik edition, *op. cit.,* reprinted by permission, pp. 138–139; Bottomore translation, *op. cit.,* p. 159.
49. MEGA I/1/1, pp. 426–427. *Ed. note:* From *Writings of the Young Marx on Philosophy and Society* translated by Lloyd D. Easton and Kurt H. Guddat, pp. 165–166. Copyright © 1967 by Lloyd D. Easton and Kurt H. Guddat. Reprinted by permission of Doubleday & Company, Inc.
50. *Ibid.,* reprinted by permission, pp. 423–424.
51. K. Marx, *The German Ideology,* MEGA I/5, pp. 418–419. *Ed. note:* See English translation in Ryazanskaya Moscow edition, part III, section entitled "Solomon's Song of Songs or the Unique," pp. 470–488.
52. *Studia Socjologiczne,* Warsaw, 1962, no. 3.

CHAPTER 2

1. K. Marx, from the manuscript "L. Feuerbach," MEGA I/5, p. 537 [my italics—A.S.]. *Ed. note:* See the different translation in Ryazanskaya edition, *op. cit.,* p. 658.
2. Reprinted by permission of International Publishers Co., Inc. Copyright © 1939. K. Marx, *The German Ideology,* Parts I and III, edited by R. Pascal, pp. 22–24. *Ed. note:* See the different translation in Ryazanskaya edition, pp. 45–47 or Easton and Guddat edition, pp. 425–426.
3. K. Marx, F. Engels, *The Holy Family,* MEGA I/3, p. 213. Dixon translation, Moscow, 1956, Foreign Languages Publishing House, p. 60.
4. K. Marx, "Communism and the Augsburg," *Allgemeine Zeitung,* MEGA I/1/1, p. 263. *Ed. note:* English translation from *Writings of the Young Marx on Philosophy and Society* translated by Lloyd D. Easton and Kurt H. Guddat, p. 135. Copyright © 1967 by Lloyd D. Easton and Kurt H. Guddat. Reprinted by permission of Doubleday & Company, Inc.
5. K. Marx, *Contribution to the Critique of Hegel's Philosophy of Right,* pp. 283–284 [MEGA I/1/1, pp. 614–615]. *Ed. note:* English translation from Easton and Guddat, *op. cit.,* reprinted by permission, pp. 257–258. See the different translation in Selsam and Martel, *Reader in Marxist Philosophy,* pp. 283–284.
6. L. Feuerbach, *Vorlesungen über das Wesen der Religion,* Stuttgart, 1908, Fromman's Verlag.
7. *Capital* (Dona Torr edition), pp. 634–635.
8. MEGA I/1/1, p. 10. See the conclusion to the Foreword of Marx's doc-

toral dissertation; English translation in Selsam and Martel edition, *Reader in Marxist Philosophy.*

9. F. Engels, "Review of Thomas Carlyle's Past and Present," *Reader,* p. 236. [MEGA I/2, p. 426].

10. *Ibid.,* p. 238 [MEGA I/2, p. 428].

11. MEGA I/5, p. 424. *Ed. note:* English translation from Ryazanskaya edition., *op. cit.,* pp. 491–492.

12. K. Marx, *Contribution to the Critique of Hegel's Philosophy of Right,* MEGA I/1/1, p. 494.

13. K. Marx, *On the Jewish Question,* MEGA I/1/1, p. 599. *Ed. note:* English translation from Easton and Guddat, *op. cit.,* reprinted by permission, p. 241. See also the different translation in Bottomore, *Early Writings,* p. 31.

14. F. Engels, *Ludwig Feuerbach and the Outcome of Classical German Philosophy,* in *Karl Marx, Selected Works,* vol. 1, New York, 1938, International Publishers Co., Inc.; see also p. 463 in Feuer edition, Marx and Engels, *Basic Writings on Politics and Philosophy,* New York, 1959, Doubleday, p. 236.

15. MEGA I/6, p. 227. *Ed. note:* Reprinted by permission of International Publishers Co., Inc. Copyright © 1964. From the Conclusion of Marx, *The Poverty of Philosophy,* edited by Dutt and Chattopadhyaya, pp. 146–147; also in Bottomore and Rubel edition, *Karl Marx Selected Writings, op. cit.,* p. 239.

16. Cf. MEGA I/6, p. 546. *Ed. note:* See the final passages of the *Communist Manifesto,* part II 'Proletarians and Communists,' as in Feuer edition, *op. cit.,* reprinted by permission, p. 29,

"When, in the course of development, class distinctions have disappeared and all production has been concentrated in the hands of a vast association of the whole nation, the public power will lose its political character. Political power, properly so called, is merely the organized power of one class for oppressing another. If the proletariat during its contest with the bourgeoisie is compelled, by the force of circumstances, to organize itself as a class, if, by means of a revolution, it makes itself the ruling class and, as such, sweeps away by force the old conditions of production, then it will, along with these conditions, have swept away the conditions for the existence of class antagonisms and of classes generally, and will thereby have abolished its own supremacy as a class.

"In place of the old bourgeois society, with its classes and class antagonisms, we shall have an association in which the free development of each is the condition for the free development of all."

17. K. Marx, F. Engels, *The Holy Family* [MEGA I/3, p. 296]. *Ed. note:* English translation in Dixon edition. Reprinted by permission of International Publishers, copyright © 1956; and Lawrence & Wishart, copyright © 1957, p. 163.

18. K. Marx, *Economic and Philosophical Manuscripts,* translated by T. B. Bottomore, in Erich Fromm, *Marx's Concept of Man,* New York, 1961, Frederick Ungar Publishing Co., pp. 95–96 [MEGA I/3, pp. 83–84], or see Bottomore edition, *Karl Marx: Early Writings,* p. 122. *Ed. note:* See the different translation in Struik edition, p. 108.

19. Roger Garaudy's interpretation of this problem (in *Humanisme marxiste,* Paris, 1957, Ed. Sociales, pp. 30–31, footnote) is, in my view, mistaken.

20. *Capital,* vol. 3, Untermann translation, Chicago, 1904, Kerr, pp. 954–955. See the somewhat more fluent translation in Bottomore and Rubel, pp. 254–255.

21. K. Marx, *Economic and Philosophical Manuscripts,* Fromm edition, p. 101 [MEGA I/3, pp. 87–88]; see also Bottomore edition, p. 127, and Struik edition, p. 113.

22. *Cf. The German Ideology,* [MEGA I/5, p. 59]. *Ed. note:* See Pascal edition, pp. 68–69 or Rayazanskaya edition, pp. 85–86.

23. K. Marx, *Economic and Philosophical Manuscripts,* Fromm edition, *op. cit.,* p. 128 [MEGA I/3, p. 115]; see also Bottomore edition, *op. cit.,* p. 156 and Struik edition, *op. cit.,* p. 136.

24. F. Engels, *The Situation of England: The Eighteenth Century,* MEGA I/4, p. 298.

25. *Loc. cit.*

26. In a fine essay, "On the Problems of Alienation" (*Studia Filozoficzne,* 1959, no. 6), Bronisław Baczko draws attention to the prophetic and chiliastic character of these views.

27. Reprinted by permission of International Publishers Co., Inc. Copyright © 1939. K. Marx, *The German Ideology,* Parts I and III edited by R. Pascal, p. 26 [MEGA I/5, p. 25]; slight variant in Ryazankaya edition, p. 47.

CHAPTER 3

1. K. Marx, F. Engels, *The Holy Family,* in *Writings of the Young Marx on Philosophy and Society* translated by Lloyd D. Easton and Kurt H. Guddat, p. 385. Copyright © 1967 by Lloyd D. Easton and Kurt H. Guddat. Reprinted by permission of Doubleday & Company, Inc. [MEGA I/3, p. 265]. *Ed. note:* See also the different translation in Bottomore and Rubel, p. 78.

2. "Life is not determined by consciousness, but consciousness by life." Reprinted by permission of International Publishers Co., Inc. Copyright © 1939. K. Marx, *The German Ideology,* Parts I and III edited by R. Pascal, p. 15 [MEGA I/5, p. 16].

3. G. Marcel, *Les hommes contre l'humain,* Paris, La Colombe, p. 173 ff.

4. *Ibid.,* p. 2.

5. K. Marx, "Comments on the Latest Prussian Censorship Instruction," MEGA I/1/1, pp. 153–154. *Ed. note:* English translation from the Easton and Guddat edition, *op. cit.,* reprinted by permission, pp. 70–71.

6. F. Engels, *Briefe an Bebel,* Berlin 1958 Dietz, Letter No. 55 [1 (-2) May, 1891] cited from pp. 177–178.

7. Bertolt Brecht, *Galileo, Ed. note:* Cited from the Charles Laughton translation (copyright Bertolt Brecht, 1952) of *Galileo* in *Seven Plays by Bertolt Brecht,* Eric Bentley, ed., New York, 1961, Grove Press, pp. 399–400. For a different version, see *The Life of Galileo,* London 1960, Methuen, p. 117.

8. I. Ehrenburg, *The Stormy Life of Lasik Roitschwanz,* London, 1965, Elek Books, p. 62. *Ed. note:* Compare the different English version, New York, 1960, Polyglot Library-Lyle Stuart, pp. 76–77.

9. *Ibid.,* pp. 62–63. New York edition, p. 77.

10. *Ibid.,* p. 70. New York edition, pp. 84–85.

11. K. Marx, *On the Jewish Question* [MEGA I/1/1, p. 599]. *Ed. note:* English translation in the Easton and Guddat edition, *op. cit.,* reprinted by permission, p. 241; see the different translation in Bottomore and Rubel, p. 241.

CHAPTER 4

1. K. Marx, *Introduction to Contribution to the Critique of Hegel's Philosophy of Right,* in Bottomore, ed., *Karl Marx: Early Writings,* reprinted by permission of C. A. Watts & Co., Ltd., London, 1963, p. 52 and McGraw-Hill, Inc., New York, 1965 [MEGA I/1/1, pp. 614–615]. *Ed. note:* See slightly different translation in Selsam and Martel, p. 284 and in Easton and Guddat, pp. 257–258.

2. K. Marx, F. Engels, *The Holy Family,* MEGA I/3, p. 179. *Ed. note:* See a slightly different translation in the Dixon edition, p. 15.

3. K. Marx, *Contribution to the Critique of Hegel's Philosophy of Right,* [MEGA I/1/1, pp. 620–621] in Bottomore, ed., *Karl Marx: Early Writings, op. cit.,* reprinted by permission, p. 59. *Ed. note:* See the different translation in Selsam and Martel, pp. 286–287, and in Easton and Guddat, pp. 263–264.

4. Bertolt Brecht, "To Posterity" from *Selected Poems,* translated by H. R. Hays. Reprinted by permission of Harcourt Brace & World, Inc., New York, 1959.

CHAPTER 5

1. K. Marx, *Economic and Philosophical Manuscripts,* Bottomore, ed., *Karl Marx: Early Writings.* Reprinted by permission of C. A. Watts & Co., Ltd., London, 1963, p. 213 and McGraw-Hill, Inc., New York, 1965 [MEGA I/3, p. 166].

2. *Ibid.,* p. 155 [MEGA I/3, p. 114].

3. K. Marx, "Critical Remarks on Prusak's Article," [MEGA I/3, p. 22.] *Ed. note:* Adapted from Easton and Guddat edition, *op. cit.,* pp. 356–357.

4. K. Marx, *The German Ideology* [MEGA I/5, p. 410]. *Ed. note:* Adapted from Ryazanskaya, *op. cit.,* pp. 475–476.

5. *Ibid.,* p. 417 [My italics—A.S.].

6. *Ibid.* [I/5, p. 417].

7. "The exclusive concentration of artistic talent in particular individuals, and its suppression in the broad mass which is bound up with this, is a consequence of division of labour. If, even in certain social conditions, everyone was an excellent painter, that would not at all exclude the possibility of each of them being also an original painter, so that here too the difference between "human" and "unique" labour amounts to sheer nonsense. In any case, with a communist organisation of society, there disappears the subordination of the artist to local and national narrowness, which arises entirely from division of labour, and also the subordination of the artist to some definite art, thanks to which he is exclusively a painter, sculptor, etc., the very name of his activity adequately expressing the narrowness of his professional development and his dependence on division of labour. In a communist society there are no painters but at most people who engage in painting among other activities." K. Marx, *The German Ideology,* [MEGA I/5, p. 373], Ryazanskaya edition, pp. 431–432.

The problem is posed with even more trenchancy in another passage from the same work:

"For as soon as labour is distributed, each man has a particular, exclusive sphere of activity, which is forced upon him and from which he cannot escape. He is a hunter, a fisherman, a shepherd, or a critical critic, and must remain so if he does not want to lose his means of livelihood; while in communist society, where nobody has one exclusive sphere of activity but each can become accomplished in any branch he wishes, society regulates the general production and thus makes it possible for me to do one thing to-day and another to-morrow, to hunt in the morning, fish in the afternoon, rear cattle in the evening, criticize after dinner, just as I have a mind, without ever becoming hunter, fisherman, shepherd or critic.

"This crystallization of social activity, this consolidation of what we ourselves produce into an objective power above us, growing out of our control, thwarting our expectations, bringing to naught our calculations, is one of the chief factors in historical development up till now." *Ibid.*, pp. 44–45 [MEGA I/5, pp. 22–23]. *Ed. note:* See a slightly different translation in the Pascal edition, *op. cit.*, pp. 22–23.

8. K. Marx, *The German Ideology* [MEGA I/5fi pp. 63–64]. *Ed. note:* Adapted from the Pascal edition, *op. cit.*, p. 74.

9. [MEGA I/6, p. 536 (My italics—A.S.)]. *Ed. note:* See for example, Feuer edition, p. 29.

10. From *Critique of the Gotha Programme,* as translated in Feuer edition, p. 119, or in Selsam and Martel edition, pp. 262–263.

11. F. Engels, *The Principles of Communism,* MEGA I/6, pp. 517–518. *Ed. note:* See the somewhat different translation by P. M. Sweezy, *Monthly Review Pamphlet No. 4,* New York, 1952, pp. 17–18.

12. F. Engels, *Socialism: Utopian and Scientific,* in K. Marx, *Selected Works,* vol. 1, New York, 1968, International Publishers, pp. 185–186. *Ed. note:* See the different translation in the Feuer edition, pp. 108–111.

13. K. Marx, Letters from the *Deutsch-Französische Jahrbücher,* [MEGA I/1/1, p. 573 (my italics—A.S.)]. *Ed. note:* Adapted from Easton and Guddat edition, *op. cit.,* p. 212.

14. Adapted from K. Marx, *The German Ideology, op. cit.,* p. 24 [MEGA I/5, p. 24].

15. *Ibid.,* p. 25 [MEGA I/5, p. 25].

Catalog

If you are interested in a list of fine Paperback
books, covering a wide range of subjects
and interests, send your name and address,
requesting your free catalog, to:

McGraw-Hill Paperbacks
330 West 42nd Street
New York, New York 10036